Ancient World Lists and Numbers

Ancient World Lists and Numbers

Numerical Phrases and Rosters in the Greco-Roman Civilizations

by DAVID MATZ

McFarland & Company, Inc., Publishers
Jefferson, North Carolina, and London

British Library Cataloguing-in-Publication data are available

Library of Congress Cataloguing-in-Publication Data

Matz, David.
    Ancient world lists and numbers : numerical phrases and
rosters in the Greco-Roman civilizations / by David Matz.
        p.   cm.
    Includes bibliographical references and index.
    ISBN 0-7864-0039-0 (lib. bdg. : 50# alk. paper) ∞
    1. History, Ancient—Registers.   2. Civilization,
Ancient—Registers.   3. Lists—History.   4. Numeration—
History.   I. Title.
D62.M37   1995
930—dc20   95-3197
                                                      CIP

Manufactured in the United States of America

McFarland & Company, Inc., Publishers
    Box 611, Jefferson, North Carolina 28640

CONTENTS

ACKNOWLEDGMENTS

I wish to thank Drs. Lee Pearcy and Anthony Papalas for reviewing the manuscript, and offering useful suggestions for its correction and improvement. Similar thanks are due to the editorial staff at McFarland.

To my parents, I extend my gratitude for reading the manuscript from the layperson's perspective, and for their supportive comments.

And most importantly, I wish to thank my wife Betsy, and my son Mike, for their patience and encouragement. For that, and for many other reasons, I dedicate this book to them.

PREFACE

This book is the product of its author's frustration over the lack of a useful reference work containing detailed information about famous (and not so famous) lists and numbers associated with the ancient civilizations, particularly the Greeks and the Romans. To find, for example, the three parts into which Caesar's Gaul was divided, one would consult a book on Roman history; an inquiry regarding the locations and descriptions of the Seven Wonders of the ancient world would necessitate the perusal of an art or architectural text; and to discover the names of the nine Muses, a dictionary on classical mythology would be the reference book of choice.

This book of lists and numbers endeavors to bring together within its pages the kind of information that perhaps only the most devoted and diligent classical scholar has committed to memory. It may serve as a ready reference that could prove equally useful to the classics or ancient history professor in need of a few details for the finishing touches on a scholarly essay or a lecture, to the student studying for an examination or looking for a term paper topic, or to the lay reader with a general interest in the ancient world.

Much of the material in this book is undoubtedly available elsewhere — if one has the command of bibliography, the time, the patience, and the inclination to search for it in a plethora of often widely scattered sourcebooks, dictionaries, anthologies, and translations. It is hoped that this volume will obviate the need for the many perambulations, both mental and physical, that currently confront the seeker of information about ancient world lists and numbers.

INTRODUCTION

A Brief History of Listmaking

Classical listmaking enjoys a long and honorable tradition. Many ancient authors included catalogues, itemizations, and numerical surveys—lists in varied forms—within the pages of their writings. The revered epic poet Homer might be considered the father of the art: his monumental catalogues in the *Iliad* of the opposing forces in the Trojan War have rightly attracted the scholarly attention of generations of professors and their students.

But the ancients' fascination with lists and numbers certainly did not end with Homer. Nearly every writer—from Hesiod and Herodotus, through the Silver Age Latin authors, and beyond—paid homage, to a greater or lesser degree, to the recording of numerical detail. To cite but four examples:

1. Callimachus (ca.305–240 B.C.), perhaps antiquity's preeminent cataloguer, assumed the daunting task of classifying, organizing, and synopsizing the holdings of the great library in Alexandria. The enormity of this project is illustrated by the vast quantity of scrolls, papyri, and other documents reputedly stored, in apparent disarray, at this famed repository, numbering about 700,000.

Several stages were involved in Callimachus's effort to transform this chaos to something resembling systematized organization:

a. He identified eight genres of literature, including epic and lyric poetry, drama, law, philosophy, history, oratory, rhetoric, and a miscellaneous category.

b. He classified every author represented in the library according to one of these eight genres. Variegated authors, whose works fit into two or more of the categories, received the appropriate multiple listings.

c. In each of the eight categories he listed the authors' names alphabetically; he also composed brief biographical sketches for each author in each list.

d. He listed the titles of each author's work(s) alphabetically, in each category. Since some of these works had multiple or varied titles, he also quoted the first words or lines of each work, to obviate potential confusion or ambiguity.

e. Finally, he recorded the length (in lines) of each literary entry.

1

This encyclopedic catalogue of the library's works—called simply *Pinaces* (*Tablets*)—consumed 120 volumes, and served as the model for all subsequent bibliographical undertakings.

   2. *Apollodorus of Athens* (second century B.C.) offered a multitude of lists in his book *Bibliotheke* (*Library*). The following is a sample:

a. Zeus's children by Hera, by Themis, by Dione, by Eurynome, by Styx, and by Mnemosyne;

b. The names of the nine Muses;

c. The names of the Argonauts;

d. The Twelve Labors of Hercules;

e. The names of Hercules' children; and

f. The names of the ten legendary kings of Athens.

Many other mythological genealogies also appear in the book.

   3. *Diogenes Laertius* (third century A.D.), also an accomplished listmaker, included in his *Lives of the Eminent Philosophers*, Book IV, information about Plato's successors at the famed Academy. The first four and the period they were in charge of the Academy were Speusippus (headed the Academy 347–339 B.C.); Xenocrates (396–314 B.C.); Polemo (314–276 B.C.); and Crates (mid-third century B.C.).

   Diogenes listed 30 titles of works attributed to Speusippus, totaling 43,475 lines. Xenocrates wrote at least 75 treatises, and Diogenes provided all 75 titles in his lists, adding that their total number of lines was 224,239. He concluded the section on Xenocrates by listing six other notable men who shared the same name. He recorded a similar list at the end of the essay on Crates, specifying ten other eminent bearers of that name.

   Diogenes wrote biographies of 82 eminent philosophers, often concluding the entries with lists of similarly named individuals, including an astounding 20 named Theodorus.

   Additional lists of titles of works by various philosophers, as compiled by Diogenes, are 17 dialogues written by Crito, Socrates' protégé; the 33 dialogues by Simon, a friend of Socrates; the 23 books by Aristippus, including one entitled *A Reply to Those Who Criticize My Love of Old Wine and Young Women*; the 36 dialogues of Plato, arranged into nine tetralogies; the 14 books of Xenophon; the 20 treatises of Zeno; the ten volumes of Antisthenes' treatises, 62 in all; the 162 works of Chrysippus; the 12 writings of Metrodorus; the 41 works of Epicurus; and Democritus's 61 treatises, which covered a wide range of topics, including philosophy, logic, astronomy, mathematics, geography, poetry, literary criticism, medicine, agriculture, and warfare.

   In the prologue to his book he presented several lists, including, the Seven Sages; the three parts of philosophy and the two divisions of philosophers; the names of 12 celebrated Greek philosophical schools and their founders; and the names of founders of eight Italian philosophical schools.

   4. *The city of Alexandria* attracted large numbers of scholars, poets, scientists, literary critics, and bibliophiles during its period of intellectual ascendancy in the fourth and third centuries B.C. Among this assemblage were to be

found Callimachus's student Aristophanes of Byzantium (ca.260–183) and Aristophanes' student Aristarchus (mid–second century). The latter two formulated what has come to be called the Alexandrian Canon: a series of quasi–top ten (or four, five, seven, etc.) lists of the best writers in the various genres, including epic poetry, lyric poetry, tragedy, comedy, oratory, and philosophy. There was but one litmus test for inclusion: the quality of the language. Criteria such as content, length, or literary or historical significance were not considered. (The Alexandrian lists appear at appropriate points in the current volume.)

Inclusion Principles

To include in the present work every list or number within the extant writings of the ancient Greeks and Romans would require a format and design of Callimachean proportions. Since this volume does not aspire to be a second *Pinaces*, it has been necessary to apply certain inclusion criteria.

Lists, and frequently synopses, of the works of most of the standard classical authors have been included, although synopses do not appear of inordinately long works. For example, to present a synopsis of the 12 books of Vergil's *Aeneid* is manageable; doing the same for the 162 books of Cato the Elder's *De Agricultura* is not. Sometimes personal preferences and biases have dictated decisions on what works to synopsize and which ones merely to list. For example, summaries of each of Horace's *Satires* have been provided; but summaries of individual *Odes*, *Epodes*, and *Epistles* have not. Likewise, it seemed pointless to synopsize works whose titles indicate clearly the content: *De Amicitia* (*On Friendship*), for example.

Authors whose works survive only in fragmentary form have generally been omitted.

In the case of prolific and highly regarded writers like Aristotle or Cicero, space and time constraints demanded that synopses be limited or excluded altogether. However, the not infrequent references to their works within the contexts of relevant lists elsewhere in the book have hopefully palliated this apparent injustice. It may, for example, seem inconsistent to offer synopses of the three surviving speeches of Aeschines, while providing nary a summary of any of Cicero's 58 orations—surely an inequity that would have keenly wounded the pride of that greatest of all Roman orators. However, the amount of attention devoted to Cicero generally in the book far outstrips the ink used on information relevant to Aeschines, a mitigating factor of which perhaps Cicero himself would have approved.

The massive amount of numerical data recorded by the ancient authors required the implementation of a winnowing process; in this regard, no claim can be made to have followed any rigid method, if indeed one could even have been devised. Greco-Roman equitableness has been attempted. A list of the kings of Rome, for example, has been balanced by a corresponding list of Athenian kings. A list of the statistics related by Suetonius in his *Life of Julius Caesar* has found its equivalent in a similar list derived from Plutarch's *Life of Alexander the Great*. Wherever possible, there has been a conscious effort to provide this rough type of equal time allowance.

Beyond that, I have endeavored to include all the obvious lists, all the natural groupings; for example, the Seven Sages; Hercules' Twelve Labors; the three parts of Caesar's Gaul; and the Nine Muses. I have also attempted to draw upon a variety of topics in the compilation of lists: literature, architecture, sports and recreation, government and politics, warfare, drama, and mythology, to cite a few. Some choices for inclusion may seem (and probably are) idiosyncratic: the eight kinds of Roman military crowns; the names of Actaeon's 33 hunting dogs; and the 29 epithets of Zeus. To those who might wonder at the logic governing the decisions to include such entries or to omit others that may have seemed more important, I can only refer to the propriety of Dr. Johnson's reply to a critic who questioned him concerning the accuracy of his definition of a fetlock: "Ignorance, madam, sheer ignorance."

Finally, a *terminus ante quem* of A.D. 300 for numbers, lists, and authors has been applied; it has been crossed in only a very few instances. And although the designations B.C.E. and C.E. have recently acquired a certain aura of political correctness, I am still enough of a traditionalist to prefer to employ the more familiar B.C. and A.D. abbreviations.

Greek and Roman Coinages

The Greeks and Roman currency systems both utilized several different denominations of coins and other measures of money. For the Greeks there were the obol, drachma, tetradrachma, mina, and talent (the latter two not coined); for the Romans there were the as, sestertius (sesterce in English), denarius, and aureus. These terms are used throughout this book.

Naturally, one would wish for some indication of equivalencies to modern currency. Unfortunately, it is a tricky business to provide these equivalencies, given that the modern economic systems are so different from ancient ones, and that a gulf of 2,000 years or more of economic vagaries separates the modern world from the ancient.

Nonetheless, it is possible to gain an idea of the value of these currencies within the context of the societies that produced them. It is known, for example, that in fifth-century Athens an average working person could expect to earn one drachma per day. One might then compare that to the average contemporary daily wage, and, from there, assign a dollar equivalency to the drachma. This much, at least, is certain:

6 obols = 1 drachma	60 minas (or 6,000 drachmas) = 1
4 drachmas = 1 tetradrachma	talent
100 drachmas = 1 mina	

A talent was obviously a huge sum of money, equivalent to hundreds of thousands of dollars. Considerations of practicality, of course, precluded the minting of talents in any denomination.

Similar cultural contexts may be adduced for the Romans. For example, the Edict of Diocletian, an early fourth-century A.D. wage-price freeze, provides an idea of the upper wage limits for a wide variety of workers, including carpenters, wagon makers, masons, teachers, artists, water bearers, camel drivers, and even sewer cleaners and shepherds; the 200–400 (per day) sesterce range seems to be the limit for most of these. Hence, as in the case of the drachma, some idea may be gained of the sesterce's modern equivalent value.

Also, in the time of Augustus a 400,000-sesterce net worth requirement was established for members of the equestrian class, Rome's prosperous upper-middle income group. From that, one might conclude that 400,000 sesterces represented, if not outlandish wealth, at least solid comfort.

The relative value of Roman coins can be broken down to the following:

4 asses = 1 sesterce   25 denarii = 1 aureus
4 sesterces = 1 denarius

Some Roman Governmental Offices

References to the following Roman governmental offices recur often in the book.

Consul. This was the highest executive office during the days of the Roman Republic; the consuls presided over the governmental machinery and commanded the Roman armies. Two were elected annually.

Praetor. This was the second most powerful executive office; praetors served as judges and also had certain important military responsibilities. The number of praetors varied; by the first century B.C. eight were elected annually.

Aedile. Aediles supervised roads and markets—in particular, weights and measures—and they were generally responsible for the security and maintenance of these areas. Four aediles were elected annually.

Quaestor. Quaestors were financial officials, often sent with the Roman army during wartime to maintain records of campaign expenditures. Originally, there were only two; by the first century B.C. there were 20, elected annually.

In addition to these four primary offices, two *censors* were elected every five years, to serve terms of 18 months. The censors had many wide-ranging powers, including the right to examine the rolls of the Roman Senate and purge those senators deemed unworthy; to compile lists of citizens for taxation purposes; and to initiate and contract for construction projects.

Finally, the ten *tribunes*, armed with veto power, protected the rights of the plebeians.

Bibliographical Notes

Nullumst iam dictum quod non dictum sit prius, as the comic playwright Terence aptly put it in his play *Eunuch* (line 41): "Nothing is said now which hasn't been said before." And this, of course, is the problem that confronts any nonfiction writer: how to say something new in a way that it has not been said before, all the while trying to avoid charges of triteness, triviality, or, worst of all, that nightmare of everyone who inputs data to diskette, plagiarism, unintentional or otherwise.

Throughout the preparation of this manuscript I have been keenly aware of the debt that I owe to numerous editors, translators, and authors of books, particularly reference works. The bibliography that appears at the end of this volume will hopefully do justice to their contributions to it. However, several of the entries appearing therein have been especially useful, and it seems appropriate to highlight those.

Much of the mythological information that appears in the current volume has been gleaned from the pages of J. E. Zimmerman's *Dictionary of Classical Mythology*. I have consistently found this little book to be the most practical and informative guide of its kind anywhere.

After I thought—naively, as it turned out—that I had completed the manuscript, I decided to check for any sins of omission that may have been lurking within it by painstakingly leafing through the 605 pages of *The Oxford Companion to Classical Literature*, edited by M. C. Howatson. This well-written and comprehensive reference book revealed several important authors whose works had not been represented in my original manuscript, in addition to supplying me with many other facts and information. To a somewhat lesser extent, Michael Grant's *Greek and Latin Authors: 800 B.C.–A.D. 1000* aided in the same manner, as did Lillian Feder's *Apollo Handbook of Classical Literature*. And, of course, *The Oxford Classical Dictionary* proved indispensible on many occasions.

There sometimes seems to exist in the scholarly world an implicit contempt for books written before the turn of the century; books that perhaps possess some quaint appeal to the bibliophile but whose practicality and accuracy have long since been eroded by the winds of more up-to-date research. This principle is undoubtedly applicable in many cases. But if, for example, the island of Naxos were 19 miles long in 1847, it seems unlikely that it could have grown or shrunk too much 150 years later. Or if 150 years ago the largest island in the Aegean were Euboea, it is most doubtful that some other island has surpassed it in the time since. Jupiter's epithet, *Optimus Maximus*, seems to have been a constant. So if these and similar facts are unchanging, does it matter if a researcher gleans them from a book written last year or one authored in 1847, such as N. W. Fiske's *Classical Antiquities*?

The cumulative erudition of the many skilled editors and translators who prepared volumes in the Loeb Classical Library series cannot be understated.

And while it would not be feasible to cite them individually here—they have been listed in the bibliography—it is certainly appropriate and necessary to pay tribute to them as a group. They have performed an inestimable service to generations of classicists and general readers alike.

Other books that I found myself referring to time and again in the gathering of facts and the compilations of lists are *Life and Leisure in Ancient Rome*, by J. P. V. D. Balsdon; *A History of Greek Literature*, by Albin Lesky (translated by James Willis and Cornelius de Heer); *A History of Rome*, by M. Cary; and *Harper's Dictionary of Classical Literature and Antiquities*.

A Note on Source Citations

Titles of ancient sources are cited in the text only when the author has more than one extant work to his credit. (Example: Plutarch *Sulla* 37.) Otherwise, only book and chapter numbers are recorded. (Example: Aulus Gellius 13.11.) The authors generally cited by book and chapter number only are

Apollodorus	Macrobius
Diodorus Siculus	Pausanias
Diogenes Laertius	Pliny (Elder and Younger)
Dionysius of Halicarnassus	Polybius
Aulus Gellius	Strabo
Herodotus	Thucydides
Livy	Vitruvius

References to Dionysius's *On the Ancient Orators* and to Pliny the Younger's *Panegyric* are so noted. Other book and chapter references are to *Roman Antiquities* and *Letters*, respectively.

A Note on the Form of Hercules' Name

There are two forms of the name Hercules: the Latin, Hercules; and the Greek, Heracles. To obviate possible confusion, the Latin form has been used throughout the book.

The THREES

The Three Accusers of Socrates

When Socrates was tried in Athens in 399 B.C. for impiety and for corrupting the youth, the formal charges were brought against him by three accusers:

1. Anytus
2. Lycon
3. Meletus

The lead prosecutor was Meletus, who, as the son of a tragic playwright, was supposedly offended by Socrates' criticisms of poets.

Three Advantages of Soldiering

In his sixteenth *Satire* Juvenal notes three advantages enjoyed by soldiers. He undoubtedly enumerated more than three, but the text of the satire is fragmentary. The three advantages are as follows:

1. Soldiers are immune to civilian punishments and, conversely, no civilian could reasonably expect to prosecute a soldier because the trial would be held under the auspices of a military court, with an army officer presiding.
2. If a soldier brings suit in a civilian court, he is not subject to the innumerable delays that beset a civilian litigant.
3. A soldier is permitted to draw up a will while his father is still alive, a privilege denied to civilians.

Three Archimedean Inventions

When the city of Syracuse was under siege by the Romans (211 B.C.), the noted engineer Archimedes reportedly invented several devices for the city's defense (and he once told Hieron, the tyrant of Syracuse, that if given a fulcrum and a place to stand, he could move the entire world). The three devices were

1. A winch whereby the Roman ships were lifted out of the water, dragged ashore, and raised up to the tops of the city walls, whereupon they were then sent careening into the sea below.

2. A catapult that could launch a boulder the size of a wagon. A number of Roman ships were sunk by means of this device.

3. A system of mirrors of various sizes and set at various angles that would concentrate the sun's rays onto the ships anchored in the harbor and incinerate them. Many scholars doubt, however, that this invention could have worked in the manner described.

The Three Architectural Marvels of Samos

According to the historian Herodotus (3.60), the island of Samos was noted for three remarkable architectural and engineering feats:

1. A tunnel nearly one mile in length, cut through a hill 900 feet high
2. A harbor enclosed by a break- water, to a length of over one-quarter of a mile
3. The largest of all known Greek temples

Nineteenth-century archaeologists discovered that the tunnel was actually only about one-half mile long, and that it contained an oddity not mentioned by Herodotus: a kink in the middle. Apparently, the tunnel was constructed by two crews of workers digging toward one another from opposite sides of the hill. When each crew reached the midpoint of the hill, they were embarrassed to find that one horizontal passageway was some 20 feet higher than the other. To rectify the error, they dug a vertical shaft connecting the two horizontal passageways.

Three Athenian Gymnasia

A gymnasium, a word that derives from the Greek adjective *gymnos* (naked), was a rectangular building constructed primarily for the use of athletes, who habitually exercised in the nude. Eventually, however, gymnasia evolved into multipurpose buildings, analogous to modern-day community centers, where nonathletes could also gather to socialize, debate, and study. Famous philosophers, such as Plato and Aristotle, became associated with the Academy and the Lyceum respectively, two of Athens's gymnasia. The third Athenian gymnasium of note was called the Cynosarges.

The Three Boasts of Favorinus

The philosopher Favorinus (ca. A.D. 80–150) wrote about 30 books, including two lengthy encyclopedic works, *Memoirs* and *Miscellaneous History* (neither extant). He boasted of three unusual accomplishments:

1. Although impotent, he was once accused of adultery
2. Although born in Gaul, he spoke and wrote fluent Greek
3. Although he sometimes offended the emperor (Hadrian), he survived and even flourished

The Three Books of Varro's De Re Rustica

The scholarly antiquarian Marcus Terentius Varro (116–27 B.C.) reputedly wrote more than 600 books, but of these only his *De Re Rustica*, on agriculture, and his *De Lingua Latina*, on the Latin language, survive. The three books of the *De Re Rustica* are

Book I. Introduction; a catalogue of literary sources; general comments on agriculture, cast in dialogue form: soils; vineyards; land surveying; placement of farm buildings; use of slave labor; farm animals; planting methods; fertilizer application; and the seasons, about which Varro asserts the following:

Season	Starting point	Duration
Spring	February 7	91 days
Summer	May 9	94 days
Autumn	August 11	91 days
Winter	November 10	89 days

Book II. Raising of livestock: prices; breeding methods; pasturing and feeding; veterinary practices; and appropriate sizes of herds. Animals considered include cattle, sheep, and goats.

Book III. Financial matters (for example, costs and profitability of farming); fish ponds and hatcheries (Varro cites the case of a certain Gaius Lucilius Hirrus, who sold his farm for 4 million sesterces, its value enhanced by its well-stocked fish ponds); beekeeping (two brothers named Veianius reportedly made 10,000 sesterces annually from honey sales); and aviaries (a certain Marcus Aufidius Lurco was said to have netted 60,000 sesterces annually from raising and selling peacocks). Also considered were the raising of ducks, geese, pigeons, and turtle doves.

Varro's other extant work, *De Lingua Latina*, originally contained 25 books; but only six survive. In these six books he discusses topics such as etymologies, vocabulary, and strange or rarely used words.

The Three Capes of Sicily

The three-cornered island of Sicily had a like number of capes:

1. Pelorias (northeastern Sicily)
2. Pachynus (southeastern Sicily)
3. Lilybaeum (western Sicily)

The Three Chief Cities of Crete

According to the geographer Strabo (10.7), the three principal Cretan cities were

1. Cnossus
2. Gortyna
3. Cydonia

The Three Column Styles

Most Greek and Roman civic and religious structures featured roofs supported by rows of stone columns. These columns were of three basic styles, differentiated by the designs at their topmost points:

1. Doric—column capitals with squared blocks of stone
2. Ionic—column capitals with spiral, volute designs
3. Corinthian—ornate column capitals, featuring acanthus leaf designs

The Three Contestants for the Golden Apple

The goddess of discord, Eris, had been omitted from the guest list for the wedding of Peleus and Thetis. In revenge, she hurled a golden apple, inscribed with the words "For the fairest," into the midst of the wedding guests. Three of the most prominent goddesses each assumed that the apple was meant for her. They were

1. Aphrodite
2. Athena
3. Hera

The ensuing quarrel was finally arbitrated by Paris, a Trojan prince, whose famous judgment tapped Aphrodite as the most worthy of the apple.

The Three-Course Roman Dinner

A formal Roman dinner usually consisted of these three courses:

1. *Gustatio*, the appetizer, consisting of olives, sausages, cheese, salad, eggs, dormice, and pomegranates
2. *Ferculum*, the main course, featuring one or more of the following: roast boar, sow, or hog; peacock; hare; various kinds of fish; sausages; bearmeat; and bread
3. *Mensa secunda*, dessert, which might include cakes of various kinds, fruits such as apples or grapes; and pastries

The Three Delphic Maxims

An uncertain number of maxims were carved into the columns and other portions of Apollo's temple at Delphi. However, three of these sayings—often attributed to the Seven Sages—have achieved lasting fame:

1. "Know thyself"
2. "Nothing in excess"
3. "Be a guarantor for debts, and ruin is at hand"

The Three Extant Speeches of Aeschines

Aeschines (393–322 B.C.), a Greek orator and rival of Demosthenes, has to his credit three surviving speeches:

1. *Against Timarchus* (345)
2. *On the False Embassy* (343)
3. *Against Ctesiphon* (330)

The third speech was an invective directed against Demosthenes, whose friend Ctesiphon had proposed that Demosthenes be awarded a golden crown for his many years of service to Athens. Demosthenes' response (*On the Crown*) criticized Aeschines and his speech; the jury voted so overwhelmingly in Demosthenes' favor that Aeschines was fined (for his failure to garner the minimum 20 percent necessary to avoid the fine). Aeschines subsequently moved to Rhodes, where he spent the remainder of his life.

He once gave an encore performance of his *Against Ctesiphon* for the Rhodians, whereupon they marveled that he did not prevail against his famed opponent. "You would not be surprised," replied Aeschines, "if you had heard Demosthenes."

The Three Extant Speeches of Andocides

The three surviving speeches of the Athenian orator Andocides (ca.440–390 B.C.) are

1. *On His Return* (407), in which he sought to be permitted to return to Athens from a period of self-imposed exile
2. *On the Mysteries* (399), in which he defended himself against a charge of profaning the Eleusinian Mysteries
3. *On the Peace* (392), in which he argued that Athens should conclude a peace treaty with Sparta

A speech attacking the flamboyant Athenian statesman Alcibiades has in the past been attributed to Andocides, but it is now thought that the oration— *Against Alcibiades*—was the work of another (unknown) orator.

The Three Extant Speeches of Dinarchus

The orator Dinarchus (360–after 292 B.C.) is said by Dionysius of Halicarnassus (*Dinarchus* 10–12) to have written more than 60 speeches; only three still survive, along with three generally thought to have been the work of others. Dinarchus's three speeches all pertain to the Harpalus affair, an unseemly incident in which Demosthenes, Aristogiton, and Philocles were all accused of accepting bribes from Harpalus, a dishonest financial official once in the employ of Alexander the Great; Harpalus had sought asylum in Athens, and the bribes he allegedly offered were designed to sway some of Athens's leading politicians and orators, possibly to defend his case. All three of Dinarchus's speeches were probably heard in 323:

1. *Against Demosthenes*
2. *Against Aristogiton*
3. *Against Philocles*

The Three Fates

The three elderly women charged with the responsibility of determining the fates and life spans for all humanity were

1. Clotho, who spins the thread of each person's life
2. Lachesis, who measures the length of the thread
3. Atropos, who cuts the thread, thereby terminating life

The Three Furies

The three Furies (also called Eumenides or Erinyes), avenging deities, played a prominent role in Aeschylus's play *Eumenides*. The three Furies were

1. Alecto (Unresting)
2. Megaera (Jealous)
3. Tisiphone (Avenger)

The Three Golden Apples

The swift runner Atalanta vowed to marry any man who could defeat her in a foot race; prospective husbands who tried and failed were executed. The suitor Hippomenes finally won her hand in marriage by dropping golden apples, three in number, at various points during the race. Atalanta's costly mistake was in stopping briefly to gather up each apple, thereby causing her to lose the contest.

The Three Gorgons

The Gorgons—hideous beasts with snakes in place of hair, gilded wings and invincible, scaly bodies—could turn to stone any mortal foolish enough to gaze upon them. Of the three, Medusa is the best known; Perseus lopped off her head by looking at her reflection in his highly polished shield as he did the deed. The three Gorgons were

1. Euryale
2. Medusa
3. Sthen(n)o

The Three Graces

These three young and beautiful goddesses, daughters of Zeus (according to some sources), were often portrayed as attendants of Aphrodite. Their names were

1. Aglaia
2. Euphrosyne
3. Thalia

The Three Harpies

The Harpies were vicious, foul-smelling hybrid monsters, half female human, half vulture, who specialized in torment and harassment. Among their victims were Phineus and Aeneas. They are usually considered three in number (but only one, according to Homer; two, according to Hesiod). Their names were

1. Aello
2. Celaeno
3. Ocypete

The Three-Headed Dog
The entrance to the Underworld was guarded by a three-headed dog, the fierce Cerberus.

The Three Historical Works of Sallust
Gaius Sallustius Crispus (Sallust, 86–34 B.C.) wrote historical accounts of the war against Jugurtha (*Bellum Jugurthinum*), the Catilinarian conspiracy (*Bellum Catilinae*), and the period 78–67 B.C. (*Historiae*). The first two monographs survive intact, the third in fragmentary form.

Sallust's treatise on Catiline, perhaps his most well-known work, is divided into 61 books:

Books I–XIX.	Introductory, including a description of Catiline's character, and a brief survey of Roman history.
Books XX–XLIV.	The unfolding of Catiline's scheme, with all its ramifications.
Books XLV–LV.	The arrest of five of Catiline's coconspirators; the debate over the appropriate punishment; and their execution.
Books LVI–LXI.	The maneuverings of Catiline's army; their defeat; and his death.

Before turning to the writing of history, Sallust made his living as a politician and orator; he also had a brief stint as one of Julius Caesar's generals during the civil war that erupted in 49 B.C. He assisted in the prosecution of Titus Annius Milo (defended by Cicero, 52 B.C.); according to Aulus Gellius (17.18, quoting Varro), a revenge motive spurred his involvement in this case: some time before he had been discovered *in flagrante* with Milo's wife, whereupon Milo publicly horse-whipped him for his adulterous behavior and, in addition, laid a heavy fine upon him.

The Three Iambic Poets of the Canon
The Alexandrian scholars ranked the following iambic poets as the best:

1. Archilochus (eighth century B.C.?)
2. Hipponax (sixth century B.C.)
3. Semonides (seventh century B.C.)

The Three Judges of the Underworld
The three judges of Hades were appointed to their posts upon their deaths by Zeus, who was impressed with the integrity with which they had conducted their lives. The three judges were

1. Aeacus
2. Minos
3. Rhadamanthus

Socrates, in his defense at his trial in 399 B.C. (Plato *Apology* 41), mentions a fourth judge, Triptolemus, but his name does not appear elsewhere as a judge.

The Law of Three Children
In order to encourage the proliferation of Roman families with children, a law (the *Lex Julia et Papia Poppaea*) was enacted in A.D. 9 at the behest of the emperor Augustus; this law bestowed special benefits upon married fathers of three or more children. The chief perquisite was the opportunity for more rapid career advancement in government posts.

Sometimes beneficent emperors conferred the status of "three children" on loyal, if childless, government servants, as Trajan did with Pliny the Younger.

The Three Long Walls
With the development of Athens's port cities of Piraeus and Phalerum in the fifth century B.C., it was decided that Athenian access to them should be protected by the construction of two parallel walls extending from Athens to the ports, a distance of about six miles. The walls were built between 461 and 456 B.C.; a third one was added a few years later, at the behest of Pericles.

The Three Parts of a Bath
The great Roman bathing establishments featured pools with three different water temperatures:

1. Tepidarium (lukewarm water)   3. Frigidarium (cold)
2. Caldarium (hot)

A bather generally paid a visit to all three pools, beginning with the tepidarium, and then on to the caldarium, before concluding the routine with a dip in the frigidarium.

The Three Parts of Caesar's Gaul
Gallia est omnis divisa in partes tres—"all Gaul is divided into three parts"—is one of the most well-known opening lines in the history of classical literature. It appears in Julius Caesar's account of the Gallic Wars, written probably in 52 and 51 B.C. The three parts of Gaul in Caesar's time were

1. Aquitania (southwestern Gaul)   3. Belgica (northeastern Gaul)
2. Celtica (central Gaul)

Later, Caesar's successor, Augustus, redivided Gaul into four parts:

1. Aquitania (western and central   3. Lugdunensis (northwestern
   Gaul)   Gaul)
2. Belgica (northeastern Gaul)   4. Narbonensis (southern Gaul)

The Three Periods of Greek Comedy

Ancient Greek comedy has been classified on stylistic and chronological grounds into the following three categories:

1. Old Comedy (fifth century B.C.). The plays written in this period often involved satirical commentary on political and public issues, as well as prominent components of both verbal and visual humor, frequently scatological in nature. The chief writers of Old Comedy were Aristophanes, Cratinus, Eupolis, and Pherecrates. Of the last three, nothing survives. Nine of Aristophanes' 11 extant plays are generally considered to have fallen within this period.

2. Middle Comedy (ca.400–323 B.C.). The political satire began to disappear, replaced by plays involving stock characters and themes drawn from daily life. The chief writers were Alexis, Antiphanes, and Eubulus. None of their plays survives. Two Aristophanic plays, *Ecclesiazusae* and *Plutus*, are thought to be representative of Middle Comedy.

3. New Comedy (ca.322–263 B.C.). Political satire almost completely vanished with New Comedy plays; instead, the action (usually set in Athens) involved events from family life, often drawing for subject matter upon love triangles, long-lost children, and unrequited love. The chief writers were Diphilus, Menander, and Philemon. No New Comedies survive completely intact, although significant portions of several of Menander's plays have come to light.

The Three Punic Wars

In the third and second centuries B.C. the Romans fought three bitter and destructive wars against the North African city-state of Carthage. The second of these involved the wily and intractable Carthaginian general Hannibal who, on several occasions, came very close to destroying his Roman opponents. (The term Punic comes from the Latin word for Carthaginian, *Punicus*.) The length of the first two wars resulted in several command changes. In each instance the leading generals are listed. The three Punic Wars were as follows:

Number	Dates	Roman commander	Carthaginian commander	Won by
First	264–241	G. Lutatius Catulus	Hamilcar Barca	Rome
Second	218–201	P. Cornelius Scipio	Hannibal	Rome
Third	149–146	Scipio Aemilianus	Hasdrubal	Rome

The Three Reference Points on the Roman Calendar

Each of the 12 Roman months contained three reference points, called the Kalends (first day), the Nones (fifth or seventh day), and the Ides (thirteenth or fifteenth). Specific calendar dates were referred to by counting forward, inclusively, to the next reference point. For example, December 25 was known to the Romans as the "eighth day before the Kalends of January."

In the months of March, May, July, and October the Nones fell on the seventh, the Ides on the fifteenth; hence, Julius Caesar's fateful day, the "Ides of March," was March 15. In the other eight months the Nones arrived on the fifth and the Ides on the thirteenth.

Three Remarkable Roman Construction Achievements

Dionysius of Halicarnassus considered the following three works to be the greatest Roman engineering achievements:

1. The aqueducts
2. The paved roads
3. The sewer system

Three for Rome versus Three for Alba Longa

When the Romans and the residents of Alba Longa were locked in an indecisive struggle for control of Alba Longa (during the reign of Rome's third king, Tullus Hostilius, 671–642 B.C.), the two sides agreed that the issue ought to be decided by a combat of three Roman youths against a like number of Albans. It so happened that an Alban man named Sicinius had fathered twin daughters; one daughter married Horatius, a Roman, while the other wedded an Alban, Curiatius. Each daughter subsequently bore triplets, six boys in all. These six were to be the combatants.

One by one each brother fell, until the final surviving Roman triumphed. But even in his hour of glory, he was not destined to have a happy outcome, for his sister had been betrothed to one of the fallen Curiatii. When she angrily reproached her brother for slaying a kinsman, she too felt the wrath of his lance, and so died.

The Three Sacred Wars

The league of tribes connected with the veneration of Apollo's temple at Delphi (the Amphictyonic Council) declared three wars against its members for various acts of disrespect toward Apollo. The three Sacred Wars were as follows:

Number/date	Chief participants
First Sacred War/ca. 590 B.C.	Thessaly, Sicyon, and Athens against Cirrha.
Second Sacred War/ca. 448 B.C.	Sparta against the Phocians; afterward Athens against Sparta.
Third Sacred War/355–347 B.C.	Phocia against the Locrians and the Boeotians. Eventually, many polises and coalitions were drawn into this conflict, including Athens, Sparta, Achaea, the Thessalians, and the Macedonians.

The Three Sirens

The mythical creatures whose song no man could resist are generally considered to be three in number:

1. Leucosia   3. Parthenope
2. Ligeia

Three Statistics on the Harbor at Ostia

Rome's port city of Ostia had two artificial harbors; the larger was constructed during the reign of Emperor Claudius (A.D. 41–54). Some statistics pertaining to Ostia's larger harbor:

1. It enclosed an area of 850,000 square yards upon its completion.
2. In A.D. 62 some 200 ships at anchor were destroyed during a storm. Part of the reason for the large-scale destruction was that the harbor was poorly protected from strong ocean winds.
3. To remedy this problem of poor protection, the emperor Trajan in A.D. 104 rebuilt Ostia's harbor in the shape of a well-fortified hexagon. Numbered docking areas, corresponding to on-shore warehouses, provided incoming ships with an organized system for discharging cargoes.

Triremes

The standard Greek warship, a trireme featured three rows or banks of oars, although the exact arrangement of oars and rowers is uncertain. A trireme was usually a little over 100 feet in length, and carried a crew of about 200 rowers, sailors, and marines.

Triumvirates

There were two notable triumvirates (associations of three men) in first-century Rome. The first of these, formed in 60 B.C., was an informal political alliance consisting of Julius Caesar, Gnaeus Pompeius Magnus (Pompey the Great), and Marcus Licinius Crassus. The so-called First Triumvirate officially ended in 53 B.C. with the death of Crassus, although relations among the three men were always tenuous.

The Second Triumvirate, organized in 43 B.C., was legally constituted with wide-ranging powers to enact legislation and nominate candidates for magistracies. The members of the second triumvirate were Mark Antony, Marcus Aemilius Lepidus, and Gaius Julius Caesar Octavianus (Octavian, later given the title Augustus).

The FOURS

The Four Ages of Mankind

Many writers, ancient and modern, claim to see a gradual decline or degeneration in the human race as time passes. The Greek and Roman mythographers were no exception; they identified four ages of mankind:

1. The Golden Age, a utopian period when humans lived in harmony with the gods
2. The Silver Age, worse than the Golden, when mortals became arrogant and disrespectful toward the gods
3. The Bronze Age, worse still than the Silver, in which people clashed and fought constantly
4. The Iron Age, the worst of all, in which mortals lived lives of ceaseless labor, a time of strife and alienation from the gods

The poet Hesiod (eighth century B.C.) inserted an Age of Heroes between the Bronze and Iron Ages.

The Four Apollonii

There were at least four writers sharing the name Apollonius, the most noted of whom is probably Apollonius of Rhodes:

Name / approximate dates	Noted for
1. Apollonius of Rhodes / 295–215 B.C.	*Argonautica*, the tale of Jason and the Argonauts
2. Apollonius of Perga / third century B.C.	Mathematical studies, especially in geometry
3. Apollonius Molon / first century B.C.	Rhetorical treatises; he gained fame as an orator, and as a teacher of both Cicero and Caesar
4. Apollonius of Tyana / first century A.D.	A fragmentary treatise on sacrifices

The Four Books of Propertius's Elegies

The Roman poet Sextus Propertius (ca. 50–16 B.C.) wrote four books of elegaics containing a total of 92 poems); much of his work was inspired by his passion for Cynthia, perhaps a real woman, perhaps a figment of his literary imagination.

Book number/number of poems	Representative sample
Book I/22 poems	Propertius laments his separation from Cynthia, who is enjoying herself at the resort town of Baiae (1.11).
Book II/34 poems	He pledges endless fidelity to Cynthia (2.20).
Book III/25 poems	He envisions attending an Augustan triumphal procession with Cynthia (3.5).
Book IV/11 poems	In the guise of a travel guide, he surveys several early Roman legends (4.10).

The Four Categories of the Works of Seneca the Younger

Lucius Annaeus Seneca (Seneca the Younger; 4 B.C.–A.D. 65), a prolific writer, and tutor of the emperor Nero, produced a wide variety of literary works.

Category I: Ten philosophical treatises (*Dialogi*, or *Dialogues*), and three moral essays.

The ten dialogues are

1. *On Providence*
2. *On the Constancy of a Wise Man*
3. *On Anger*
4. *Consolation to Marcia*
5. *On the Happy Life*
6. *On Leisure*
7. *On the Tranquillity of the Mind*
8. *On the Shortness of Life*
9. *Consolation to Polybius*
10. *Consolation to Helvia, his Mother*

The three moral essays are

1. *On Clemency*
2. *On Benefits*
3. *Moral Epistles*

The latter is a collection of 124 letters, all addressed to Seneca's friend Lucilius. The topics are many and varied—such as using time wisely; the advantages of mental training over physical; retirement; fearing the worst, or the unlikely; and festivals. Many letters deal with facets of Seneca's stoic philosophical principles.

Category II: *Naturales Quaestiones*, or *Natural Questions*, on natural phenomena, in seven books; with a summary of their contents, are

Book I.   On lights, or fire, in the sky: comets and shooting stars; halos; and rainbows. Properties of mirrors.
Book II.   The three divisions of the study of the universe: 1. astronomy; 2. meteorology; and 3. geography. Lightning and thunder.

Book III.   The earth's waters: rivers, underground springs, oceans and seas, and hot springs. The circumstances under which a catastrophic flood might destroy the world.

Book IV.   The Nile River. Hail and snow.

Book V.   Definition, origins, and descriptions of winds.

Book VI.   Numerous theories on the causes of earthquakes. (Seneca believed that earthquakes occurred when rapidly moving air was forced into fissures in the earth, leading to underground confinement. There the air raged and shook the earth's surface, until it could create an outlet for itself, thus terminating the earthquake.)

Book VII. The nature and origins of comets.

Category III: Nine tragic plays, most based on Euripidean or Sophoclean models:

1. *Agamemnon*
2. *Hercules Insane*
3. *Hercules Oetaeus*
4. *Medea*
5. *Oedipus*
6. *Phaedra (Hippolytus)*
7. *Phoenician Women*
8. *Thyestes*
9. *Trojan Women*

A tenth play, *Octavia* (concerning Nero's divorcing of Octavia in A.D. 62), is sometimes ascribed to Seneca.

Category IV: *Apocolocyntosis*, or *Pumpkinification*, a satire on the deification of the emperor Claudius.

Seneca's father, known as Seneca the Elder (55 B.C.–ca. A.D. 41) was also a noted writer. Of his many works, only two rhetorical treatises survive: *Controversiae*, or *Debates*, in ten books, and *Suasoriae*, or *Argumentation*, in two books.

The Four Children of Agamemnon and Clytemnestra

The Mycenean warlord Agamemnon, leader of the Greek forces at Troy, and his wife, Clytemnestra, had four children, three daughters and one son:

1. Chrysothemis
2. Iphigenia
3. Electra
4. Orestes (the one son)

This family's deeds (and misdeeds) form the basis for numerous myths, legends, tragic dramas, and poems. According to one myth, Agamemnon sacrificed Iphigenia to placate the goddess Artemis, who had delayed his fleet's voyage to Troy by sending contrary winds.

The Four Children of Oedipus and Jocasta

Oedipus, the tragic figure who unwittingly killed his father and married his mother, Jocasta, fathered two sons and two daughters by way of this incestuous union. They were

1. Eteocles
2. Polynices
3. Antigone
4. Ismene

The Four Crown Festivals

Of the hundreds of athletic festivals held annually in ancient Greece, four eventually emerged as the most popular and prestigious. They were called "crown festivals" because the only reward offered to winners was a leaf crown; most of the other Greek athletic events presented cash awards or other valuable prizes to victorious athletes.

Name/approximate date of founding	Location	Biennial, quadrennial
1. Isthmian games/581 B.C.	Corinth	Biennial
2. Nemean games/573 B.C.	Nemea (on the Peloponnesus)	Biennial
3. Olympic games/776 B.C.	Olympia (on the Peloponnesus	Quadrennial
4. Pythian games/582 B.C.	Delphi	Quadrennial

The Four Elegaic Poets of the Canon

The four best elegaic poets, according to the Alexandrian scholars, were

1. Callimachus (ca.310–240 B.C.)
2. Callinus (seventh century B.C.)
3. Mimnermus (seventh century B.C.)
4. Philetas (born ca.320 B.C.)

The Four Elements of the Universe

In the mid–fifth century B.C. the Greek philosopher Empedocles suggested that the universe was composed of the following four basic elements:

1. Earth
2. Air
3. Fire
4. Water

The Four Emperors in One Year

The year A.D. 69 was a particularly chaotic one in the history of the Roman Empire, with an ongoing civil war replete with frequent coups d'état. Since four men ruled in 69, the year is commonly known as the year of the four emperors.

1. Servius Sulpicius Galba (ruled from June 68 to January 69)
2. Marcus Salvius Otho (ruled from January to April)
3. Aulus Vitellius (ruled from April to December)
4. Titus Flavius Vespasianus (commonly called Vespasian; ruled from December 69 to 79)

A six-emperor year occurred in A.D. 238, when Maximinus, Gordian I, Gordian II, Pupienus Maximus, Balbinus, and Gordian III all had a share of imperial power. Gordian I was proclaimed emperor at age 83, after the death of Maximinus; he named his son Gordian II as coregent. When the son died in battle, Gordian I committed suicide; his reign lasted less than a month. They were succeeded by the coregents Pupienus and Balbinus, who were both assassinated soon after the demise of Gordian I. Gordian III, grandson of Gordian I, became, at age 13, the sixth emperor of the year.

The Four Factions

Roman charioteers were organized into teams called factions. Faction owners supplied horses, chariots, and all other equipment necessary for the races. Originally, there were only two factions, the Red and the White. Sometime in the first century B.C., however, the numbers were increased to four by the addition of the Green and the Blue factions. During the reign of the emperor Domitian (A.D. 81–96), two more factions were added, the Purple and the Gold, but these two vanished shortly after Domitian's death.

The Four Horses of the Sun God

According to Greek mythology, the sun made its way across the sky each day courtesy of the pulling power of four powerful horses, trained and driven by the sun god, Helios. The sun god's four horses were called

1. Pyrois
2. Eous
3. Aethon
4. Phlegon

The Four Humors

Ancient Greek physicians believed that the human body was composed of four elements called humors, and that a proper balance of these humors was necessary for the maintenance of good health. The four humors were

1. Blood
2. Air (or phlegm)
3. Yellow bile
4. Black bile

Four Julias of Note

At least four noted Roman women shared the name Julia:

1. The sister of Julius Caesar, and grandmother of the future emperor, Augustus.
2. Julius Caesar's daughter, who was briefly (59–54 B.C.) married to Pompey, a marriage arranged to strengthen the political ties between her father and her husband.
3. Augustus's daughter, whose lascivious behavior and lifestyle deeply disappointed her father. Ultimately, he exiled her.
4. Augustus's granddaughter, who also incurred his wrath because of her loose morals.

So profound was the estrangement between Augustus and both Julias that he forbade either to be buried in the family mausoleum.

Four Jumping-Off Points to Britain

According to Strabo (4.5), those wishing to journey from mainland Europe to Britain generally selected one of four points of departure, all at the mouths of rivers (and all located in modern-day France or Germany). These four rivers are

1. The Rhine
2. The Sequana
3. The Liger
4. The Garumna

Four Legs, Two Legs, and Three Legs

Perhaps the ancient world's most famous riddle — what walks on four legs in the morning, two at midday, and three in the evening? — was posed by the fearsome Sphinx to residents of Thebes; it devoured any who could not answer. The tragically flawed Oedipus saved himself and the city by providing the correct response: a human being (who crawls on all fours as an infant, walks upright as an adult, and requires the assistance of a cane in old age).

The Four Macedonian Wars

The Romans fought a series of four wars against the Macedonians, mostly brought on by unrest in Greece and the adventurism of several Macedonian kings.

Number	Dates	Roman commander	Macedonian commander	Victor
First	214–205 B.C.	Valerius Laevinus	Philip V	Inconclusive
Second	200–197 B.C.	T. Quinctius Flamininus	Philip V	Rome
Third	171–168 B.C.	L. Aemilius Paulus	Perseus	Rome
Fourth	150–148 B.C.	Q. Caecilius Metellus	Andriscus	Rome

The Four Philostrati

There were four noted Greek authors, probably from the same family, and all bearing the name Philostratus.

Name/approximate dates	Noted work(s)
1. Verus Philostratus/ second century A.D.	None extant
2. Flavius Philostratus/ca. A.D. 170–249	*Life of Apollonius of Tyana; Lives of the Sophists*
3. Philostratus of Lemnos/ born ca. A.D. 190	*Eikones* (*Images*), a discussion/description of 65 wall paintings
4. Philostratus the Younger/third century A.D.	*Eikones*, descriptions of 17 wall paintings

It is thought that Flavius Philostratus was the son of Verus and the father-in-law of Philostratus of Lemnos; and that Philostratus the Younger was the grandson of Philostratus of Lemnos.

Four Requirements for a Successful Dinner Party

The success of a dinner party, so says Varro (quoted by Aulus Gellius 13.11), depends upon the fulfillment of four criteria:

1. A congenial group of guests
2. An appropriate place
3. A convenient time
4. Appropriate preparations (which apparently refers to items such as the furniture, the menu, and the serving dishes)

Four Sacred Caves

Occasionally, caves appear in literature and mythology as sacred sanctuaries. Four of the most famous are as follows:

1. The cave of Zeus, in Crete (on Mount Dicte), thought by some to have been his birthplace.

2. The Cave of Trophonius, in northern Boeotia, the site of an underground oracle. (The procedure for consulting this oracle is described in some detail by Pausanias [Book IX]).

3. The Corcyrian Cave on Mount Parnassus, near Delphi, thought to be sacred to Pan and the nymphs.

4. The Cave of the Lupercalians, on the Palatine Hill in Rome, where the religious rites of the Lupercalian celebrants were conducted each February 15.

Four Ways to Make Money

Cato the Elder was once asked about the best way for a family to prosper. He replied:

1. Graze the cattle well
2. Graze them pretty well
3. Graze them badly
4. Start plowing

The FIVES

The Five Amazon Queens

The Amazons were a race of fierce female warriors who lived in the Black Sea region. Many well-known mythological characters did battle with them, including Hercules, Perseus, and Theseus. The word Amazon means "no breast" in Greek, from the custom of these women of excising their right breasts, to facilitate the shooting of a bow. Five of their most famous queens were

1. Antiope (possibly the same as Hippolyta, or possibly her sister)
2. Hippolyta (Hercules' Ninth Labor was to obtain Hippolyta's girdle)
3. Lampeto
4. Marpesia
5. Penthesilea

The Five Books Extant of Polybius's Histories

The historian Polybius (ca. 200–after 118 B.C.) authored a lengthy compendium of Roman and Greek history. Of the 40 books originally contained in this treatise, only the following five have survived intact. These are listed below, along with a summary of their contents:

Book I.   Introduction; First Punic War (264–241 B.C.).
Book II.   The years (238–220 B.C.) between the First and Second Punic wars.
Book III.   Events of the Second Punic War to the Battle of Cannae (216 B.C.).
Book IV.   Events in Greece 220–216 B.C.
Book V.   A continuation of the topics begun in Book IV.

Portions of several other books are extant, including Book VI, which contains Polybius's well-known laudatory essay on the Roman constitution, as well as a lengthy survey of the tactics and organization of the Roman army in the second century B.C.

The Five Books of Statius's Silvae

Publius Papinius Statius (ca. A.D. 40–95) wrote a collection of five books (containing a total of 32 poems) entitled *Silvae*, addressed to various friends.

27

Book number/ number of poems	Dedicated to	Representative sample
Book I/ 6 poems	Stella	A description of the celebration of the Saturnalian Festival (1.6).
Book II/ 7 poems	Melior	A consolation addressed to Melior on the death of his talking parrot (2.4).
Book III/ 5 poems	Pollius	A poem addressed to his wife Claudia, whom he tries to persuade to return with him from Rome to Naples for their retirement years (3.5).
Book IV/ 9 poems	Marcellus	The building of a new coastal road to Naples (4.3).
Book V/ 5 poems	Abascantus	Several poems dealing with losses of family members, including a consolation to Abascantus on the death of his wife (5.1).

Statius also wrote *Thebaid*, a 12-book epic poem on the Seven against Thebes, and a fragmentary work *Achilleid*, on Achilles' early life and his conscription into the force to be sent to Troy.

The Five Categories of Aristotle's Works

To synopsize, or even to categorize, the extant writings of Aristotle (384–322 B.C.) is a task of herculean proportions. Several different classification systems may be employed; perhaps the most practical grouping is by subject matter, as follows:

1. Logic
2. Metaphysics
3. Natural science
4. Ethics and political science
5. Literature

Category I: Treatises on logic and reasoning

1. *Categories*
2. *On Interpretation*
3. *Prior Analytics*
4. *Posterior Analytics*
5. *Topics*
6. *Sophistical Refutations*

These six works are generally grouped together under the title *Organon* (*Instrument*, or *Tool*).

Category II: Metaphysical treatise

Aristotle's treatise entitled *Metaphysics* (the lone entry in this category) is divided into 14 books. It covers topics such as the definition, problems, and scope of metaphysics; truth; reality; ontological questions; form and substance; the potential and the actual; and mathematics and number theories.

Category III: Treatises on natural science, especially biology

1. *Physics*
2. *On the Heavens*
3. *On Coming to Be and Passing Away*
4. *Meteorological Phenomena*
5. *Inquiry into Animals*
6. *Parts of Animals*
7. *Movement of Animals*
8. *Progression of Animals*
9. *Generation of Animals*
10. *On the Soul*
11. *Parva Naturalia*, or *Short Essays on Natural History*

The most significant work in this category is perhaps the *Inquiry into Animals*, in which Aristotle's notions on matters of taxonomy are presented in compelling detail. He also provides physical and anatomical descriptions of numerous species of mammals, birds, fish, and reptiles. *Inquiry into Animals* is divided into ten books, although some scholars consider the tenth book to be non–Aristotelean.

Category IV: Treatises on government, politics, ethics

1. *Nicomachean Ethics*
2. *Eudemian Ethics*
3. *Politics*

The *Politics* (apparently not fully extant), containing eight books, features discussions on topics such as the nature of the state; the family; slavery (which Aristotle conditionally defends); the origin of money; the various kinds of governments and constitutions, including those of Sparta, Crete, and Carthage; citizenship, revolutions; the best kind of state; and the nature and importance of education.

In Book IV Aristotle enumerates the three elements of government — legislative, executive, and judicial — a list that has a modern ring to it.

Category V: Treatises on poetry and rhetoric

1. *Rhetoric*
2. *Poetics*, which includes analyses and assessments of tragic and comic playwriting, as well as poetry per se. The *Poetics* stands as the earliest known classical treatise entirely on literary criticism.

Five Categories of Revolutionaries

In his second speech against Catiline (in November 63 B.C.), Cicero mentioned five categories of men most prone to join Catiline in the revolution he was plotting:

1. Debtors who owned large tracts of real estate, but who were unwilling to sell their lands to raise funds for debt liquidation.
2. Debtors who were awaiting a revolution in the hope that they could thereby gain control of the government and the legal machinery of the state.
3. Older men who may have been debt-free, but who remained active and robust, and who apparently hoped to profit through the anticipated proscriptions that a revolution would bring.

4. The fourth category consisted of slackers, people who had never been solvent or responsible citizens.

5. The lowest of the low: murderers, parricides, and violent criminals.

Coincidentally, five of Catiline's chief lieutenants had been captured, imprisoned and were awaiting their fate at the time that Cicero delivered his Catilinarian orations. (All five were executed for their complicity in the plot.) Their names were

1. Cassius
2. Cethegus
3. Gabinius
4. Lentulus
5. Statilius

The Five Closings of the Temple Gates

The open gates of the Temple of Janus indicated that the Romans were at war (the open gates symbolizing the departure of the army from the city). Prior to the time of Augustus, the gates had been closed—symbolizing peace—only twice in the 700-year history of Rome: once during the reign of King Numa (714–671 B.C.), and again at the conclusion of the First Punic War in 235 B.C. The emperor Augustus is said to have closed the gates three times during his reign: in 31 and 25 B.C., and a third time, date unknown.

The Five Days of the Ancient Olympics

The ancient Olympic games were celebrated over a period of five days. The specific events that occurred on each day are uncertain, but the schedule may have been something along these lines:

Day One: Sacrifices to Zeus and other religious ceremonies; administration of the Olympic oath.

Day Two: Chariot and horse races; pentathlon.

Day Three: Events for boys (contestants aged 18 and under): foot races, wrestling, and boxing.

Day Four: Events for men—foot races, wrestling, boxing, and pankration.

Day Five: Closing ceremonies; awarding of prizes; feasts and celebrations.

Five Difficult Questions

At the conclusion of his seventh *Satire*, Juvenal mocks zealous parents who demand omniscience of their children's teachers. These parents may accost a teacher at almost any time, even in a social setting, and bombard him with virtually unanswerable questions, such as:

1. Who was the nurse of Anchises?
2. What was the name of Anchemolus's stepmother?
3. What country was she from?

4. How many years did Acestes live?
5. How many jugs of Sicilian wine did Acestes give to the Trojans?

These questions, all based on various passages in the *Aeneid* and all designed to embarrass the teacher, cannot be answered with certainty. For example, Vergil suggests that Acestes (question 4) is *aevi maturus*, "advanced in years," but the poet does not provide a specific age. He also mentions that Acestes loaded wine onto the Trojan ships (question 5), but he does not state the quantity.

Juvenal concludes by noting that a teacher's annual pay would never exceed the amount that could be earned by a charioteer for winning a single race.

The Five Ephors

Several Greek cities, most notably Sparta, were governed by officials called ephors. In Sparta they were five in number, elected annually.

The Five Epic Poets of the Canon

The five best epic poets, according to Alexandrians, were

1. Antimachus (born ca.444 B.C.)
2. Hesiod (eighth century)
3. Homer (eighth century)
4. Panyas(s)is (fifth century)
5. Pisander (seventh or sixth century)

The Five Events of the Pentathlon

The ancient Greek athletic festivals featured an event called the pentathlon, consisting of five contests:

1. Discus throw
2. Javelin throw
3. Long jump
4. Foot race
5. Wrestling

The Five Good Emperors

After the occasionally turbulent times of the first century A.D., the Romans were fortunate to enjoy a respite in the second century, when they were ruled by five effective and just emperors in succession. The so-called five good emperors were

1. Nerva (reigned A.D. 96–98)
2. Trajan (A.D. 98–117)
3. Hadrian (A.D. 117–138)
4. Antoninus Pius (A.D. 138–161)
5. Marcus Aurelius (A.D.161–180)

The Five Hyades

In his infancy the god Dionysus was tended by five nurses called the

Hyades; later, Zeus transformed them into stars. The names of the five Hyades were

1. Bacche   4. Macris
2. Bromie   5. Nysa
3. Erato

Five Important Events in 63 B.C.

The year 63 B.C. was a momentous one in Roman history, to say the least. Many significant events occurred that year, including the following:

1. January: Marcus Tullius Cicero takes office as one of the consuls for the year.
2. Early in the year: Cicero defends the aged senator Gaius Rabirius Postumus against a charge that 37 years earlier he had been involved in the murder of a tribune. Although Cicero wins the case, the favorable publicity accruing to the instigator and prosecutor—Julius Caesar—would help to keep Caesar's name in the forefront of people's minds.
3. March: Julius Caesar is elected pontifex maximus (chief priest), the highest office in the Roman religious hierarchy.
4. September: The future emperor Gaius Octavius (later known as Augustus) is born.
5. November-December: Cicero delivers perhaps his most famous speeches, a series of four orations denouncing the frustrated office seeker and bankrupt aristocrat Catiline, who had organized an abortive conspiracy to overthrow the Roman government.

Five Liturgies

In fifth- and fourth-century (B.C.) Athens, the wealthier citizens were expected (and sometimes required) to make various kinds of contributions to the city, for the common welfare. These annual contributions were called liturgies; at least five different liturgies could be undertaken.

1. The trierarchy, in which the contributor financed the maintenance and repair of a trireme, at a cost of (according to the orator Lysias) 40–60 minas. About 400 Athenians (per year) served as trierarchs in the early stages of the Peloponnesian War.
2. The *choregia*, in which the contributor funded the production of a play.
3. The gymnasiarchy, in which the contributor paid for supplies and personnel connected with the administration of gymnasia (buildings primarily for athletes).
4. The presentation of a *hestiasis*, in which the contributor provided a dinner for the members of his tribe.
5. The *architheoria*, in which the contributor covered the costs associated with sending Athenian representatives to a foreign festival (for example, the Olympic games).

The burden of a liturgy fell upon Athenian citizens (and resident aliens, or *metics*) whose net worth exceeded three talents. If a citizen felt that he had been unfairly assigned a liturgy, he could take the matter to court. There he could challenge another citizen (whom he deemed more financially able) either to assume the liturgy in his place or to exchange properties with him. The process was called an *antidosis* ("exchange").

One of Lysias's surviving speeches (*Defense on a Charge of Bribetaking*) deals with an *antidosis*. The speech is particularly noteworthy in that the (unnamed) plaintiff begins by listing his previous benefactions to Athens, thus revealing that liturgies could become quite burdensome:

Liturgy (or similar obligation) / approximate date B.C.	Amount of money plaintiff spent to perform it
1. A tragic play / 410	3,000 drachmas
2. Another tragic play / 410	2,000 drachmas
3. A display of pyrrhic (war) dancers / 409	800 drachmas
4. A tragic play, plus the tripod commemorating the victory of the play in the dramatic competitions for the year / 409	5,000 drachmas
5. Cyclic (circular) chorus, for a ceremony probably connected with the god Dionysus / 408	300 drachmas
6. Outfitting warships, for seven years / dates not stated	36,000 drachmas
7. "Special levy" / not stated	3,000 drachmas
8. Another "special levy" / not stated	4,000 drachmas
9. Torch races / 405	1,200 drachmas
10. Chorus of children / not stated	1,500 + drachmas
11. A comic play / 404	1,600 drachmas
12. Pyrrhic dancers / 404	700 drachmas
13. Victorious warship in a boat race / not stated	1,500 drachmas
14. Ceremonial processions during the celebration of the Panathenaic festival / not stated	3,000 + drachmas
Total:	63,600 drachmas

The plaintiff states that the ships he outfitted were the best in the Athenian navy; as proof, he notes that Alcibiades—a man whose military instincts were of the highest order—chose to sail on one of the ships that he (the plaintiff) equipped. The plaintiff also claims that had he opted to interpret the law strictly, he would have been legally responsible for less than one-fourth of the expenses enumerated above. Finally, he notes that at the Battle of Aegospotami (405 B.C., in which the Spartans defeated the Athenians in the decisive battle of the

Peloponnesian War) only 12 warships escaped undamaged (of about 200, according to Plutarch [*Alcibiades* 37], who said eight escaped). Of those 12, the plantiff had outfitted two.

Five Neoteric Poets

In the first century B.C. in Rome there arose a literary movement that scorned traditional models of epic and drama, instead turning to new meters, themes, language, and style. Cicero sarcastically dubbed the practitioners of this movement *hoi neoteroi* ("the new ones," or "the moderns"). The term caught on, and survives to the present day. Five leading neoteric poets were

1. Gaius Valerius Catullus (84–54)

2. Gaius Licinius Calvus (82–47)

3. Gaius Helvius Cinna (died 44)

4. Marcus Furius Bibaculus (born 103)

5. Publius Valerius Cato (born 100)

Only Catullus's works survive to the present time, although there are fragments of poetry from several of the others.

The Five Plebeian Secessions

The first three centuries of the Roman Republic (founded 509 B.C.) were fraught with class struggles between the moneyed, influential families (patricians) and the masses (plebeians). One of the techniques used by the plebeians to gain concessions from the patricians involved a mass exodus, usually to some nearby location, or to the Aventine Hill; this was called a *secessio plebis*, or secession of the plebeians. The secessions generally succeeded, since the patricians needed plebeian soldiers to man the ranks of the army.

Five of these secessions are mentioned in the ancient sources, although some scholars doubt the historical authenticity of the first three.

1. 494 B.C.: The Roman Senate (composed exclusively of patricians at this time) had reneged on a promise to provide debt relief, thus precipitating the first secession. The plebeians returned when the patricians consented to the creation of five (later ten) tribunes to protect plebeian interests.

2. 449 B.C.: The plebeians, upset that the newly published law code (the Twelve Tables) did not sanction their legislative assemblies, retreated to the Aventine Hill until the patricians yielded on this issue.

3. 445 B.C.: In the third secession the plebeians demanded, and were granted, the right to intermarry with patricians.

4. 342 B.C.: The fourth secession, actually a military mutiny, occurred when plebeian troops became disenchanted with fighting a lengthy war (the First Samnite War) a great distance from Rome.

5. 287 B.C.: The fifth and final secession—to the Janiculum Hill— occurred in support of a plebeian demand that their plebiscites be considered legal and binding. The patricians acceded.

Dionysius of Halicarnassus (6.69), who covered the first secession in great detail, added that the patricians sent ten men to negotiate with the plebeians, including the following eight (the other two names having been lost):

1. Agrippa Menenius Lanatus
2. Manius Valerius
3. Publius Servilius
4. Publius Postumius Tubertus

5. Titus Aebutius Flavus
6. Servius Sulpicius Camerinus
7. Aulus Postumius Balbus
8. Aulus Verginius Caelimontanus

Five Price Tags for Expensive Roman Dinners

Wealthy Romans often entertained their dinner guests in grand style, as the following list suggests:

1. Seneca remarks that a newly appointed Roman priest might have to spend 1 million sesterces on a dinner commemorating the occasion.
2. Seneca also states that the emperor Caligula once spent 10 million sesterces on a single dinner.
3. A banquet given for 12 diners by Lucius Verus cost 6 million sesterces. Among the gifts given to the guests were one servant (each); platters, carvers, and live animals; crystal goblets; gold, silver, and bejeweled cups; golden perfume boxes; and carriages, with draft animals, and drivers.
4. The emperor Elagabalus (reigned A.D. 218–222) spent a minimum of 100,000 sesterces on the dinners he gave, and sometimes the bill ran as high as 3 million sesterces.
5. The first-century B.C. politician-general Lucius Licinius Lucullus never spent less than 200,000 sesterces on a formal dinner.

The Five Rivers of Hades

The boatman Charon ferried dead souls across the Underworld's most famous river, the Styx, the same river in which Achilles' mother, Thetis, dipped him to imbue him with invulnerability. The five rivers in Hades were

1. Acheron
2. Cocytus
3. Lethe

4. Phlegethon
5. Styx

The Five Spartoi

King Cadmus, the legendary founder of Thebes, killed a dragon sacred to the god Ares. Athena advised him to sow the dragon's teeth; when he did so, armed men sprang forth from the ground. These warriors fought one another, until only five survivors remained; these five, the *Spartoi* ("sown men"), became the progenitors of the Theban nobility. Pausanias and Apollodorus provide their names:

1. Chthlonius   4. Pelorus
2. Echion   5. Udaeus
3. Hyperenor

Pausanias (9.5) adds that Echion was the strongest of these, and hence considered a worthy son-in-law for Cadmus.

The Five Tragic Poets of the Canon

The Alexandrian scholars considered the five following tragic poets to be the best representatives of the genre:

1. Achaeus (fifth century B.C.)   4. Ion (fifth century B.C.)
2. Aeschylus (525–456 B.C.)   5. Sophocles (ca.496–406 B.C.)
3. Euripides (ca.485–406 B.C.)

Five Unusual Punishments

The concept of eternal punishment, prominent in some branches of Christian and other religious thought, was not of primary importance in Greek mythology. In fact, there are only five notable examples of mythological characters who received unusual, eternal punishments:

1. Forty-nine of the 50 daughters of Danaus killed their husbands on their wedding nights. For this treachery, the Danaides, as they were called, were forced to endlessly fill leaking jars with water.

2. Ixion, a murderous king of Thessaly, hoped to seduce Hera, wife of Zeus. Zeus learned of the plot, and sent to Ixion a cloud-like phantom resembling Hera. After Ixion consummated his love with the cloud, Zeus decreed that he be fastened to a continuously rotating wheel in the Underworld.

3. For showing a lack of respect to the god Hades, Sisyphus was sentenced to eternally roll a large rock up a hill. Each time he reached the summit, the rock slipped from his grasp and rolled back to its starting point, requiring him to begin his journey anew.

4. Tantalus attempted to trick the gods at a banquet by arranging for his own son Pelops to be the main course at the meal. For this outrage, Tantalus was doomed to stand forever in a pool of water, with the branches of a fruit tree just overhead. Every time he bent to take a drink, the water receded; whenever he tried to pluck the fruit, a breeze blew the branches out of his reach.

5. Tityus insulted the goddess Leto. As a result, he was bound to a rock in the Underworld, where vultures chewed at his liver, which continually regenerated itself.

The Five Wives of Mark Antony

The notorious Mark Antony (82–30 B.C.), well known for his ill-fated love affair with Cleopatra, had five wives in all; most of these he married for political reasons. The five were

1. Fadia   4. Octavia
2. Antonia   5. Cleopatra
3. Fulvia

Antony's contemporary, Julius Caesar, also had a proclivity for marrying frequently. He numbered three wives: Cornelia, Pompeia, and Calpurnia. He was engaged at least once, to a certain Cossutia, although the marriage never took place; he also sought to divorce Calpurnia in 52 B.C., in order to marry the daughter of his rival, Pompey, another abortive union.

In 61 B.C. he divorced Pompeia, who was allegedly involved in an adulterous affair with Publius Clodius, on the grounds that members of his family must be above suspicion of wrongdoing.

The SIXES

The Six Books of Lucretius's De Rerum Natura

Unlike many classical authors, Titus Lucretius Carus (ca.99–55 B.C.) wrote only one book: *De Rerum Natura* (*On the Nature of Things*). However, this lone treatise has achieved lasting fame as an expression of Lucretius's devotion to the principles of epicureanism. Scattered throughout *De Rerum Natura* are words of praise for Epicurus (342–270 B.C.) and his philosophical principles. The six books are summarized below.

Book I.   This begins with an invocation to Venus; and then goes on to describe the atomic theory, which held that the universe is composed of voids and infrangible particles, or atoms, a Greek-based word meaning "not split(able)."

Book II.   Here is described the motion of atoms, which collide, cling, and thereby produce matter. The possibility is raised of the existence of life forms in other parts of the universe.

Book III.   This volume develops the proposition that the soul is composed of atoms, and is therefore mortal.

Book IV.   Sensory perception is described, and various bodily functions. The book concludes with a polemic against sexual love.

Book V.   The finite nature of the universe is described, along with the beginnings of animal and human life, and the origins of civilization.

Book VI.   The causes of various natural phenomena, including thunder, lightning, clouds, rain and snow, earthquakes, volcanoes, magnetism, and diseases are detailed. The book concludes with a description of the great plague which ravaged Athens ca.430 B.C.

The Six Books of Ovid's Fasti

The Roman poet Ovid wrote a poem, entitled *Fasti*, in which he described the religious and historical importance of the various days on the calendar. The work (probably) originally contained twelve books—one for each month—but only the first six are extant. The list below provides six examples of the content of the *Fasti*, for each of the six months:

Month/date	*Representative sample*
January 13	The emperor Gaius Julius Caesar Octavianus received the title Augustus (27 B.C.).
February 15	A description of the ancient rite of purification, the Lupercalian Festival, held annually on this date.
March 15	Julius Caesar was assassinated on this date in 44 B.C.
April 21	A description of the Parilian Festival, an ancient religious rite whose date, April 21, eventually became associated with the founding of Rome (753 B.C.).
May 15	Spring ends; summer begins.
June 1	The founding of the Temple of Juno Moneta on the Capitoline Hill is described.

The Six Cities of the Dorian Hexapolis

A hexapolis, or league consisting of six cities, was formed among six of the principal cities located in the area of southwestern Asia Minor:

1. Camirus
2. Cnidus
3. Cos
4. Halicarnassus
5. Ialysus
6. Lindus

The Six Diadochi

After the death of Alexander the Great, his empire was divided among six of his officers, called *diadochi* ("successors"). They were

1. Antigonus I
2. Antipater
3. Cassander
4. Lysimachus
5. Ptolemy I
6. Seleucus I

The Six Elements of an Aristophanic Play

The plays of the comic playwright Aristophanes generally (but not always) contained the following elements:

1. A prologue, in which the main characters are introduced and the basis of the plot is outlined.

2. The *parodos*, in which the chorus enters the action of the play for the first time.

3. A series of comic scenes, involving debates and arguments between characters; a good deal of slapstick comedy is usually present. There is also further character delineation and plot explication in this portion of an Aristophanic play.

4. The *parabasis*, a direct address to the audience, spoken by the chorus leader. Aristophanes generally used the parabasis as a vehicle for the expression of an opinion on some controversial issue of the day.

5. Additional comic scenes, leading to a resolution of conflicts or questions raised in the play.

6. The *exodos*, a concluding celebration, usually in the form of a banquet, a dance, or a party.

The Six Fora of Rome

Ancient Rome's business district—a type of downtown section of the city—was called the forum. Originally, Rome had only one forum, but Julius Caesar and several emperors built additional fora, ultimately bringing the total number to six:

1. Forum Romanum (the original forum)
2. Forum Julium (begun 54 B.C. by Julius Caesar)
3. Forum Augustum (completed 2 B.C. by the emperor Augustus)
4. Forum Vespasiani (completed A.D. 75 by the emperor Vespasian; alternatively called the Forum Pacis)
5. Forum Nervae (completed A.D.97 by the emperor Nerva; alternatively called the Forum Transitorium)
6. Forum Trajani (completed A.D. 114 by the emperor Trajan).

The Six Lexiarchoi

The six *lexiarchoi* were the officials in Athens responsible for entering the names of newly enfranchised young citizens in the proper registries.

The Six Librarians of Alexandria

The city of Alexandria could boast of many famous landmarks, but the most prominent of all were probably the two libraries. The larger of these, founded during the reign of Ptolemy I (ca.367–282 B.C.), eventually contained some 700,000 manuscripts. The first six chief librarians were

1. Zenodotus of Ephesus (ca.325–234 B.C.); librarian 284–260
2. Apollonius of Rhodes (third century B.C.); librarian 260–247
3. Eratosthenes (ca.275–194 B.C.); librarian 247–194
4. Aristophanes of Byzantium (ca.257–180 B.C.); librarian 194–180
5. Apollonius the Classifier (second century B.C.); librarian 180–153
6. Aristarchus of Samothrace (ca. 215–145 B.C.); librarian 153–145

There was also a noted library in Pergamum, containing some 200,000 volumes. Rome is said to have ultimately boasted of 26 public libraries. Oddly, there seems to have been a dearth of public libraries in Greece, although private individuals such as Pisistratus, Euripides, and Aristotle owned large personal collections of manuscripts. Aulus Gellius (7.17) states that Pisistratus established the first public library in Athens, and that other Athenians augmented its holdings.

Six Months in the Underworld

Persephone, daughter of the goddess Demeter, was kidnapped by Hades, thus causing her grieving mother to neglect her harvest responsibilities. The ensuing famine moved Zeus to intervene in the matter. It was ultimately arranged that Hades could retain Persephone in the Underworld for six months of the year (some sources say four months), with Demeter allowed to enjoy her daughter's presence for the remaining months.

Six Mythological Hybrid Monsters

Hybrid monsters figure prominently in a number of ancient myths and legends. Six of the most famous of these gruesome creatures were

1. Centaurs: half-man and half-horse
2. Chimeras: head of a lion, body of a goat, and a snake-like tail
3. Griffins: half-lion and half-eagle
4. The Minotaur: head of a bull and body of a man
5. Scylla: woman's body from the waist up; the lower part composed of six heads of vicious dogs
6. The Sphinx: head of a woman and body of a dog, with bird's wings and lion's paws.

The Six Plays of Terence

The Roman comic playwright Publius Terentius Afer (Terence, ca.190–ca.159 B.C.) wrote six plays, all of which survive.

1. *The Brothers* (160 B.C.): Two brothers are raised in separate homes.
2. *The Eunuch* (161 B.C.): The story of a love triangle involving an Athenian youth, a courtesan, and a soldier is recounted in this play.
3. *The Mother-in-Law* (166 B.C.): The young Athenian Pamphilus learns to love Philumena, his father's choice of a wife for him.
4. *Phormio* (161 B.C.): The parasite Phormio assists a pair of young lovers in their efforts to marry.
5. *The Self-Tormentor* (163 B.C.): The older farmer Menedemus labors from dawn to dusk in order to rid himself of the guilt he feels for forcing his son to join a mercenary army.
6. *The Woman of Andros* (166 B.C.): Simo, an Athenian, disapproves of the plans of his son to marry Glycerium, a woman from Andros.

The Six Poems Extant of Callimachus

Callimachus (ca.305–240 B.C.), a Greek poet and scholar born in the North African town of Cyrene, immigrated to Alexandria as a young man. There he was assigned the herculean task of cataloguing and synopsizing the hundreds of thousands of holdings (mostly scrolls) in the great library. His catalogue, called the *Pinaces*, eventually filled 120 volumes. This surely tedious undertaking acquainted him with nearly every significant author and genre in Greek literature, which, in turn, very likely spurred his own creative imagination. In the *Pinaces* he established eight categories of writers:

1. Dramatists
2. Epic and lyric
   poets
3. Lawgivers
4. Philosophers

5. Historians
6. Orators
7. Rhetoricians
8. Writers on
   miscellaneous
   topics

He supposedly wrote 800 books, dealing with a vast range of topics, in the form of catalogues, encyclopedias, and anthologies. He also authored numerous collections of poems, epigrams, and aphorisms.

Of this monumental output, only six poems — hymns to various deities or sacred places — survive intact, although fragments (including those of some 60 epigrams) of several of his other poetic endeavors are extant. The six hymns are

1. To Zeus
2. To Apollo
3. To Artemis
4. To Delos

5. On the baths
   of Pallas
6. To Demeter

Six Provisions of the Lex Gabinia

In 67 B.C. the tribune Aulus Gabinius proposed a law granting wide powers to Pompey the Great to clear the seas of pirates. Six of the (numerically significant) provisions of the *Lex Gabinia* are

1. That Pompey be granted a three-year allotment of time to complete the task
2. That he be given powers equal to those of provincial governors, to a distance of 50 miles inland
3. That he be granted an expense account of 6,000 talents
4. That he be granted the use of 500 ships
5. That 120,000 foot soldiers be assigned to him
6. That he be given the right to appoint 24 *legati*, or generals, to serve under his command. (This far exceeded the usual number of two to fifteen.)

This proposal generated a great deal of heated controversy in the Roman Senate, where many notables strongly opposed it. Eventually, however, the measure was approved.

Six Reforms of Lucius Cornelius Sulla

Sulla ruled Rome as its dictator from 81 to 79 B.C., and while in that office he proposed and enacted several important measures, including the following six:

1. Sulla increased considerably the size of the Roman Senate, to perhaps as many as 500 members; the traditional number was 300.

2. This "new" Roman Senate included a significant contingent of men drawn from native Italian stock (rather than strictly or mostly Roman).

3. Sulla attempted to emasculate the tribunate by limiting tribunes' legislative powers, by restricting their veto power, and by debarring them from running for any other high government office.

4. He increased the number of praetors from six to eight, and the number of quaestors from 12 to 20.

5. He transformed northern Italy into the province of Cisapline Gaul.

6. He made a number of judicial reforms, the most important of which was probably the establishment of special courts or commissions (*quaestiones*) to try criminal cases. (Prior to this time, such cases were adjudicated by the Assemblies.) He created seven of these *quaestiones*, for the following crimes:

1. *Quaestio maiestatis*: treason
2. *Quaestio peculatus*: embezzlement of public funds
3. *Quaestio ambitus*: electoral bribery
4. *Quaestio repetundarum*: provincial extortion
5. *Quaestio de sicariis et veneficis*: murder, poisoning
6. *Quaestio de falsis*: counterfeiting and forgery, especially of wills
7. *Quaestio de iniuriis*: incitement of civil violence; assault

Sulla's judicial reforms attained the greatest degree of permanence.

The Six Residences of Cicero

Marcus Tullius Cicero owned at least six homes and villas, located in the following places:

1. An expensive home on the Palatine Hill in Rome, a residence that once belonged to Marcus Licinius Crassus.

2. A house once owned by the dictator Lucius Cornelius Sulla in Tusculum. One of Cicero's well-known philosophical treatises, *Tusculan Disputations*, arose out of a five-day conference held in Tusculum, with some of his learned friends.

3. Antium, site of his library.

4. Arpinum, his hometown.

5. Astura, an island off the coast of Latium.

6. Campania, on the coast.

The Six Satires of Persius

The Roman poet Aulus Persius Flaccus (A.D. 34–62) has to his credit six surviving satires:

Satire I. In this satire Persius attacks what he views as a decline in the quality of contemporary Roman literature and the sophistication of its admirers.

Satire II. Persius discusses and criticizes the kinds of prayers offered to the gods.

Satire III. This satire progresses from the consideration of a specific case of a lazy young man to a general discussion of the propriety and value of the study of philosophy.

Satire IV. The theme of this satire revolves around the ramifications of the famous Delphic maxim "Know thyself."

Satire V. The fifth satire, considered by critics to be Persius's best, focuses upon the issues of freedom and slavery from a Stoic philosopher's point of view.

Satire VI. The theme of this somewhat obscure satire seems to be that one should enjoy the delights of the present age.

The Six Scriptores Historiae Augustae

A series of biographies of Roman emperors (from Hadrian to Numerianus) was compiled by a group of six writers. These works collectively were known as the *Scriptores Historiae Augustae*. The names of these writers and the emperors about whom they wrote follows:

Writer	*Emperors*
1. Aelius Spartianus	Hadrian, Aelius (Lucius Aelius Caesar was adopted by Hadrian as his successor, but died before assuming the emperorship), Didius Julianus, Septimius Severus, Pescennius (Gaius Pescennius Niger Justus was proclaimed emperor by his legions in Syria, after the murder of the emperor Pertinax in 193; he was defeated in battle and executed before reaching Rome to formally take office), Caracalla, Geta
2. Julius Capitolinus	Antoninus Pius, Marcus Aurelius, Lucius Verus, Pertinax, Clodius Albinus (Decimus Clodius Albinus, governor of Britain, was hailed as emperor by his troops in A.D. 192; like Pescennius, however, he was killed [in Gaul] before he could claim the emperorship), Macrinus, Maximinus, Gordian I, Gordian II, Gordian III, Pupienus Maximus, Balbinus
3. Vulcacius Gallicanus	Avidius Cassius (Avidius Cassius proclaimed himself emperor in Syria in A.D. 175, apparently motivated by an erroneous belief that Marcus Aurelius had died; he was assassinated shortly thereafter)
4. Aelius Lampridius	Commodus, Diadumenianus, Elagabalus, Severus Alexander

5. Trebellius Pollio	Philip, Decius, Trebonianus, Aemilianus, Valerianus, Gallienus, Claudius Gothicus
6. Flavius Vopiscus	Aurelian, Tacitus, Probus, Firmus, Carus, Carinus, Numerianus

Six Teachers of Hercules

Apollodorus (2.4) states that Hercules was tutored in various arts and skills by the following teachers (Chiron's name does not appear in Apollodorus's catalogue, but he is elsewhere attested as a teacher of Hercules):

Teacher	Art/skill
1. Amphitryon	Chariot driving
2. Autolycus	Wrestling
3. Castor	Sword fighting
4. Chiron	Polite behavior
5. Eurytus	Archery
6. Linus	Lyre playing

Linus supposedly once employed corporal punishment to reprimand his famous but recalcitrant student, whereupon Hercules picked up his lyre and struck Linus on the head with it, killing him. Hercules was later acquitted of murder, on the grounds that he had sufficient provocation.

The Six Vestal Virgins

The Roman hearth goddess Vesta was served originally by four and later by six priestesses called Vestal Virgins. Their chief duty involved maintaining Vesta's temple, and especially tending the sacred flame. Vestal Virgins were selected at a very young age—6 to 10. They were required to serve for a period of 30 years, during which time they had to remain chaste. Should they violate the celibacy rule, they might be stoned to death or buried alive.

During her 30-year commitment, it was expected that a Vestal Virgin would spend the first 10 years learning her duties, the second 10 years performing them, and the third 10 years training her eventual successor.

Other qualifications required of a prospective Vestal Virgin, according to the legal writers Antistius Labeo and Ateius Capito, were as follows:

1. Both of her parents must be living.
2. She cannot have a speech impediment, poor hearing, or any physical defect.
3. Her father must be a Roman citizen in good standing.
4. Neither parent can be from a servile family, nor can they have been involved in *negotiis sordidis*, "disreputable businesses."
5. Her parents must reside in Italy.
6. A girl who has two or more siblings cannot be selected.

The Six Victims of Theseus

Theseus, the most famous of the legendary kings of Athens, was born in Troezen, a small town in the Peloponnesus almost directly across the Saronic Gulf from Athens. As a young man Theseus traveled to Athens to claim the throne. However, instead of sailing across the gulf, he chose the longer, more dangerous overland route (in an attempt to prove his worthiness and also to emulate his hero, Hercules). In the course of the journey he encountered six formidable purveyors of violence, often subduing them in the manner in which they had been accustomed to dispatch their victims. Plutarch (*Theseus* 8.11) describes several other Thesean conquests en route to Athens, but these six are the most well known. The six were as follows:

1. Periphetes, the club-bearer. Theseus killed him and took his club, no doubt mindful of the similar weapon brandished by Hercules.

2. Sinis, the pine-bender. This highwayman placed his victims on a doubled-over pine tree; when the tension on the tree was released, it catapulted Sinis's victims through the air, where they were splattered against a nearby cliff face. Theseus did likewise to Sinis.

3. Phaea, a murderous woman, called the Sow both because of her appearance and her lifestyle. Unfortunately, Plutarch does not specify the manner in which Theseus overcame Phaea.

4. Sciron, a common mugger, used to force his victims to wash his feet; as they were engaged in this unseemly task, he would kick at them until they fell over a cliff into the sea.

5. Cercyon, a wrestler. Theseus engaged him in a wrestling contest, and killed him.

6. Procrustes, a thief and a highwayman. Procrustes habitually compelled his victims to lie in an iron bed. If the victim were too tall, Procrustes would cut off his feet or legs until the fit was perfect. On the other hand, should the victim be too short, Procrustes stretched him to the desired height. (Hence the modern word "procrustean.") Theseus overcame Procrustes by arranging his anatomy to fit the dimensions of his famous bed.

The Six Works Extant of Antiphon

The learned Athenian orator Antiphon (ca.480–411 B.C.) began his legal career as a logographer, or ghostwriter of courtroom speeches for various litigants. Eventually, he composed, delivered, and published speeches under his own name. Six of these survive, including three tetralogies, concerning hypothetical murder cases, in which Antiphon wrote two speeches each for accusers and defenders.

The Tetralogies:

First tetralogy: A man and his slave are assaulted; the master dies immediately, but the slave implicates the attackers before he, too, expires. Can the slave's testimony be considered in the murder trial that follows?

Second tetralogy: While practicing the javelin throw in a gymnasium, an athlete accidentally strikes and kills a bystander with the javelin. The father of the deceased brings the matter to court to determine the appropriate punishment for the offender (if any).

Third tetralogy: A young man kills an older companion during an argument at a drinking party: murder, or self-defense?

The Speeches:

On the Chorus Singer (date uncertain; possibly 418), in which he defends a *choregus* (financial sponsor of a play) against a charge of murder, for accidentally causing the death of one of the chorus singers, a boy named Diodotus. (Diodotus had drunk a potion that was supposed to improve the quality of his voice; instead, it poisoned him.)

Against the Stepmother for Poisoning (ca.416), in which he prosecutes a woman for killing her husband, Philoneos, and a friend with poisoned wine. Antiphon undertook the case at the request of Philoneos's son, who believed that the slave originally executed for the murders was innocent, and that his own stepmother was the true culprit.

On the Murder of Herodes (ca.414), in which Antiphon defends a man, Euxitheus, implicated in the mysterious disappearance (presumably the result of foul play) of his traveling companion, Herodes.

Antiphon is thought to have written as many as 60 speeches. Papyrus fragments have been discovered of his final oration: a defense of his actions during the short-lived rule of the Four Hundred in Athens in 411. When he was praised for the eloquence of this speech, he is reported to have replied that he would rather please one refined man than an infinite number of illiterate dolts.

The Six Works Extant of Arrian

Flavius Arrianus (Arrian; second century A.D.), a Romanized Greek, wrote treatises on a variety of subjects. Six of these survive, either wholly or in part:

1. *Anabasis*, on the expeditions of Alexander the Great, considered Arrian's most important surviving work.

2. *Indica*, a description of India and the customs of its people.

3. *Enchiridion*, a short manual summarizing the stoic philosophy of Epictetus.

4. *Discourses*, the published form of the notes that Arrian compiled during Epictetus's lectures.

5. *Circumnavigation of the Black Sea*, a naval handbook.

6. *On Hunting*, modeled after Xenophon's treatise of the same name.

The Six Works Extant of Hyperides

Like a number of his oratorical contemporaries, Hyperides (389–322 B.C.) began his career by ghostwriting speeches for his fellow citizens to present in court cases. Eventually, however, he gained fame as a pleader in his own right;

some 52 speeches are attributed to him, all lost until a nineteenth-century papyrus find revealed significant portions of six of them.

Hyperides was an eclectic orator, one who argued all kinds of cases for all sorts of clients. He was also known as a womanizer, famous for the three mistresses he simultaneously maintained. One of his assuredly most interesting cases was his defense of a prostitute named Phryne, who had been accused of impiety. At a dramatic moment in his oration he exposed her breasts to display their comeliness to the jury. Unfortunately, his speech for Phryne is not listed among the six surviving works.

> 1. *Against Athenogenes*. Athenogenes had sold under false pretenses a debt-ridden perfume business to Hyperides' client, who then became responsible for the debts.
>
> 2. *Against Demosthenes*. In a celebrated case of 323, Hyperides was one of the prosecutors of Demosthenes, who was accused of accepting a large bribe from a wealthy Macedonian financial official named Harpalus.
>
> 3. *For Euxenippus*. Euxenippus had been asked to sleep in a temple of the god Amphiaraus, with the expectation that, during the night, the god might reveal to him the solution to a dispute between two tribes over certain property rights. Euxenippus was subsequently accused of accepting a bribe to lie about the information supposedly imparted to him by the god.
>
> 4. *For Lycophron*. The orator defended Lycophron against a charge of adultery.
>
> 5. *Against Philippides*. Hyperides argued that Philippides had illegally proposed a decree honoring King Philip and certain other Macedonians.
>
> 6. *Funeral Speech*. This was given in honor of Athenian soldiers who died in the Lamian War against Macedonia (323–322 B.C.).

Longinus (reputed first-century-A.D. author of *On the Sublime*, a work of literary criticism in 44 extant chapters) makes the interesting observation (in chapter 34) that Hyperides was like a pentathlete: good in many events (or oratorical techniques), the best in none.

The SEVENS

The Septemviri *of Rome*

A *septemvir* was a member of a board or a commission composed of seven men. Two of the most important such boards were

    1. In 44 B.C. a board of seven was organized to distribute public lands to veteran soldiers and other people in need.

    2. A college of seven priests oversaw the preparation of sacred festivals.

The Seven Against Thebes

Oedipus had grimly prophesied that his two sons, Eteocles and Polynices, would kill one another. A dispute over the kingship of the city of Thebes arose between the two of them, with Eteocles forcing his brother into exile. Polynices journeyed to Argos, where he recruited six other warriors to join him in an attack on Thebes. Collectively, they came to be known as the Seven against Thebes:

1. Adrastus	5. Parthenopaeus
2. Amphiaraus	6. Polynices
3. Capaneus	7. Tydeus
4. Hippomedon	

The sons, and hence successors, of the Seven were called the Epigonoi. There are generally considered to have been seven of these successors:

1. Aegialeus	5. Promachus
2. Alcmaeon	6. Sthenelus
3. Amphilochus	7. Thersander
4. Diomedes	

Seven Celebrations of the Secular Games

At the close of a generation (*saeculum*, a period of 100, or according to some sources, 110 years), the Romans held a religious ceremony to commemorate the event. The first such celebration may have occurred in 449 B.C. The second, third, and fourth were observed in 348, 249, 149 B.C. The fifth was postponed until its revival by Augustus in 17 B.C. (a postponement that was occasioned by the civil war raging in 49 B.C.).

Another celebration of the Secular Games occurred in A.D. 47 (supposedly 800 years, or eight 100-year *saecula*, since Rome's founding, and again in A.D. 88 (based roughly on the time elapsed since the Augustan revival).

The Secular Games of 17 B.C., a three-day affair, were the inspiration for a poem by Horace, the *Carmen Saeculare*. This poem was sung during the ceremony by two specially selected choruses, one consisting of 27 young men, the other 27 young women.

Seven Cities Claiming to Be Homer's Birthplace

The birthplace of the epic poet Homer is problematic at best; many cities in the ancient world claimed the honor, but the following seven are the most credible:

1. Athens
2. Argos
3. Chios
4. Colophon
5. Rhodes
6. Salamis
7. Smyrna

Seven Cities Named Caesarea

Just as there were numerous ancient cities named Alexandria (in honor of Alexander the Great), so too several existing cities were renamed Caesarea, in honor of Julius Caesar or one of his successors (also called Caesar). Seven of these are

City	Location	Approximate date of renaming
1. Caesarea	Cappadocia (Asia Minor)	Between 13 and 9 B.C.
2. Caesarea	North Africa	25 B.C.
3. Caesarea	Western Asia Minor	26 B.C.
4. Caesarea by Anazarbus	Cilicia (Asia Minor)	A.D. 19
5. Caesarea Philippi	Syria	4 B.C.
6. Caesarea in Pisidia	Asia Minor	25 B.C.
7. Caesarea Maritima	Judaea	10 B.C.

Seven Construction-Minded Friends of Augustus

The twenty-ninth chapter of Suetonius's biography of the emperor Augustus is concerned with some of the construction projects undertaken during the emperor's reign. At the end of the book Suetonius lists seven of Augustus's friends and associates who oversaw the completion of certain buildings in Rome. They were

Name	Project
1. Marcius Philippus	Temple of Hercules and the Muses
2. Lucius Cornificius	Temple of Diana
3. Asinius Pollio	Hall of Liberty
4. Munatius Plancus	Temple of Saturn
5. Cornelius Balbus	A theater (subsequently known as the Theater of Balbus)
6. Statilius Taurus	An amphitheater
7. Marcus Agrippa	*Complura et egregia* ("many distinguished structures")

Seven Consulships

By custom, and presumably by law, no Roman politician was supposed to hold the office of consul more than once within any ten-year span. But Gaius Marius (157–86 B.C.) shattered that tradition by gaining the office seven times: six consecutive terms (105–100), and a seventh term in 86.

Seven Cycladic Islands of Fame

The Cycladic Islands, or Cyclades, are located in the Aegean Sea, south and east of Athens. The name derives from the Greek word for wheel, since the islands are roughly situated in the shape of a large circle. Greek geographers identified at least 15 Cycladic islands. Seven of the most famous include

Name	Approximate size	Reason for fame
1. Andros	21 miles long; 8 miles wide	Andros was famous for its wine, and hence was sacred to the god of wine, Dionysus.
2. Ceos	14 miles long; 10 miles wide	Ceos was the birthplace of two of the most prominent Greek lyric poets: Simonides and Bacchylides.
3. Delos	5 miles in circumference	The smallest yet most famous of the Cyclades, Delos was traditionally thought to be Apollo's birthplace; it was the site of a celebrated shrine of Apollo.
4. Melos	14 miles long; 8 miles wide	In 416 B.C. Athens demanded the surrender of Melos; when the islanders refused the Athenians decimated the populace. A noteworthy account of the preattack negotiations—the Melian Dialogue—appears in Book V of Thucydides' treatise on the Peloponnesian War.
5. Naxos	19 miles long; 15 miles wide	Naxos was the largest, most powerful, and the most fertile of the Cyclades. Some

Name	Approximate size	Reason for fame
		versions of Theseus and the labyrinth myth state that Theseus deserted Ariadne on this island.
6. Paros	36 miles in circumference	The second largest Cycladic island, Paros was famous for the fine white marble quarried there.
7. Tenos	15 miles long	Tenos was noted for its high quality garlic, and for a spring whose water supposedly would not mix with wine.

Other Cycladic islands include Cimolos, Cyaros, Cynthos, Myconos, Oliaros, Prepesinthos, Seriphos, Siphnos, and Syros.

The Seven Daughters of Atlas

The seven daughters of Atlas, more commonly known as the Pleiades, were

1. Alcyone
2. Celaeno
3. Electra
4. Maia
5. Merope
6. Sterope
7. Taygeta

Seven Days to Nest

According to Aristotle, the number seven bears particular significance for the female partridge, for she constructs a nest in seven days, lays her eggs seven days thereafter, and spends seven days raising her hatchlings.

Seven Destroyers of Monsters

Tales of heroes who battled and subdued fearsome monsters were popular in the myths of the Greeks. Seven of the most famous battlers of monsters were

1. Apollo: killed Python, a serpent.
2. Bellerophon: destroyed the Chimera, a hybrid beast—part lion, part goat, and part serpent.
3. Hercules: killed or disabled numerous monsters, especially those associated with the Twelve Labors.
4. Odysseus: blinded Polyphemus, the one-eyed giant of the race called Cyclopes.
5. Oedipus: solved the monstrous Sphinx's riddle, whereupon she killed herself in despair.
6. Perseus: slew the Gorgon Medusa, whose face could turn an onlooker to stone.
7. Theseus: killed the cannibalistic Minotaur, half-man, half-bull denizen of the labyrinth.

Seven Feet of Snow

The winter of 400–399 B.C. was unexpectedly severe in Rome, where snow in any amount seldom falls. But in this winter seven feet of show descended upon the city. Some of the notable consequences were the death from starvation or exposure of many people and animals; the destruction of numerous fruit-bearing trees; and the collapse of houses due to the weight of the snow on their roofs. According to Dionysius of Halicarnassus (12.8), this was the only occurrence in Roman history of such a meteorological anomaly.

The Seven Hills of Rome

Rome, the "city built on seven hills," actually encompassed more than a dozen named hills and ridges. The seven major ones, however, are generally considered to be the following:

1. Aventine
2. Caelian
3. Capitoline
4. Esquiline
5. Palatine
6. Quirinal
7. Viminal

Seven Kings of Rome

Tacitus (*Annals* 1.1) reports that in the beginning Rome was ruled by kings. There were seven of these rulers:

1. Romulus (reigned 753–714 B.C.)
2. Numa Pompilius (714–671 B.C.)
3. Tullus Hostilius (671–642 B.C.)
4. Ancus Marcius (642–617 B.C.)
5. Tarquinius Priscus (617–579 B.C.)
6. Servius Tullius (579–535 B.C.)
7. Tarquinius Superbus (535–509 B.C.)

With the expulsion of the seventh king, the monarchy was abolished and replaced by a republican form of government.

Seven Lakes of Fame

Name	Location	Reason for fame
1. Lake Benacus	Northern Italy	The largest lake in Italy; the peninsula of Sirmio, at its southern end, was a favorite haunt of the poet Catullus.
2. Lake Copais	Greece (Boeotia)	Its eels, which upscale Athenians considered a dinner delicacy.

3. Lake Fucinus	Central Italy	The largest lake in central Italy; its frequent inundations of the surrounding countryside resulted in a celebrated attempt by the emperor Claudius to have it drained, an 11-year (A.D. 41–52) project with mixed results.
4. Lake Larius	Northern Italy	A long, narrow, and deep lake; Pliny the Younger owned several villas on its shores.
5. Lake Regillus	Central Italy	Site of a famous battle (ca. 496 B.C.) between Latins and Romans.
6. Lake Stymphalus	Greece (Peloponnesus)	The mythical home of the bronze-clawed, man-eating birds dispersed by Hercules—his sixth Labor.
7. Lake Trasimene	Central Italy	A large, shallow, weedy lake; the site of a terrible Roman defeat at the hands of Hannibal in 217 B.C.

The Seven Liberal Arts

The notion that a free man ought to possess certain kinds of knowledge apparently dates to Aristotle. The seven branches of this requisite knowledge were as listed below, with the Roman antiquarian Varro adding medicine and architecture to the list:

1. Literature
2. Rhetoric
3. Dialectic
4. Arithmetic
5. Geometry
6. Music
7. Astronomy

Seven Mountains of Fame

Name	Approximate altitude in feet	Reason for fame
1. Mt. Olympus (Greece)	9,000	The mythical home of the twelve major deities.
2. Mt. Parnassus (Greece)	8,200	The peak that towers over Delphi, site of Apollo's famous oracle and a prestigious quadrennial athletic festival.

Name	Approximate altitude in feet	Reason for fame
3. Mt. Taygetus (Greece)	7,900	A mountain near Sparta, where young Spartans engaged in much of their physical training.
4. Mt. Pangaeus (Greece)	6,000	Natural resources: timber, gold, and silver.
5. Mt. Helicon (Greece)	5,900	Mythical home of the Muses.
6. Mt. Vesuvius (Italy)	4,000	Its volcanic eruption in A.D. 79 buried the cities of Pompeii and Herculaneum.
7. Mt. Pentelicus (Greece)	3,600	White marble, used in most of the famous Athenian sculptures and temples.

Seven Novels of Antiquity

Seven identifiable novels (five Greek and two Latin) survive from antiquity. The Greek novels are generally romantic tales involving hardships (kidnapping, piracy, or abandonment by parents) overcome by pairs of young lovers.

Author/approximate date	Title/synopsis
1. Achilles Tatius/second century A.D.	*Leucippe and Clitophon*: about the melodramatic adventures of two young lovers.
2. Chariton/second century A.D.	*Chaereas and Callirhoe*: a romantic adventure set in fifth-century B.C. Syracuse, at the time of the Athenian invasion.
3. Heliodorus/third century A.D.	*Aethiopica*: the longest of the surviving Greek novels; details the travels and travails of the Ethiopian princess Chariclea, and her Thessalian lover Theagenes.
4. Longus/third century A.D.	*Daphnis and Chloe*: a pastoral romance with the two protagonists ultimately marrying and living happily ever after.
5. Xenophon of Ephesus/ second century A.D.	*Anthea and Habrocomes*: concerning their marriage, their (unwanted) separation during a sea voyage, and their eventual reunification.

6. Petronius/first century
   A.D.

Satyricon: about the (mis)adventures of two vagabonds, Encolpius and Ascyltus. Included in this novel is the celebrated description of Trimalchio's dinner party.

7. Apuleius/second century A.D.

Metamorphoses, concerning the protagonist's escapades and experiences while in the form of a donkey.

The Seven Plays Extant of Aeschylus

One of the greatest tragic playwrights in Athenian history, Aeschylus (525–456 B.C.) wrote about 90 plays, of which only seven survive:

1-3. *Oresteia* (458 B.C.), the only extant trilogy, contains the following plays:

Agamemnon, which treats the return of Agamemnon from Troy, and his treacherous murder at the hands of his wife, Clytemnestra, and her lover, Aegisthus.

Libation Bearers, a tale of vengeance for Agamemnon's death, carried out by his son, Orestes.

Eumenides, the consequences borne by Orestes for his act of matricide.

4. *Persians* (472 B.C.), the only surviving historical tragedy from ancient Greek times, describes the downfall of the Persian king Xerxes at the Battle of Salamis (480).

5. *Prometheus Bound* (date uncertain), the story of Prometheus's theft of fire — which he gave to mankind — and the punishment that he suffers for this act.

6. *The Seven against Thebes* (467 B.C.), a tragedy based upon the attack on Thebes by seven warriors under the leadership of Oedipus's son Polynices.

7. *The Suppliants* (492 B.C.), a play based upon the proposal of marriage made by the 50 sons of Aegyptus (king of Egypt) to the 50 (unwilling) daughters of Danaus.

The Seven Plays Extant of Sophocles

The playwright Sophocles (ca.496–406 B.C.) is generally regarded, along with Aeschylus and Euripides, as one of ancient Athens's greatest tragedians. He is thought to have written some 120 plays, although only seven of these have survived to the present day. Sophocles' seven extant plays are as follows:

1. *Ajax* (ca.447 B.C.): When Ajax and Odysseus compete for ownership of the slain Achilles' armor, and Odysseus wins, Ajax goes insane and kills a number of sheep and cattle (which he mistook for the Greek leaders who deprived him of the armor). He ultimately commits suicide.

2. *Antigone* (ca.442 B.C.): Antigone, the sister of the slain Polynices, must decide whether to obey King Creon's order denying the rite of burial to her brother.

3. *Electra* (ca.418–414 B.C.): Electra, daughter of Agamemnon and Clytemnestra, wishes for vengeance against her mother, the one who murdered her father, for whom she grieves deeply. Her brother, Orestes, carries out the matricide.

4. *Oedipus at Colonus* (ca.409 B.C.): Oedipus, old and blind, a deposed king who hates the sons born to him in his incestuous marriage, at last dies in peace. (When Sophocles' own son was endeavoring to have his elderly father declared mentally incompetent, the 90-year-old playwright read a choral passage from this play to demonstrate his acuity. The reading so deeply moved the jury that they threw the son's case out of court.)

5. *Oedipus the King* (ca.430 B.C.): Often considered the finest extant Greek tragedy, this play deals above all with hubris, particularly as it is displayed in the powerful and arrogant Oedipus, the man who believes that he can defy fate and the gods by continuing to rule Thebes, despite his incestuous marriage.

6. *Philoctetes* (409 B.C.): Philoctetes, the slayer of Paris, remains on the island Lemnos for nearly the entire span of the Trojan War, until persuaded by Neoptolemus, Odysseus, and ultimately Hercules, to set sail for Troy.

7. *The Women of Trachis* (ca.413 B.C.): This play deals with Hercules' slaying of the centaur Nessus and the consequences of that act, particularly its effects on Deianira, Hercules' wife.

Seven Rivers of Fame

Name	Reason for fame
1. Alpheus (Greece)	The river near Olympia, site of the ancient Olympic games.
2. Aufidus (Italy)	In 216 B.C., near the banks of this river, Hannibal decimated the Romans (Battle of Cannae).
3. Ebro (Spain)	This river formed the putative boundary between Roman and Carthaginian spheres of influence in Spain.
4. Rhone (France)	Hannibal tricked his reluctant elephants into crossing this river by camouflaging rafts with dirt and tree branches.
5. Rubicon (Italy)	The boundary between Italy and the provinces; returning generals were supposed to dismiss their armies before crossing the river. When Caesar did not do so — the

occasion of his famous remark
"the die is cast" (in 49 B.C.)—a
civil war resulted.

6. Tiber (Italy)   The river on whose banks the city
                                         of Rome was built.

7. Scamander (Turkey)   The river that flowed near the an-
                                         cient city of Troy.

Seven Sacred, Magical, or Powerful Numbers

The Greeks and Romans both believed that certain numbers possessed
various kinds of sacred or magical properties. The most common seemed to be
three, four, five, seven, eight, nine, and twelve. The following are some examples:

> Three. Deities were often grouped in threes: the Three Fates or the
> Three Graces; and triads such as Zeus, Athena, and Apollo, or Jupiter,
> Mars, and Quirinus. The Pythagorean philosophers considered three to be
> the perfect number, symbolizing a beginning, a middle, and an end.
>
> Four. Tradition suggests that the legendary founder of the Olympic
> games, Hercules, specified that it be a quadrennial festival in honor of his
> four brothers. Four was the number sacred to the god Hermes. A prayer
> repeated four times seems to have had some significance in Roman
> religious observances. Also, four was noteworthy to the Pythagoreans, as
> the first square after one.
>
> Five. The number five also seems to have had importance in Roman
> religious ritual. It is thought that the number five may also have had
> some significance in that it corresponded to the number of fingers on a
> hand.
>
> Seven. This was Apollo's sacred number; it was—like three—a number
> for traditional groupings: the seven planets, for example, or the Seven
> Sages.
>
> Eight. At the end of his biography of Theseus, Plutarch describes the
> unique properties of the number eight: the first cube of an even number
> $(2 \times 2 \times 2)$, and also double the first square of an even number (2×4).
> The Pythagoreans considered the number eight to be the symbol of
> justice, in that it could be divided evenly into fours, which could in turn
> be divided into twos, which ultimately yielded a pair of ones.
>
> Nine. The sacred number three, when squared, created another sacred
> number, nine, as well as another number evocative of traditional group-
> ings: the nine Muses for example, or the nine Curetes (young men who
> protected Zeus shortly after his birth).
>
> Twelve. Twelve was another common grouping in myth and legend: the
> 12 Olympian gods; Hercules' Twelve Labors; and the 12 signs of the Zodiac.

Marcus Varro devoted the first book of his treatise *On Portraits* (no longer
extant) to the various powers and peculiarities of the number seven. A summary
is preserved in Aulus Gellius (3.10):

Seven stars in the constellations called the Greater and Lesser Bears

Seven Pleiades

Seven planets

Seven circles in the heavens

The summer solstice occurs in the seventh sign of the Zodiac from the winter solstice, and conversely, the winter in the seventh sign from the summer. The same proportional relationship holds true for the vernal and autumnal equinoxes.

Kingfishers nest in the water for seven days.

A complete revolution of the moon around the earth requires four times seven days. This number (28) can also be obtained by adding the numbers one through seven inclusively (that is, $1 + 2 + 3 + 4 + 5 + 6 + 7 = 28$).

Seven days after conception, a fetus begins to take shape; in seven times seven days the fetus has assumed a definite form. A baby born before the seventh month will not be healthy.

Seven feet represents the limit of human growth, although traditionally Orestes reached a height of seven cubits (a little over 12 feet).

A baby's teeth erupt in the seventh month, seven at a time in both the upper and lower jaws. The baby teeth begin to fall out in seven years, while the permanent teeth generally appear within twice times seven years.

The sound produced by a seven-stringed lyre can aid in one's circulation, according to some physicians.

Serious diseases sometimes reach critical points on the seventh days (and also on the fourteenth and twenty-first days).

Those who commit suicide by starvation usually expire on the seventh day.

At this point in the narrative Gellius records several other Varronian observations, which he labels *frigidiuscula*, a charming word that defies exact translation; literally, it means something like "pretty chilly little things," that is, observations that are rather trite or insignificant, "a reach" in modern parlance:

The Seven Wonders

The Seven Sages

Seven as the standard number of laps in a chariot race

The Seven against Thebes

That he had reached the twelfth seven-year cycle of his life when he completed this book, and that he had written 7×70 books in his lifetime.

The Seven Sages of Greece

The list of the seven wisest men of ancient Greece varies, but it most commonly contains the seven listed below. A famous story concerns the discovery by some fishermen of a golden tripod that had become entangled in their nets. The dispute that arose over ownership of the prize was mediated by Apollo's priestesses at Delphi, who declared that the tripod must be given to the wisest man in Greece. Hence, it was conveyed to Thales, who refused to accept it, saying that Bias was a wiser man than he. Bias also declined, and so the tripod was sent in turn to the other sages, all of whom demurred. Ultimately, it was dedicated to Apollo. The Seven Sages were

1. Bias of Priene (sixth century B.C.)
2. Chilon of Sparta (sixth century B.C.)
3. Cleobulus of Lindos (sixth century B.C.)
4. Periander of Corinth (seventh–sixth century B.C.)
5. Pittacus of Mitylene (seventh century B.C.)
6. Solon of Athens (seventh–sixth century B.C.)
7. Thales of Miletus (seventh century B.C.)

Other prominent figures sometimes considered worthy to be included on a list of sages were Anacharsis of Scythia; Myson of Chenea; Pherecydes of Syros; Epimenides of Crete; and Pisistratus of Athens.

Seven Victims of the Morbus Pedicularis

In chapter 36 of his biography of Sulla, Plutarch lists seven well-known figures who contracted and succumbed to a gout-like disease called *morbus pedicularis*. The seven were

1. Acastus, son of Pelias; he was one of the Argonauts.
2. Alcman, a seventh-century B.C. poet from Sparta.
3. Callisthenes of Olynthus, a historian who accompanied Alexander the Great on his expeditions. (Other sources state that Callisthenes was executed by Alexander.)
4. Eunus, a runaway slave who led a slave revolt in Sicily 135–132 B.C.
5. Mucius Scaevola, a lawyer and jurist.
6. Pherecydes, a sixth-century B.C. mythographer and one of the first Greek prose writers.
7. Perhaps the most noted name on the list is that of (Lucius Cornelius) Sulla himself, a statesman and general who established a brutal dictatorship in Rome (81–79 B.C.), and lived a notoriously dissolute life in retirement.

The Seven Wives and Seven Mistresses of Zeus

Much ink has been consumed in mythology texts detailing the tales of Zeus's womanizing. This busy god also married seven times. The wives (in order) were

1. Metis
2. Themis
3. Eurynome
4. Demeter
5. Mnemosyne
6. Leto
7. Hera

Additionally, Zeus found the time and the opportunity to have affairs with numerous mistresses; seven of the most famous of these paramours were

1. Alcmene (mother of Hercules by Zeus)
2. Danae (to whom Zeus appeared in a shower of gold, and they became the parents of Perseus)
3. Europa (to whom Zeus appeared in the guise of a white bull, and they begat the famous lawgiver Minos)
4. Io (whom Zeus transformed into a heifer to allay Hera's suspicions)
5. Leda (to whom Zeus appeared as a swan, and they parented Helen and Polydeuces)
6. Maia (the mother of Hermes by Zeus)
7. Semele (the mother of Dionysus by Zeus)

The Seven Wonders of the Ancient World

Of the seven architectural and artistic wonders of the ancient world, only the pyramids still stand. The Seven Wonders were

1. The Egyptian Pyramids.
2. The Hanging Gardens of Babylon: a series of walls carved into a mountainside with bushes and trees draped over the walls.
3. The Statue of Zeus at Olympia: a chryselephantine statue reputedly 40 feet tall.
4. The Colossus of Rhodes: a 100-feet-tall statue of Apollo that overlooked the harbor at Rhodes.
5. The Temple of Artemis at Ephesus: a huge temple—one of the largest known in the ancient world—it measured 342 feet in length.
6. The Mausoleum at Halicarnassus, an elaborate tomb built for Mausolus, a ruler of Halicarnassus (in modern southwestern Turkey).
7. The Lighthouse at Alexandria, a 400-feet-tall structure with a flame that could be seen for miles by sailors approaching the coast of North Africa.

The EIGHTS

The Eight Accused Generals

After the naval battle of Arginusae (406 B.C.), the Athenian generals decided not to attempt to rescue the wounded or stranded survivors; the inclement weather, they said, rendered such an effort impossible. That explanation did not satisfy the authorities in Athens, who ordered the generals to stand trial. Two of the eight—Protomachus and Aristogenes—fled; the other six returned to Athens to face their accusers (Pericles was the son of the famous statesman of the same name). All were found guilty and executed. The six who were tried were:

1. Aristocrates
2. Diomedon
3. Erasinides
4. Lysias
5. Pericles
6. Thrasyllus

The Eight Books of Caesar's Gallic Wars

Julius Caesar organized his famous commentary on the Gallic Wars into eight books, one book for each of the eight years of warfare.

Book number/ year covered, B.C.	Content summary
Book I/58	Demographic and geographic survey of Gaul; campaigns against the Helvetians and the German king Ariovistus.
Book II/57	Campaigns against the Nervians and the Aduatucians.
Book III/56	Campaigns in the Alps and in Aquitania.
Book IV/55	The crossing of the Rhine (including a famous description of the temporary wooden bridge built across the river); the first invasion of Britain.
Book V/54	The second invasion of Britain; turmoil in Gaul.
Book VI/53	Rebellions in Gaul; a description of Gallic and Germanic culture.
Book VII/52	The rise to power of the Gallic chieftain Vercingetorix; Caesar's encounters with him.
Book VIII/51	Final campaigns; conclusion.

Most authorities believe that the eighth book was written by Aulus Hirtius, one of Caesar's officers.

Some select statistics from Caesar's book on the Gallic Wars are as follows:

Seventeen of Caesar's Most Prominent Officers (Legati)

1. Gaius Fabius
2. Lucius Roscius
3. Publius Licinius Crassus
4. Gaius Trebonius
5. Quintus Pedius
6. Gaius Antistius Reginus
7. Aulus Hirtius
8. Lucius Minucius
9. Publius Sulpicius
10. Quintus Tullius Cicero (brother of the famous orator)
11. Titus Labienus (Caesar's principal staff officer for the entirety of the war)
12. Lucius Munatius Plancus
13. Servius Sulpicius Galba
14. Marcus Silanus
15. Titus Sextius
16. Marcus Antonius (Mark Antony)
17. Gaius Caninius Rebilus

59 Gallic, British, and German Tribes Encountered by Caesar Gallic Tribes

Name of Gallic tribe	Aquitanian, Belgian, or Celtic	Name of Gallic tribe	Aquitanian, Belgian, or Celtic
1. Aduatucians	Belgian	24. Morinians	Belgian
2. Aeduans	Belgian	25. Nantuates	Belgian
3. Ambianians	Belgian	26. Nervians	Belgian
4. Andes	Celtic	27. Paemanians	Belgian
5. Arvernians	Celtic	28. Parisians	Celtic
6. Atrebates	Belgian	29. Pictones	Celtic
7. Aulercians	Celtic	30. Rauracians	Celtic
8. Bellovacians	Belgian	31. Remians	Belgian
9. Bituriges	Celtic	32. Rutenians	Celtic
10. Boians	Celtic	33. Sedunians	Belgian
11. Cadurcians	Celtic	34. Sequanians	Belgian
12. Caeroesians	Belgian	35. Sotiates	Aquitanian
13. Caletians	Belgian	36. Suessiones	Belgian
14. Carnutes	Celtic	37. Tarusates	Aquitanian
15. Condrusians	Belgian	38. Treverians	Belgian
16. Curiosolites	Celtic	39. Tulingians	Celtic
17. Eburones	Belgian	40. Turonians	Celtic
18. Eburovices	Celtic	41. Veliocasses	Belgian
19. Helvetians	Celtic	42. Venetians	Celtic
20. Latobrigians	Celtic	43. Veragrians	Belgian
21. Lexovians	Celtic	44. Viromanduians	Belgian
22. Lingones	Belgian	45. Vocates	Aquitanian
23. Menapians	Belgian		

German tribes	*British tribes*
46. Batavians	53. Ancalites
47. Frisians	54. Bibrocians
48. Suebians	55. Cantians
49. Sugambrians	56. Cassians
50. Tencterians	57. Cenimagnians
51. Ubians	58. Segontiacians
52. Usipetes	59. Trinobantes

Select numbers and statistics from each of the eight books are given below.

Book I

368,000: Caesar provides a census list in Book I of the various components of the Helvetian camp. The grand total was 368,000, itemized as follows:

263,000 Helvetians	23,000 Rauracians
36,000 Tulingians	32,000 Boians
14,000 Latobrigians	

He also notes that the total included 92,000 men capable of bearing arms.

Book II

100,000: The Bellovacians, most warlike of the Belgian Gauls, were reputed to have a 100,000-man army. Other Belgian tribes, and their troop strength were as follows:

Suessiones	50,000	Ambianians	10,000
Nervians	50,000	Caletians	10,000
Morinians	25,000	Veliocasses	10,000
Aduatucians	19,000	Viromanduians	10,000
Atrebates	15,000	Menapians	7,000

In addition, the cumulative troop strength of the Condrusians, Caeroesians, Eburones, and Paemanians was 40,000.

After subduing the Aduatucians, Caesar records that 53,000 of their nation were sold as slaves. When the news of Caesar's military exploits reached Rome, an unprecedented 15-day period of thanksgiving was decreed.

Book III

50,000: A Gallic army consisting of 50,000 Aquitanians and Cantabrians fell to the Caesarian legions.

30,000: Servius Galba's forces defeated 30,000 Nantuates, Veragrians, and Sedunians in the Alps.

220: Caesar's navy overcame 220 ships of the Venetians (located in modern-day northwestern France), despite the fact that the Venetian craft were better suited to naval conflict in the north Atlantic. (Caesar also provided in this book a detailed description of the mode of ship construction employed by the Venetians.)

Book IV

430,000: The German tribes (excepting the Suebians) living near the Rhine River had at their disposal some 430,000 soldiers.

100: The Suebians, most numerous and bellicose of the Germanic peoples encountered by the Caesarians, were organized into 100 clans, which provided 1,000 men each for military purposes.

80: A foray into Britain is described in Book IV; 80 ships conveyed two legions across the English Channel. An additional 18 ships were allotted to the cavalry.

Book V

7,000: Quintus Cicero's camp was besieged by 60,000 Gauls, who broke off their blockade when Caesar approached with a much smaller force — about 7,000 men.

600: During the winter of 55–54 B.C., Caesar's troops in Gaul constructed over 600 ships for the purpose of making a second voyage to Britain. Combined with the still serviceable ships from the previous year, Caesar sailed to the island with some 800 vessels, a sight that terrified the British forces. About 40 of the ships were subsequently destroyed at anchor by a fierce storm, and many others sustained heavy damage. However, Caesar quickly organized work crews, with the result that the damaged ships were all repaired within ten days.

Book VI

300 defenders: A fortification defended by a mere 300 Roman soldiers (and even they were not in fighting condition, having just recently recovered from injury and illness) was nearly overrun by an advancing German army. Only Caesar's fortuitous arrival on the scene saved the situation. Three unusual kinds of animals were found in the Hercynian Forest (in Germany):

1. Oxen shaped like deer, with single horns protruding from the foreheads;
2. Goat-shaped elk;
3. "Aurochs," huge, vicious animals that resembled bulls, and were nearly as large as elephants.

The full extent of this forest was unknown to Caesar, but he claimed that it was so vast that even the swiftest traveler would require nine days' time to traverse it.

Two classes of Gauls: Throughout all of Gaul, according to Caesar, there existed only two classes of men: Druids (priests) and knights (soldiers). Some Druids spent 20 years in training and in memorizing sacred texts.

Book VII

250,000 Gauls under Vercingetorix: Perhaps the most intractable Gallic chieftain with whom Caesar had to contend was the Arvernian Vercingetorix. In the year 52 B.C. Caesar had pursued Vercingetorix as far as the town of Alesia, where the latter took refuge. Caesar commenced siege operations, constructing a series of sophisticated fortifications (see below) around Alesia with a double purpose: to prevent Vercingetorix's escape and to provide protection for Caesar's troops against the 250,000-man Gallic army en route to relieve Vercingetorix. According to Caesar, the following lists the various Gallic contingents and their troop strength:

Tribe	Troop strength
Aeduans (with their allies the Segusiavians, Ambivaretians, Brannovices, and Blannovians)	35,000
Arvernians (with their allies the Eleutetians, Cadurcians, Gabalians, and Vellavians)	35,000
Sequanians, Senones, Bituriges, Santones, Rutenians, and Carnutes	12,000 each
Bellovacians and Lemovices	10,000 each
Pictones, Turonians, Parisians, and Helvetians	8,000 each
Suessiones, Ambianians, Mediomatricians, Petrocorians, Nervians, Morinians, Nitiobriges, and Cenomanians	5,000 each
Atrebates	4,000
Veliocasses, Lexovians, and Eburovices	3,000 each
Rauracians and Boians	1,000 each
Curiosolites, Redones, Ambibarians, Caletes, Osismians, Venetians, (coastal) Lemovices, and Venellians	30,000 altogether

Caesar also mentions that the Bellovacians did not send their full complement of troops because they were not willing to submit to another tribe's authority. However, they did provide a token force of 2,000 men. Shortly after this enumeration, Caesar states that the Gallic army consisted of 8,000 cavalry and about 250,000 infantry. However, the list above totals 271,000 (minus the 8,000 Bellovacians). No explanation for the discrepancy is offered.

Roman fortification techniques at Alesia: Sharpened tree trunks, in rows of five, were interconnected and set firmly into trenches, dug to a depth of five feet. In front of the trenchwork were dug pits, three feet in depth, with sharpened stakes concealed within them. These pits were arranged in groups containing eight rows, separated by a distance of three feet.

When the news of Caesar's ultimate success at Alesia reached Rome, a 20-day period of thanksgiving was decreed.

800 Gallic survivors: The Roman siege of the city of Bourges ended with the massacre of all but 800 of its 40,000 residents. (Caesar justified the slaughter on the ground that it avenged a similar, albeit smaller scale, Gallic attack on Roman citizens living in the town of Cenabum.)

20 cities set on fire: Vercingetorix and his war council set fire to 20 cities of the Bituriges, apparently to prevent them from falling into Caesar's hands.

Six feet of snow: Caesar claimed that on his march northward from Italy to Gaul to confront Vercingetorix, the route that he had selected was blocked by six feet of newly fallen snow. Never one to be slowed by such an obstacle, Caesar merely ordered his men to clear a path; they did so, and he proceeded.

Book VIII

12,000 Andian casualties: The leader of the Andes, Dumnacus, lost 12,000 of his soldiers in an attack on a portion of the Roman army commanded by Gaius Fabius.

Caesar also authored a three-book commentary on the civil war that erupted after his crossing of the Rubicon River with his army intact, in January 49 B.C. His account focuses on the events of 49 and 48.

Book number/ years covered B.C.	Content summary
Book I/49	The consequences of the crossing of the Rubicon; Pompey's flight to Greece; and Caesar's journey to Spain,
Book II/49	Caesar's subjugation of Spain; and the defeat of a Caesarian force in North Africa under the command of Gaius Curio.
Book III/48	Caesar's pursuit of Pompey in Greece; the Battle of Pharsalus; and Pompey's flight to and death in Egypt.

The Eight Books of Celsus's De Medicina

Aulus Cornelius Celsus (first century A.D.) wrote an encyclopediac work covering agriculture, medicine, military affairs, oratory, and philosophy. But only the portion on medicine (*De Medicina*) survives intact. The treatise was so highly regarded that it earned its author laudatory epithets such as the "Roman Hippocrates" and the "Cicero of Physicians." The eight books are as follows:

Book I.   An overview of the history of medicine; description and definition of good health; suggestions on maintaining health; and methods of strengthening areas of physical weakness.

Book II.   General description of diseases; effects of the seasons and
            weather on health (Celsus states that spring is the most
            healthful season, autumn the least); general and specific
            physical harbingers of disease; prognoses of various kinds of
            ailments; and methods of treatment.

Book III.   The four classes of disease (acute, chronic, diseases that are com-
            binations of acute and chronic, and diseases that are neither);
            and treatments for various kinds of fevers, mental deficiencies,
            water retention, malnutrition, epilepsy, jaundice, elephan-
            tiasis, and paralysis.

Book IV.   A survey of the various parts of the body: head, mouth, tongue,
            windpipe, liver, lungs, stomach, intestines, kidneys, and
            bladder; and descriptions of and remedies for ailments that
            afflict these body parts.

Book V.   Drugs and their uses: descriptions of drugs that inhibit
            bleeding, cause clotting, reduce inflammation, fight infection,
            cleanse, disperse or expel diseased matter, decongest, promote
            scab formation, soothe, and soften. Methods of drug prepara-
            tion; a description of antidotes; and pills (for sleeping, for
            headaches, stomach aches, and toothaches, and for chest pains
            and coughing). Lesions, including a lengthy and detailed
            discussion of numerous kinds of wounds and other traumata
            and their treatment.

Book VI.   Disorders that afflict specific body parts: scalp, eyes, ears, nose,
            teeth and gums, tonsils, mouth, fingers, navel, and reproduc-
            tive organs. (The section on the eyes is particularly detailed.)

Book VII.   Surgical procedures for dislocations or hemorrhaging; abscesses;
            wounds suffered in warfare—especially those caused by spears,
            arrows, or leaden balls; and tumors of the head and neck.
            Surgical procedures for disorders of the eyes and eyelids, ears,
            nostrils, mouth—including tooth extraction, tonsils, thyroid,
            navel area, intestines exposed due to trauma, abdominal wall,
            genital region, and bladder—including extraction of kidney
            stones. Methods for removing a deceased fetus from the
            uterus. Treatments for the disorders of the legs and fingers,
            including gangrene.

Book VIII. Matters relating to bones: skull, teeth, spine, ribs, sternum, arm
            bones, hip, leg bones, ankles, heels, and other bones of the
            feet. Descriptions of diseased bone and cartilage, and bone
            excision. Treatments for head, nose, and ear injuries. A
            general description of fractures and dislocations.

The Eight Books of Thucydides' Peloponnesian War

The historian Thucydides (ca.460–400 B.C.) wrote a monumental history
of the Peloponnesian War, a treatise whose influence and importance have not
diminished with the passage of time. The work is divided into eight books, as
follows:

Book number/years covered B.C.	Content summary
Book I / Prehistory–431	Introduction; conflicts and disputes that set the stage for the Peloponnesian War; and the Pentecontaetia.
Book II / 431–429	The beginning of the war; the Plague; Pericles' Funeral Oration; and initial military engagements.
Book III / 428–426	Rebellion in Mytilene; Plataea's capitulation to the Spartans; and events in Corcyra, Sicily, and Greece.
Book IV / 425–423	Victory for Athens at Pylos, and defeat at Delium; and Spartan occupation of Amphipolis.
Book V / 422–416	Peace of Nicias; Athenian alliance with Argos; Melian Dialogue; and Athenian subjugation of Melos.
Book VI / 415	Debate over the Sicilian Expedition; the decision to invade Sicily; and subsequent military activities in Sicily.
Book VII / 414–413	Athenian setbacks in Sicily; and the ultimate destruction of the Athenian forces.
Book VIII / 412–411	Persian involvement in the war; and the rise and fall of the Four Hundred in Athens.

Thucydides' narrative ends abruptly in the middle of Book VIII; it seems likely that he had intended to write about the entirety of the war, to 404 B.C. The most plausible (although not the only) explanation for this sudden end is that he died before he was able to complete the project.

The Eight Books of Valerius Flaccus's Argonautica

The poet Valerius Flaccus (first century A.D.) wrote an epic poem about the voyage of Jason and the Argonauts, entitled *Argonautica*. The work is divided into eight books:

Book I.　Introduction; the building and launching of the *Argo*.
Book II.　The *Argo* sails east.
Book III.　A battle in Cyzicus; and the story of Hercules and Hylas.
Book IV.　Hercules departs for Troy; and the *Argo*'s voyage continues.
Book V.　The Argonauts land in Colchis, and conclude an alliance with the king, Aeetes; and Jason meets Medea.

Book VI.   Accounts of battles.
Book VII.   Medea's dilemma: love for Jason versus loyalty to her father.
Book VIII.   Jason obtains the Golden Fleece and leaves Colchis, taking
          Medea with him.

The Eight Bridges of Rome
The ancient Romans developed and perfected the art of bridge building.
Ultimately, eight bridges spanned Rome's Tiber River:

1. Pons (bridge) Aelius
2. Pons Aemilius
3. Pons Agrippae
4. Pons Cestius

5. Pons Fabricius
6. Pons Mulvius
7. Pons Neronianus
8. Pons Sublicius

The Eight Events of the Funeral Games for Patroclus
In the twenty-third book of the *Iliad*, Homer recounts the athletic festival
sponsored by Achilles, in honor of his recently slain friend, Patroclus. The two
wrestling contestants, Ajax (son of Telamon) and Odysseus, battled to a draw, and
were declared cowinners. Each received a tripod. The two contestants for the javelin
throw were Agamemnon and Meriones. Since it was acknowledged that Agamemnon was the far superior thrower, the contest was canceled and the magnanimous
Agamemnon allowed Meriones to claim the prize. The eight contests of this
festival, including the two just mentioned, were

Event	Winner	Prize(s)
1. Chariot race	Diomedes	A servant woman and a tripod
2. Boxing	Epeius	A six-year-old mule
3. Wrestling	—	A large tripod
4. Foot race	Odysseus	A silver mixing bowl
5. Sword fight	Diomedes	A silver sword
6. Discus throw	Polypoites	The iron discus used in the contest
7. Archery	Meriones	Ten steel axe heads
8. Javelin throw	—	A decorated cauldron

Eight Litter Bearers
It was considered the epitome of Roman decadence for a person to be carried
in a litter with eight bearers, a luxurious mode of transportation provided for the
emperor Caligula (who reigned A.D. 37–41). Cicero mentions that the corrupt
Sicilian governor Gaius Verres was borne by eight men in a litter furnished with
a large cushion stuffed with rose petals. And the epigrammatist Martial refers to
a certain Philippus who, although perfectly healthy, rode about in an eight-bearer
litter.

The Eight Military Crowns

According to Aulus Gellius (5.6), the Romans awarded eight different kinds of crowns for various acts of military valor.

Name/material	Awarded to
1. Triumphal/gold	A victorious general, for his triumphal procession (granted after a major victory over a dangerous or aggressive enemy).
2. Siege/grass	A general who liberated the citizens of a besieged city.
3. Civic/oak leaves	A soldier who saved a comrade's life in battle.
4. Mural/gold	The first soldier to breach the walls of an enemy city.
5. Camp/gold	The first soldier to penetrate an enemy's camp.
6. Naval/gold	The first soldier to board an enemy ship during a naval battle.
7. Ovation/myrtle leaves	A victorious general, for an ovation (a smaller-scale triumphal procession, usually because the defeated enemy was considered second-rate).
8. Olive/olive leaves	Those who were not directly involved in a particular battle, but still procured the honor of participating in a triumphal procession.

Eight Priestly Colleges

The second king of Rome, Numa Pompilius, is reported by Dionysius of Halicarnassus (2.64, 70, 72, 73) to have established the following priestly colleges:

1. *Curiones*: priests who presided over the 30 *curiae*, or voting districts.

2. *Flamines*: priests assigned to the veneration of a specific deity; for example, the *flamen Dialis*, priest of Jupiter.

3. *Celeres*: priests assigned to protect the king.

4. *Augures*: priests whose responsibilities involved the interpretation of omens, especially as revealed by birds.

5. *Vestal Virgins*: priestesses who tended to the rites and temple of the goddess Vesta.

6. *Salii*: priests of the god Mars.

7. *Fetiales*: priests who represented the Roman people in foreign affairs.

8. *Pontifices*: priests who established and interpreted religious law; they also served as judges in cases involving religious matters, and meted out punishments for sacrileges.

Eight Reforms of Gaius Sempronius Gracchus

In 123–122 B.C. a reform-minded Roman tribune by the name of Gaius Sempronius Gracchus proposed a number of measures, some highly controversial. Eight of Gracchus's proposals were as follows:

1. An endorsement of a land redistribution plan passed in 133 (at the urging of Gaius's brother, Tiberius).
2. The construction of new roads to benefit farmers who had been allotted land under the provisions of the land redistribution law.
3. The founding of a new colony in North Africa, on the site of ancient Carthage.
4. Regulations on the price and availability of the corn supply in Rome.
5. A prohibition on recruiting for military service young men under the age of 17.
6. A prohibition on the convening of special courts with powers of capital punishment.
7. A measure specifying that juries, instead of being made up of senators, were to be composed of equestrians (the so-called merchant, or middle class).
8. A proposal admitting Italic peoples to full Roman citizenship.

Most of these proposals—which must have seemed dangerously revolutionary to conservative and even moderate politicians of the day—did not pass into law. Gaius Gracchus and some 3,000 of his adherents were executed or murdered in the aftermath of the violence spawned by his legislative program.

Eight Requirements for Happiness

The poet Martial lists the following as the eight necessities for personal happiness:

1. An innkeeper
2. A butcher
3. A bath
4. A barber
5. A gameboard (with gaming pieces)
6. A few books of his own choice
7. An educated friend
8. Two servants, a boy and a girl

Eight Spartan Sayings

The ancient Spartans were noted for their economy of speech; indeed, the district in which Sparta was located, Laconia, has provided the English language with the word "laconic." Plutarch collected and published several hundred well-known Spartan sayings (*Moralia* 208–236), including the following eight:

1. When someone praised the courage of the soldiers of Argos, a Spartan remarked: "In Troy." (That is, centuries earlier. The implication is that Spartan soldiers had become preeminent.)
2. When the poet Pindar wrote "Athens: Greece's bulwark," a Spartan noted that with a bulwark like that, Greece would surely fall.

3. When someone viewed a painting showing Athenians overcoming Spartans and commented, "Courageous Athenians!" a Spartan standing nearby chimed in with "In the picture."

4. When King Philip, upon entering Laconia, wrote to the Spartans to inquire whether they preferred him to approach as friend or enemy, they replied, "Neither."

5. Some travelers had a chance encounter with a group of Spartans on the road. The travelers said, "You're lucky. A band of muggers has just now hightailed it for the woods." The Spartans retorted, "We're not the lucky ones, by god. They are."

6. When King Philip issued orders to the Spartans in a letter, they wrote back, "Re your orders to us: No."

7. After the Spartan general Lysander had defeated Athens in battle and occupied the city (404 B.C.), he sent this message to Sparta, "Athens is taken." The Spartan leaders, in typical laconic fashion, remarked, "'Taken' would have sufficed."

8. When a physician examined King Pausanias (reigned 408–394 B.C.) and found nothing wrong with him, the king replied, "That is because you are not my doctor."

The Eight Winds

The first-century B.C. architect Andronicus of Cyrrha (in Syria) is said to have constructed in Athens an octagonal marble tower with artistic representations of the eight winds on each of its sides. The names of the eight were

1. Boreas: north wind
2. Caicias: northeast wind
3. Apeliotes: east wind
4. Euros: southeast wind
5. Notos: south wind
6. Lips: southwest wind
7. Zephyros: west wind
8. Sciron: northwest wind

The Roman counterparts (according to Vitruvius [1.4]):

1. Septentrio: north wind
2. Aquilo: northeast wind
3. Solanus: east wind
4. Eurus: southeast wind
5. Auster: south wind
6. Africus: southwest wind
7. Favonius: west wind
8. Caurus: northwest wind

The Eight-Year Year

The so-called Greek "Great Year," or "Eternal Year," represented an eight-year cycle wherein certain events were traditionally thought to have taken place. Hercules, for example, reputedly completed his Twelve Labors within an Eternal Year; this was likewise the length of servitude placed upon Cadmus (for killing the dragon) and Apollo (for dispatching the Cyclopes). In historical times eight years of servitudinal exile was the commonly prescribed sentence for a murderer, and it is thought that this practice was derived from the mythological precedents.

The NINES

The Nine Archons of Athens

The chief magistrates of Athens were called archons; nine were chosen each year, by lot. The title *archon eponymous* devolved upon the leading archon, and the year in which he served was named for him. The second and third in rank were called, respectively, *archon basileus* (king archon) and *polemarchos* (war archon). Each of the other six received the somewhat generic title *archon thesmothetes* (lawgiver). The archons lost much of their power and influence with the rise of the Athenian democracy in the fifth century B.C.

The Nine Books of Oppian (Four on Hunting and Five on Fishing)

The poet Oppian (early third century A.D.) wrote a treatise on fishing (*Halieutica*), and one on hunting (*Cynegetica*), although scholarly consensus suggests that the latter was written by a different author, perhaps, in fact, by another writer also bearing the name Oppian.

The four books on hunting are as follows:

Book I.   Introduction; hunter's equipment; and breeds of horses and dogs, and their uses in hunting.

Book II.   Descriptions of various kinds of game, including deer, sheep, elephants, panthers, and apes.

Book III. A continuation of Book II, including descriptions of lions, bears, tigers, wild boars, crocodiles, and rabbits.

Book IV. Methods of hunting lions, leopards, bears, rabbits, gazelles, and foxes.

The five books on fishing are as follows:

Book I.   Introduction; and descriptions of various kinds of fish and other sea creatures, including eels, turtles, mullets, dolphins, seals, and oysters.

Book II.   A continuation of Book I, including descriptions of squid, crabs, starfish, lobsters, and stingrays.

Book III. Methods of fishing; best times and seasons to fish; hooks and baits; and strategies employed by various kinds of fish to elude capture.

Book IV. Catching certain species of fish by using live bait of the same species and or opposite sex; and various other methods of catching fish.

Book V. A description of large denizens of the depths, especially whales. Included in this book is an interesting discussion on the immorality of catching and killing dolphins.

The Nine Books of Theophrastus's **Plant Researches**

The fourth-century B.C. essayist Theophrastus wrote on numerous topics, including a treatise on botany. Its nine books contain the following topics:

Book I.	Classification and composition of plants.
Book II.	Propagation and cultivation of plants.
Book III.	Wild trees (including fir, maple, ash, willow, elm, oak, and poplar).
Book IV.	Plants native to specific regions (for example, Egypt, Libya, and Asia).
Book V.	Kinds of timber and their uses, especially in ship and house construction.
Book VI.	Shrubbery.
Book VII.	Herbaceous plants.
Book VIII.	Herbaceous plants (continued).
Book IX.	Juices, resins, and medicines obtained from plants.

Nine Days of Mourning

The traditional mourning period for a deceased Roman was nine days. On the ninth day a memorial ceremony was held, followed by a banquet.

The Nine Greeks in the Wooden Horse

One of the most famous stories in Greek mythology describes the end of the 10-year Trojan War, won by the Greeks through the treachery of the Wooden Horse. The crafty and cunning Odysseus suggested that the Greeks construct a wooden horse, with a hollow belly large enough to contain nine men. This they did; they brought the horse to the walls of Troy, claiming that it was a gift to the Trojans from Athena, and that they (the Greeks) had decided to break off their siege of Troy and return home. After some debate, the Trojans dragged the horse into their city, and then enjoyed a festive celebration occasioned by the putative end of the war. That night, after the Trojans had fallen prey to a mass drunken stupor, the Greeks concealed in the body of the horse emerged, opened the city's gates to let in their waiting comrades, and together they destroyed Troy. According to Vergil (*Aeneid* 2.261–264) the nine Greeks in the horse were

1. Acamas   2. Epeus   3. Machaon

4. Menelaus	6. Odysseus	8. Thessandrus
5. Neoptolemus	7. Sthenelus	9. Thoas

A Nine Jet Fountain

Located on the Acropolis was a fountain with nine jets, originally called the Callirhoe, but later known as the Enneacrunus. Archaeological research has indicated that the springs feeding this fountain were used as a water source by the Athenians. Thucydides (2.15) suggests that the tyrant Pisistratus constructed the nine-jet fountain, which drew its water from these subterranean springs.

Nine Logographers

In the earliest days of Greek literature, history, mythology, geneological information, and the like were transmitted from one generation to the next by means of an oral tradition in a poetic format. The first historians who attempted to write these accounts in prose were called logographers (prose writers). At least nine of these logographers are known by name, although their works survive today only in fragmentary form.

Name/approximate dates, B.C.	Topic(s)
1. Acusilaus of Argos/sixth century?	Geneologies
2. Cadmus of Miletus/540	The founding of Miletus; the colonization of western Asia Minor
3. Charon of Lampsacus/mid-fifth century	Persian history; history of Lampsacus
4. Dionysius of Miletus/dates unknown	Persian history
5. Hecataeus of Miletus/550–476	Geography; geneologies
6. Hellanicus of Lesbos/480–400	Mythology; geography; Athenian history
7. Hippys of Rhegium/dates unknown	Italian and Sicilian history
8. Pherecydes of Athens/d. 400	Early Attic myths
9. Xanthus of Sardis/fifth century	History of Lydia

The term logographer (*logographos*; alternatively, *logopoios*) also applied to rhetoricians who served as ghostwriters for courtroom orators.

The Nine Lyric Poets of the Canon

The Alexandrian scholars regarded the following as among the best lyric poets:

1. Alcaeus (b. ca.620 B.C.)	2. Alcman (654–611 B.C.)

3. Anacreon (b. ca.570 B.C.)
4. Bacchylides (fifth century B.C.)
5. Ibycus (mid-sixth century B.C.)
6. Pindar (518–438 B.C.)

7. Sappho (sixth century B.C.)
8. Simonides (ca.556–468 B.C.)
9. Stesichorus (ca.630–555 B.C.)

The Nine Muses

These mythological figures were viewed as sources of inspiration for writers, musicians, and scientists. Each Muse was identified with a specific area of endeavor:

1. Calliope: epic poetry
2. Clio: history
3. Erato: love poetry
4. Euterpe: lyric poetry
5. Melpomene: tragedy

6. Polyhymnia: sacred music
7. Terpsichore: choral dancing
8. Thalia: comedy
9. Urania: astronomy

So highly regarded was the Greek poet Sappho (sixth century B.C.) that she was sometimes styled the Tenth Muse. Very little of the seven books of her poetry has survived to the present day; while only one complete poem remains intact.

The Nine Principal Works of Galen

Galen (A.D. 129–199), an eminent physician, was also a prolific writer. His treatises deal primarily with medicine; his influence was widespread, not only in his own day but well into the Middle Ages, where his writings served as standard medical texts. His principal works are as follows:

Title	Topic
1. *On the Use of the Parts of the Human Body*	Anatomy
2. *On Anatomical Procedure*	Anatomy
3. *On the Natural Faculties*	Physiology
4. *On the Teachings of Hippocrates and Plato*	Philosophy of Medicine
5. *On Tumors*	Pathology
6. *Therapeutical Method*	Therapeutics
7. *On the Mixing and Efficacy of Drugs*	Pharmacology
8. *On the Diagnosis of Different Pulses*	Diagnosis/prognosis
9. *Protrepticus*	Handbook for medical students

Additionally, Galen annotated several of Hippocrates' medical writings; he also produced works on a number of nonmedical topics, including grammar and word studies, comic plays, philosophy, and rhetoric.

Nine Towns in Nine Days

When an alliance of Praeneste and eight other towns moved against Rome (ca. 380 B.C.), the dictator Titus Quinctius Cincinnatus rallied the Romans and put down the threat, capturing all nine towns in nine days. Livy (6.29) states that Cincinnatus resigned his dictatorship on his twentieth day in office.

The TENS

The Ten Attic Orators

In the first century A.D. a scholar named Caecilius of Calacte composed a list of the ten Greek orators who were presumably the best practitioners of the art. The ten who made the list were

1. Antiphon (ca.480–411 B.C.)
2. Andocides (ca.440–390 B.C.)
3. Lysias (ca.458–380 B.C.)
4. Isocrates (436–338 B.C.)
5. Isaeus (420–350 B.C.)
6. Lycurgus (390–325 B.C.)
7. Aeschines (393–322 B.C.)
8. Demosthenes (384–322 B.C.)
9. Hyperides (389–322 B.C.)
10. Dinarchus (360–after 292 B.C.)

The Board of Ten Generals

One of the reforms enacted in fifth-century B.C. Athens involved the annual election of ten military leaders, collectively called the Board of Ten Generals. Ambitious men like Pericles used their membership in this body as a springboard to political power.

The Ten Books of Apicius's Treatise On Cooking

A first-century A.D. gourmet named Marcus Gavius Apicius wrote extensively on foods, cooking, and recipes. These writings were later collected (probably in the third century A.D.) and published under the title *De Re Coquinaria* (*On Cooking*). The *De Re Coquinaria* is divided into ten books, each containing a variety of culinary themes:

Book I. Wine, spices; and methods of preserving various kinds of food.

Book II. Minces, puddings, and sausage.

Book III. Vegetables, including asparagus, squash, melons, cabbages, beets, and carrots.

Book IV.   Recipes for various kinds of appetizers, delicacies and desserts.
Book V.   Peas, beans, and chickpeas.
Book VI.   Ostrich, crane, duck, peacock, pheasant, goose, and chicken dishes.
Book VII. Specialty dishes, including sow's belly, fig-fed pork, truffles, snails, and eggs.
Book VIII. Wild boar, venison, gazelle, beef, veal, hare, and dormouse dishes
Book IX.   Seafood dishes, including shellfish, oysters, sardines, and mussels; and fish sauces.
Book X.   More on seafood dishes—eel, sea scorpions, perch, mullet, and red snapper; and fish sauces.

Several writers, including Seneca and Martial, report that Apicius spent 100 million sesterces on his gourmandizing and other extravagances. When Apicius took an inventory of his finances and discovered a balance of "only" 10 million sesterces, he reputedly poisoned himself (at a banquet, of course) because he believed that no gourmet worth his salt could possibly live appropriately on such a paltry sum.

The Ten Books of Curtius's History of Alexander

Quintus Curtius Rufus (first century A.D.) wrote a narrative of the campaigns of Alexander the Great, the only book-length treatment of Alexander's career by a Roman historian. Books I and II survive only in epitomized form.

Book III.   A description of the Persian king Darius's (III) preparations of his forces at the Euphrates River (333 B.C.); and subsequent sieges, marches, and battles.
Book IV.   Siege of Tyre; and the Battle of Gaugamela.
Book V.   Capture of Persepolis; and the death of Darius.
Book VI.   A revolt (against Macedonian rule) in Greece; and a conspiracy against Alexander, allegedly masterminded by Philotas, a disenchanted Macedonian army officer.
Book VII.   The subjugation of the Sogdiani and the Scythians.
Book VIII. Another conspiracy against Alexander, this one led by Hermolaus, one of the royal pages. Also implicated was the historian Callisthenes, who was executed for his suspected involvement; and the Battle of the Hydaspes River.
Book IX.   A description of Alexander's travels and battles in India; and a military mutiny of his war-weary soldiers.
Book X.   Another mutiny; the founding of cities; and Alexander's death in Babylon.

The Ten Books of Diogenes Laertius's Lives of the Philosophers

Diogenes Laertius (third century A.D.) wrote accounts of the lives and philosophical teachings of numerous Greek thinkers. His compilation is divided into ten books, each narrating the lives of certain philosophers. Following is a sample listing from each book:

Book I.	Thales; Solon; Periander; and Anacharsis.
Book II.	Anaximander; Socrates; Xenophon; and Aristippus.
Book III.	Plato (the sole entry in this book).
Book IV.	Xenocrates; Arcesilaus; and Bion.
Book V.	Aristotle; Theophrastus; Demetrius of Phalerum; and Heraclides.
Book VI.	Antisthenes; and Diogenes the Cynic.
Book VII.	Zeno; Cleanthes; and Chrysippus.
Book VIII.	Pythagoras; and Empedocles.
Book IX.	Heraclitus; Democritus; and Pyrrho.
Book X.	Epicurus (the sole entry in this book).

The Ten Books of Lucan's Pharsalia

The Roman poet Marcus Annaeus Lucanus (Lucan, A.D. 39–65) authored a large number of poetic works in his brief life, of which only one, *Pharsalia*, survives. *Pharsalia* (or *Civil War*, as it is alternatively titled) covers the conflict between Pompey and Caesar in 49–48 B.C. A summary of the ten books follows:

Book I.	Background information; and character delineations of Pompey and Caesar.
Book II.	Character delineation of Cato the Younger; and Pompey's flight to Greece.
Book III.	Caesar in Rome and Massilia; and Pompey's activities in Greece.
Book IV.	Caesar in Spain; and the defeat of Caesarian forces in Illyricum and North Africa.
Book V.	Pompey's leavetaking of his wife, Cornelia; and Caesar's dictatorship.
Book VI.	The Battle of Dyrrhachium.
Book VII.	The Battle of Pharsalus.
Book VIII.	Pompey's subsequent flight to Egypt and his assassination.
Book IX.	Cato's movements; and Caesar's arrival in Egypt.
Book X.	Caesar and Cleopatra. [Book X was not finished when Lucan died.]

The Ten Books of Pausanias's Description of Greece

Pausanias (second century A.D.) traveled widely throughout Greece, and wrote a lengthy book describing in great detail the topography, history, legends, and monuments of the places that he visited. The work is divided into ten books:

Book I. Attica	Book VI. Elis (Part II)
Book II. Corinth	Book VII. Achaea
Book III. Laconia	Book VIII. Arcadia
Book IV. Messenia	Book IX. Boeotia
Book V. Elis (Part I)	Book X. Phocis

In Books V and VI Pausanias cites the names of over 200 Olympic athletes, sometimes adding cursory biographical data. (Elis was the district in southwestern Greece in which Olympia was located.)

The Ten Books of Vergil's Eclogues

Vergil's *Eclogues*, a series of pastoral poems, was divided into ten books:

Book I.   A lament over lands lost by farmers during the Roman civil war.

Book II.   A shepherd's unrequited love.

Book III.   A singing contest between the shepherds Menalcas and Damoetas.

Book IV.   The so-called "Messianic" *Eclogue*, in which Vergil describes the birth of a child who will usher in a new golden age. Some Christian scholars see in this poem a foretelling of Christ's birth.

Book V.   A singing contest featuring two shepherds, Menalcas and Mopsus.

Book VI.   The shepherd Silenus sings of the world's creation.

Book VII.   Another singing contest, this time between the shepherds Corydon and Thyrsis.

Book VIII.   A song about a girl who regains her lost lover.

Book IX.   A poem about a farmer's lost lands.

Book X.   A poem about the love of Vergil's friend Gallus for Lycoris.

The Ten Books of Vitruvius's De Architectura

The Roman architect Vitruvius (early first century A.D.) wrote a technical manual on architecture, the only one of its kind surviving from antiquity. The topics of its ten books are as follows:

Book I.   Background information; and city planning.

Book II.   Materials; and construction methods.

Book III.   Ionic temples.

Book IV.   Doric and Corinthian temples.

Book V.   Public buildings — theaters and baths.

Book VI.   Private homes.

Book VII.   House decoration — pavements; plastering; wall painting; and colors

Book VIII.   Water — quality; testing; and aqueduct and pipe construction.

Book IX. Measurements; acoustics; and geometry.
Book X.   Civil and military machines.

Decarchies

After the victory by the Spartans in the Peloponnesian War (431–404 B.C.), they customarily established councils of ten men—decarchies—to administer the affairs of cities that had been allied to Athens.

Decemviri (Ten Men)

Councils or Boards of Ten Men were organized in ancient Rome to perform a number of official functions. The following are some examples:

1. A Board of Ten was empaneled to determine for the courts whether a man was free or slave.

2. A Board of Ten prepared the text of the Twelve Tables.

3. A Board of Ten was entrusted to care for the Sibylline Books, records of prophesies made by the ten Sibyls (see below). This board originally consisted of two members (IIviri sacris faciundis). By the terms of the Licinian Law of 367 B.C., the number was increased to 10 (5 patricians, 5 plebeians). Later, the number was raised once again, this time to 15. The date of this final augmentation is unknown, although Marcus Caelius, in a letter to Cicero dated August 51 B.C., refers to the appointment of Publius Cornelius Dolabella to the "Fifteen."

Decennia

Spans of ten years to delineate or measure events occur in a variety of historical contexts in the Greek and Roman world. Ten examples are listed here:

1. The Trojan War lasted ten years.

2. The Greek hero Odysseus wandered for ten years after the Trojan War before returning to his island home of Ithaca.

3. After the Athenian statesman Solon reformed the laws of Athens in 594 B.C., he requested a period of ten years to travel abroad.

4. For a period in the fifth century B.C. the Athenians held an annual ostracism vote, in which they exiled from the city a politician or general who seemed to be too ambitious, arrogant, or tyrannical. The length of exile was ten years.

5. A span of ten years (556–546 B.C.) separated the first and second tyrannies of the Athenian statesman Pisistratus (d. 527 B.C.).

6. A span of ten years separated the two great invasions of Greece by the Persians. The first of these, under King Darius, occurred in 490 B.C.; the second, led by Darius's son Xerxes, took place in 480.

7. The Roman siege of the town of Veii—a Roman "Trojan War"—lasted for ten years (405–396 B.C.).

8. The Roman poet Vergil spent ten years writing his classic epic Aeneid.

9. In 46 B.C. Julius Caesar was granted a ten-year dictatorship.
10. The emperor Vespasian ruled Rome for ten years (A.D. 69–79).

The Ten Diners at Trimalchio's Banquet

Nine people, seated by threes at three different couches, would generally be found at formal Roman dinner parties. In Petronius's (first century A.D.) entertaining account of a dinner party given by the flamboyant Campanian freedman Trimalchio, there were ten diners seated at the three couches:

1. Trimalchio	5. Ascyltos	8. Fortunata
2. Agamemnon	6. Habinnas	9. Proculus
3. Hermeros	7. Scintilla	10. Diogenes
4. Encolpius		

In one of his *Satires* (2.8) the poet Horace describes the more typical arrangement of a dinner party, with nine diners:

1. Fundanius	4. Servilius Balatro	7. Nometanus
2. Viscus	5. Vibidius	8. Nasidienus
3. Varius	6. Maecenas	9. Porcius

The learned encyclopedist Varro (quoted in Aulus Gellius 13.11) suggests that the number of guests at a dinner party ought not to be less than three (the number of Graces), nor more than nine (the number of Muses).

In his biography of Lucius Verus (5.1), Julius Capitolinus notes that Verus organized a banquet for 12 diners, despite the (supposedly) familiar aphorism *septem convivium, novem vero convicium*: "seven, just right; nine, a fight." However, Capitolinus's biography contains the only known reference to the propriety of seven (not nine) dinner guests.

The Ten Events of the Ancient Olympics

In the first celebration of the ancient Olympics—the traditional date is 776 B.C.—the only event was a 200-yard sprint. Other events were added gradually, until the total reached ten:

1. Stade race, a 200-yard dash.
2. Diaulos race, a 400-yard dash.
3. Dolichos race, a long-distance race of varying lengths.
4. Hoplite race, a race in which the competitors carried shields and wore helmets.
5. Boxing, much like modern boxing, except that in the ancient version there were no rounds, no weight classes and no point systems. Victory was decided when one boxer yielded.
6. Wrestling, in which the object was to throw the opponent to the ground.
7. Pankration, a brutal combination of boxing and wrestling.
8. Pentathlon, a single contest composed of five events: long jump, javelin, discus, wrestling, and a foot race.

9. Horse racing.
10. Chariot racing.

The Ten Historians of the Canon
The Alexandrians rated the following ten historians as the most skilled:

1. Anaximenes (ca.380–320 B.C.)
2. Callisthenes (fourth century B.C.)
3. Ephorus (ca.405–330 B.C.)

4. Hellanicus (ca.500–415 B.C.)
5. Herodotus (ca.490–425 B.C.)

6. Philistus (d. 356 B.C.)
7. Polybius (ca.200–after 118 B.C.)
8. Theopompus (fourth century B.C.)
9. Thucydides (ca.460–400 B.C.)
10. Xenophon (ca.430–354 B.C.)

The Ten Kings of Athenian Legend
In its earliest days Athens was reputedly ruled by ten legendary kings; the following list is drawn from the third book of Apollodorus's *Library*:

1. Cecrops
2. Cranaus
3. Amphictyon
4. Erichthonius

5. Pandion
6. Erechtheus
7. Cecrops (son of Erechtheus

8. Pandion (son of Cecrops)
9. Aegeus
10. Theseus

Ten Platonic Categories
Plato categorized many aspects of life into various kinds of divisions (usually of three, four, or five). The following are ten examples:

1. Three kinds of goods: mind; body; and external goods.
2. Three kinds of friendship: natural; social; and guest/host.
3. Five kinds of government: democratic; aristocratic; oligarchical; monarchical; and tyrannical.
4. Three kinds of justice: pertaining to gods; pertaining to humans; and pertaining to the deceased.
5. Three kinds of knowledge: practical; productive; and theoretical.
6. Five kinds of medicine: pharmaceutical; surgical; nutritional; diagnostic; and curative.
7. Five kinds of speech: political; rhetorical; colloquial; dialectical; and technical.
8. Three kinds of music: vocal; instrumental; and vocal and instrumental (as when, for example, a harpist sings and accompanies himself on the harp).
9. Six kinds of rhetoric: persuasion, dissuasion, accusation; defense; panegyric; and invective.
10. Three kinds of craftsmanship: production (for example, a miner who provides metal); fabrication (a blacksmith who creates a weapon from the metal); and use (a soldier who uses the metal weapon).

The Ten Plays of Menander

The plays of Menander (342–292 B.C.) were lost until the middle of the twentieth century, when papyrus finds revealed one nearly complete play (*Dyskolos*), and substantial portions of nine others.

He is thought to have authored about 100 plays over the course of his career. The ten survivors are

1. *Aspis* (Shield)
2. *Colax* (Flatterer)
3. *Dis Exapaton* (Twice a Swindler)
4. *Dyskolos* (Grouch)
5. *Epitrepontes* (Men in Arbitration)
6. *Georgos* (Farmer)
7. *Misumenos* (Hated Man)
8. *Perikiromene* (Shorn Hair)
9. *Samia* (Woman from Samos)
10. *Sicyonios* (Man from Sicyon)

The plot of the almost intact play, *Dyskolos*, revolves around Knemon, a surly old misanthrope who initially rebuffs the attempts of young Sostratus to ask for his daughter's hand in marriage, but who eventually consents, after many schemes and machinations have been implemented by Sostratus and his friends.

The Ten Poletai

The *poletai* were Athenian financial officials, whose primary duty was the supervision of sales and rentals of state-owned property, including land, buildings, and confiscated goods. In Aristotle's time (fourth century B.C.) there were ten such officials.

Ten Repartees of Diogenes

The quirky Athenian philosopher Diogenes the Cynic (ca.400–325 B.C.) was a master of the quick repartee, the sarcastic putdown. The following are ten examples (culled from Diogenes Laertius [6.2]):

1. Diogenes was once accosted by a creditor named Midias, who claimed that Diogenes owed him 3,000 drachmas. Diogenes immediately strapped on a pair of boxing gloves and, after pummeling Midias, tauntingly exclaimed, "And now *you* owe *me* 3,000 punches!"

2. Upon seeing a prostitute's son throwing stones into a crowd of people, Diogenes said, "Careful! You wouldn't want to hit your father."

3. One day when Diogenes was eating breakfast in a public square, some onlookers began insulting him and calling him a dog. His reply was, "*You're* the dogs, staring at me like that while I eat!"

4. One bright morning when Diogenes was sunbathing, Alexander the Great approached him and said, "Ask me for anything you wish." Diogenes answered, "Move out of my sunlight."

5. Upon seeing some temple officials apprehending a petty thief, Diogenes remarked, "The little crook is being led off by the big crooks."

6. Having visited an unsanitary public bathing establishment, he said, "After people have washed here, where can they go to wash?"

7. One day he was observed begging a statue for a handout. When asked the reason, he replied, "I'm practicing getting turned down."

8. Diogenes was once asked whether he had any servants; he said that he did not. "Well, if you should die then, who would bury you?" Diogenes answered, "Anyone who wants the house."

9. A fellow patron in a tavern once criticized his drinking. He retorted, "Well, what do you expect? After all, I go to a barbership to get a haircut."

10. Diogenes is perhaps most famous for walking around Athens in broad daylight carrying a lantern, searching, as he put it, for "an honest man."

Ten Roman Families of Note

A Roman *gens*, or clan, shared the same last name theoretically derived from a common ancestor. The family name appeared second in the typical three-part Roman name; for example, Gaius Julius Caesar, where Julius was the *gens*, or family name. Sometimes people sharing the same family name were only remotely related, if at all (just as today, not everyone named Smith, for example, hails from the same nuclear family).

Ten of the most famous family names in ancient Rome, along with three of each family's most noted members were as follows:

1. Aemilius
   a. Marcus Aemilius Lepidus: As consul in 187 B.C. he initiated the construction of the road that bears his name, the Via Aemilia.
   b. Lucius Aemilius Paulus: A Roman general who won the decisive Battle of Pydna (168 B.C.) in the Third Macedonian War.
   c. Marcus Aemilius Lepidus: A consul in 46 B.C., and a member of the Second Triumvirate (with Octavian and Mark Antony).

2. Claudius
   a. Appius Claudius Caecus: He held the offices of censor (312 B.C.), and consul (307 B.C.); he was associated with the construction of an aqueduct (Aqua Appia), and the celebrated Appian Way (Via Appia).
   b. Publius Claudius Pulcher: As consul in 249 B.C. he led the Roman fleet to a disastrous defeat at the Battle of Drepana, supposedly the result of Claudius's disregard of the verdict of the Sacred Chickens, who refused to eat their corn (a bad omen, according to the dictates of Roman augury).
   c. Nero Claudius Caesar: Perhaps the most well known of those first-century A.D. Roman emperors who were characterized by bizarre behavior, Nero ruled from 54–68.

3. Cornelius
   a. Publius Cornelius Scipio: Publius Cornelius Scipio defeated Hannibal at the Battle of Zama in North Africa (202 B.C.), and for this tremendous achievement he was granted the honorary title "Africanus."

    b. Lucius Cornelius Sulla: Sulla, who held the office of dictator from 81 to 79 B.C. (in violation of the six-month term limit), imposed numerous judicial and political reforms on the Romans during his tenure in the dictatorship.

    c. Publius Cornelius Dolabella: A military commander during the civil wars of 49 B.C. and following, he first sided with Caesar, and then (after Caesar's death), with Mark Antony. He was married for a time to Cicero's daughter, Tullia.

4. Julius

    a. Gaius Julius Caesar: The famed general, memoirist, and conqueror of Gaul, Caesar probably influenced the course of Roman history more dramatically than any Roman of his day or any other day.

    b. Gnaeus Julius Agricola: Agricola, a Roman military commander in Britain in the late first century A.D., was the subject of a biography written by his son-in-law, the well-known historian Tacitus.

    c. Sextus Julius Frontinus: Frontinus wrote two technical treatises that still survive: one on the Roman aqueduct system and another on military strategy.

5. Junius

    a. Lucius Junius Brutus: Junius Brutus was instrumental in destroying the Roman monarchy and establishing the republic (ca.509 B.C.).

    b. Decimus Junius Brutus: As consul in 138 B.C. he won several military victories in Spain. Later he was a staunch opponent of the Gracchan reforms.

    c. Marcus Junius Brutus: A leader in the conspiracy to assassinate Julius Caesar (44 B.C.), and the subject of Caesar's (probably apocryphal) dying words "*Et tu, Brute*." He was soon after killed in the Battle of Philippi (42).

6. Marcius

    a. Ancus Marcius: The fourth of the seven legendary kings of Rome (reigned 642–617 B.C.).

    b. Gaius Marcius Coriolanus: A Roman military commander/ adventurer, and stubborn enemy of plebeian rights and power in the early fifth century B.C.

    c. Quintus Marcius Rex: He was responsible for initiating the construction of one of Rome's celebrated aqueducts, the Aqua Marcia, named in his honor (144 B.C.).

7. Quinctius

    a. Lucius Quinctius Cincinnatus: As dictator in 458 B.C. he led the relief force that extricated a surrounded Roman army.

    b. Titus Quinctius Flamininus: As consul in 198 B.C. he freed Greece from the dominance of Macedonia.

    c. Publius Quinctius: Defended by Cicero (81 B.C.), the case on behalf of Quinctius was Cicero's first.

8. Sulpicius

    a. Publius Sulpicius Galba: As consul in 200 B.C. he spearheaded the drive to declare war on King Philip of Macedonia, thus initiating the first of four Macedonian Wars.

b. Servius Sulpicius Rufus: He served as consul in 51 B.C., and was much respected as a jurist and mediator.

c. Sulpicia: The daughter of Sulpicius Rufus, she was one of the few identifiable "women of letters" in ancient Rome (although only 43 lines of her poetry survive).

9. Terentius

a. Marcus (or Gaius?) Terentius Varro: An impetuous, hot-headed military commander, it was his eagerness for battle that led to the terrible Roman defeat at Cannae (216 B.C.), at the hands of Hannibal and the Carthaginians.

b. Terentia: Cicero's wife and confidante, he addressed several of his extant letters to her. After some thirty years of marriage, they divorced, partially, it is said, because of Cicero's lack of trust in his wife's management of their money.

c. Marcus Terentius Varro: Over the course of Varro's long life (116–27 B.C.) he found time to soldier, to teach, to become involved in politics, and to build libraries; he also wrote a number of treatises on various topics, including two that remain to the present day, on agriculture, and on the Latin language.

10. Valerius

a. Publius Valerius Poplicola: Poplicola—the name means "cultivator of the people"—was traditionally thought to be one of the first consuls in the new Roman republic (509 B.C.).

b. Lucius Valerius Flaccus: A friend, neighbor, and political mentor to the famed censor and consul Cato the Elder, Valerius Flaccus held several important governmental and military posts in the early second century B.C.

c. Marcus Valerius Martialis: Martial, the celebrated first-century A.D. epigrammatist, emigrated from Spain to Rome, where he spent some 35 years churning out his witty, occasionally ribald, commentaries on Roman life and society.

The Ten Sibyls

The Sibyls were women thought to have been granted special powers to intercede with the gods on behalf of human beings. The Sibyls also recorded prophecies, typically on palm leaves; these prophecies were transcribed and preserved in three volumes called the Sibylline Books. The ancient authors do not agree on the number of Sibyls, but ten is the most commonly accepted figure.

These ten supposedly live in the following places:

1. Persia
2. Libya
3. Delphi
4. Cumae
5. Samos
6. Cimmeria
7. Erythrae
8. Tibur
9. Marpessus
10. Phrygia

The Ten-Talent Dowry

When the flamboyant Athenian statesman Alcibiades married his wife, Hipparete, his new father-in-law, Hipponicus, presented him with a dowry of ten talents. Later, when a child was born to the couple, Alcibiades attempted to extort from Hipponicus an additional ten talents, claiming that there was a prenuptial agreement between the two of them, to the effect that ten more talents would be payable to Alcibiades upon the birth of children.

The Ten Tribes of Athens

The Athenian lawgiver/reformer Clisthenes (in about 510 B.C.) divided the citizens of Athens into ten districts called tribes. The names of Athens's ten tribes were as follows:

1. Erechtheis	5. Acamantis	8. Hippothontis
2. Aigeis	6. Oineis	9. Aiantis
3. Pandionis	7. Cecropis	10. Antiochis
4. Leontis		

Ten Tribunates

Gaius Licinius Stolo, who held the office of tribune an astonishing ten times in the fourth century B.C., was tried (in 357) for evading the provisions of a law (which he himself had proposed some ten years earlier) specifying that no citizen could own more than 500 iugera (about 130 acres) of land. He held 1,000, jointly with his son. He was convicted and compelled to pay a fine of 10,000 asses (Roman unit of money).

The Ten Tribunes

Early in the fifth century B.C. the tribunate was established in Rome to protect the rights of the plebeians. Tribunes had extensive power to obstruct legislation or debate that was inimical to plebeian interests. Initially, there were five tribunes, elected annually; later, the number was raised to ten.

The ELEVENS

The Eleven

In ancient Athens the officials in charge of prisons and punishments of criminals were called "The Eleven." One official was selected from each of the ten Athenian tribes; additionally, a secretary was assigned to them, bringing the total to 11.

The Eleven Aqueducts of Rome

The Tiber River, which flowed through Rome, was too polluted to be considered a dependable source of water for drinking, bathing, or washing. Hence, the Romans built a series of aqueducts that diverted clean water into the city from springs and rivers in the Apennine Mountains. Eventually, 11 aqueducts were constructed. The longest of the aqueducts was the Marcia, about 56 miles in length; and the shortest was the Appia, about ten miles long.

1. Aqua Appia (built 312 B.C.)
2. Aqua Anio Vetus (272–270 B.C.)
3. Aqua Marcia (144–140 B.C.)
4. Aqua Tepula (125 B.C.)
5. Aqua Julia (33 B.C.)
6. Aqua Virgo (19 B.C.)
7. Aqua Alsietina (A.D. 10)
8. Aqua Claudia (A.D. 38–52)
9. Aqua Anio Novus (A.D. 38–52)
10. Aqua Traiana (A.D. 109)
11. Aqua Alexandrina (A.D. 226)

The Eleven Books of Lucius Apuleius's Metamorphoses

Lucius Apuleius (second century A.D.) was the author of various essays and translations (Greek to Latin), but he is best known for his novel — the only surviving Latin example of the genre — entitled *Metamorphoses* (sometimes also called *The Golden Ass*). The work is divided into 11 books:

Books I–III. A first-person account of how the protagonist (named Lucius), while traveling in Thessaly, encounters a slave girl named Fotis. Magical powers are attributed to her. Unfortunately, when Lucius prevails upon her to transform him into an owl, she bungles the job, and instead changes him into a donkey.

Books IV–VIII. Lucius the donkey learns that the antidote to his four-legged predicament is the eating of roses. But before he is able to consume any, he is kidnapped by robbers and taken to their lair, along with a fellow captive, a young girl named Charite. A servant of the kidnappers regales Charite with fantastic stories, including the famous tale of Cupid and Psyche.

Books VIII–XI. Lucius, still in donkey form, escapes from the robbers, but to a life filled with tragic and difficult experiences and adventures. Eventually, however, the Egyptian goddess Isis appears to him in a dream, promising him a resolution of his problems. The next day a priest of Isis offers him roses. When he resumes his human form, he becomes a worshipper of the goddess.

The Eleven Districts of Italy

To facilitate Roman imperial administration of Italy, the emperor Augustus divided it into 11 districts, as follows:

The areas of Italy included in each of the 11 districts	General location/comments
1. Latium, Campania	West central Italy; Rome is located in Latium; Capua, Pompeii, and Mount Vesuvius in Campania.
2. Apulia, Calabria	Southeastern Italy; Calabria, located in the heel of the Italian boot, was the site of the important port city of Brundisium.
3. Lucania, Bruttium	The southernmost areas of Italy.
4. Samnium and adjacent areas	Central Italy, primarily in the Apennine mountain range.
5. Picenum	East central Italy.
6. Umbria	Northeastern Italy.
7. Etruria	Western Italy, north of Latium and home to the Etruscans, early and powerful inhabitants of Italy.
8. Cisalpine Gaul	The northernmost areas of Italy.
9. Liguria	West of Cisalpine Gaul.
10. Venetia, Istria	Northeastern Italy, north of Umbria.
11. Transalpine Gaul	Outside the boundaries of modern Italy, in southern France. Site of Massilia (modern Marseilles).

Eleven Philosophical Works Extant of Cicero

The literary talents of the Roman orator Marcus Tullius Cicero were not confined to the writing of legal briefs and political speeches. He also authored a number of philosophical essays on various topics. Eleven of these survive; Cicero wrote nine of them between 46 and 44 B.C., shortly before his death in the year 43.

Latin title	English title	Approximate date of composition
1. *De Re Publica*	*Concerning the Republic*	54–51
2. *De Legibus*	*Concerning the Laws*	52
3. *Paradoxa Stoicorum*	*Stoic Paradoxes*	46
4. *Academica*	*Academics*	45
5. *De Finibus Bonorum et Malorum*	*On the Chief Good and the Chief Evil*	45
6. *Tusculanae Disputationes*	*Tusculan Disputations*	45–44
7. *De Natura Deorum*	*On the Nature of the Gods*	44
8. *De Divinatione*	*Concerning Prophecy*	44
9. *De Fato*	*Concerning Fate*	44
10. *De Senectute*	*Concerning Old Age*	44
11. *De Officiis*	*Concerning Duties*	44

The Eleven Plays Extant of Aristophanes

The Greek comic playwright Aristophanes (ca.445–385 B.C.) wrote over forty plays. Of these, 11 survive:

1. *Acharnians* (425 B.C.), in which a farmer attempts to arrange a private peace treaty to keep the warring Spartans and Athenians off his land.
2. *Birds* (414 B.C.), a fantasy play in which two Athenians, tired of life in Athens, decide to found a new city in the heavens.
3. *Clouds* (423 B.C.), a satirical attack on the philosopher Socrates.
4. *Ecclesiazusae* (392 B.C.), in which the women of Athens take over the Assembly.
5. *Frogs* (405 B.C.), a satire on the quality of tragic playwriting and, specifically, the playwright Euripides.
6. *Knights* (424 B.C.), an attack on the politician Cleon.
7. *Lysistrata* (411 B.C.), in which the women of Athens and Sparta resort to a sex strike to force their men to end the Peloponnesian War.
8. *Peace* (421 B.C.), an appeal for an end to the Peloponnesian War; "Peace" (personified) has been buried in a pit by War, and the Greek farmers and workers must rescue her.
9. *Plutus* (388 B.C.), a morality play on wealth and its consequences.
10. *Thesmophoriazusae* (411 B.C.), a criticism of the plays of Euripides.
11. *Wasps* (422 B.C.), a satire on the Athenian court system and the litigiousness of the Athenians.

The Eleven Speeches Extant of Isaeus

The orator Isaeus (ca.420–350 B.C.) wrote some fifty speeches, of which 11 survive intact. All 11 pertain to cases involving inheritances and the rights of heirs. As such, they provide important evidence about Athenian legal procedures in this area. The 11 titles are given below, along with the approximate date, if known:

1. *On the Estate of Apollodorus*; date unknown
2. *On the Estate of Aristarchus*; date unknown
3. *On the Estate of Astyphilus*; date unknown
4. *On the Estate of Ciron*; date unknown
5. *On the Estate of Cleonymus*; date unknown
6. *On the Estate of Dicaeogenes*; 389 B.C.
7. *On the Estate of Hagnias*; date unknown
8. *On the Estate of Menecles*; date unknown
9. *On the Estate of Philoctemon*; date unknown
10. *On the Estate of Nicostratus*; 374 B.C.
11. *On the Estate of Pyrrhus*; date unknown

The TWELVES

The Twelve Books of the Aeneid

The *Aeneid*, a classic epic poem by the Roman poet Vergil (70–19 B.C.), describes the founding of the Roman race by the hero Aeneas. The poem is divided into 12 chapters, or books.

Book I.   After many adventures and mishaps, Aeneas of Troy and some of his Trojan friends land in North Africa, near Carthage.

Book II.   Aeneas tells the story of his sufferings to Dido, queen of Carthage.

Book III.   A continuation of Aeneas's tale.

Book IV.   Aeneas leaves Carthage; Dido (who had fallen in love with him) is grieved and angered over his departure. She commits suicide.

Book V.   Aeneas holds funeral games in Sicily, in honor of his deceased father, Anchises.

Book VI.   The Trojans arrive in Italy; Aeneas visits the Underworld.

Book VII.   The Trojans make their way to the Tiber River; and war breaks out between the Trojans and the native peoples of the region, principally the Latins and the Rutulians.

Book VIII. Other indigenous peoples are not hostile to the Trojans, however, and Aeneas is able to enlist the aid of some of these for the war.

Book IX.   The Trojans suffer several military setbacks.

Book X.   Aeneas defeats in single combat the Rutulian leader Mezentius.

Book XI.   The tide of battle against the Latins begins to turn in favor of the Trojans.

Book XII.   Aeneas and the Latin king, Turnus, meet in single combat and Aeneas prevails.

The *Aeneid* ends with the death of Turnus. However, after that event, Aeneas fulfills his destiny by establishing the new race, the Romans.

Vergil also wrote ten books of pastoral poems (*Eclogues*), and four books of poetry on farming (*Georgics*).

The Twelve Books of Columella's De Re Rustica

Lucius Junius Moderatus Columella (first century A.D.), a Romanized Spaniard, wrote a treatise on farming (*De Re Rustica*), in 12 books. Columella also wrote a short essay on trees (*De Arboribus*). The books of *De Re Rustica* are listed below:

Book I.　　　Preface; review of Greek and Roman authors who wrote on agricultural topics; factors to consider when buying a farm; size of buildings; and the acquisition of farmhands and slaves.

Book II.　　Methods of plowing, planting, and fertilization, for various kinds of grains and legumes; and harvesting.

Books III/IV.　Planting, grafting, and care of vineyards. In Book III the author mentions that the start-up cost for planting seven iugera (about four acres) with grapevines was 29,000 sesterces, as follows:

　　　　8,000: to purchase a slave skilled as a vine-dresser
　　　　7,000: for the land, at the rate of 1,000 sesterces for 1 iugerum
　　　　14,000: to purchase the plants and the trellises on which they must be grown.

Book V.　　Detailed descriptions of various methods of measuring land; and the cultivation of vines, olive trees, and other varieties of fruit-bearing trees.

Book VI.　　Training and care of oxen; and the breeding and care of cattle, horses, and mules.

Book VII.　　Breeding and care of sheep, goats, pigs, and dogs.

Book VIII.　Kinds of poultry and their care—hens, pigeons, thrushes, geese, and ducks; and fish and fish ponds.

Book IX.　　Bee cultivation.

Book X.　　Horticulture. (Book X is written in hexameter verse, and is intended as a supplement to Book IV of Vergil's *Georgics*.)

Book XI.　　Duties of a *vilicus* (foreman); weather and climatic conditions for each month of the year, and the agricultural work appropriate to each of the months; and the cultivation of cabbage, lettuce, parsley, radishes, asparagus, cucumbers, and similar crops.

Book XII.　　Storage of furniture and tools; procedures for preserving farm produce; and recipes for making wine and olive oil.

The Twelve Books of Martial's Epigrams

The poet Marcus Valerius Martialis (Martial, ca. A.D. 40–104) wrote over 1,500 poems during his career, most of them published under the title *Epigrams*. He was a social critic and satirist, a poet whose pithy (and often very short) epigrams mocked the flaws and foibles of his fellow Romans. The list below includes an example of the content of one epigram for each of the 12 books:

Book I (epigram number 10). Martial chides the fortune-hunter Gemellus for marrying an ugly, old rich woman with a bad cough.

Book II (epigram number 52). Martial notes that a certain lady named Spatale is so well endowed that when she attends the public baths she has to pay triple the going rate.

Book III (epigram number 9). This epigram views from a writer's perspective the age-old debate over the noise (or lack thereof) made by a falling tree in an uninhabited forest. Can a writer truly be called a writer if no one ever reads his writing?

Book IV (epigram number 24). A certain hardy woman named Lycoris has outlived all her friends, and Martial laments that his own wife is not numbered among the friends of Lycoris.

Book V (epigram number 81). "The rich get richer and the poor get poorer" is Martial's complaint in this epigram.

Book VI (epigram number 82). Martial mocks his own modest wardrobe, and offers it as proof that one cannot become wealthy by writing for a living.

Book VII (epigram number 77). An unscrupulous man named Tucca wants copies of Martial's poems, not to read them but to try to sell them.

Book VIII (epigram number 27). Martial ridicules Gaurus, who lavishes his generosity on a rich old man, remarking that Gaurus hopes for the old man's imminent demise and a prominent place in his will.

Book IX (epigram number 68). Martial complains about a loud-mouthed, boring teacher, claiming that even the crowds in the Coliseum make less noise.

Book X (epigram number 86). The athlete Laurus, a star in his prime, has "lost it."

Book XI (epigram number 93). Theodorus, a particularly inept poet, has lost his house in a fire, and Martial wonders why the gods did not destroy Theodorus at the same time.

Book XII (epigram number 10). Martial derides a greedy fortune-hunter, already a millionaire, who strives for still more wealth.

(Martial wrote two collections of poems about giving and receiving gifts at the Saturnalian festival. These collections were appended to the *Epigrams* as a thirteenth book and a fourteenth book.) Total number of epigrams per book is listed below:

Book I.	118	Book VIII.	82
Book II.	93	Book IX.	103
Book III.	100	Book X.	104
Book IV.	89	Book XI.	108
Book V.	84	Book XII.	98
Book VI.	94	Book XIII.	127
Book VII.	99	Book XIV.	223

Additionally, Martial commemorated the dedication of the Coliseum in A.D. 80 in a work entitled *Liber Spectaculorum* (*Book of Spectacles*). It contains 33 short poems, most praising the emperor Titus for his role in the construction of the amphitheater.

The Twelve Books of Quintilian's Institutes of Oratory

The Roman writer-educator Quintilian (ca. A.D. 35–95) wrote a lengthy treatise on the method and content of a course of training for a Roman orator. The work is divided into 12 books:

Book I.   Educational principles; grammar; spelling; composition; word usage; and diction.

Book II.   Teaching methods; definitions, and descriptions of oratory.

Book III.   The various kinds of speeches and cases.

Book IV.   Introduction of a case; and statement of facts.

Book V.   Proofs; and kinds of evidence.

Book VI.   Methods of influencing judges; and use of humor.

Book VII.   The ambiguities, contradictions, and intent of law.

Book VIII.   Styles and word usages appropriate to oratory.

Book IX.   Figures of speech and thought; and prose rhythms.

Book X.   Importance of reading widely; writing; revision; composition; and extemporaneous speeches.

Book XI.   Relevance; memory; gesture; and dress.

Book XII.   Intellectual and personal qualities necessary for an orator; oratorical styles; and retirement.

The Twelve Books Extant of Tacitus's Annals

The Roman historian Cornelius Tacitus (ca. A.D. 55–117) wrote his *Annals*, a history of Rome spanning the years A.D. 14–68, in 18 books. Twelve of the 18 are extant. The surviving books are as follows, with the period they cover and a summary of their contents:

Book I (A.D. 14–15).   The topics include a summary of the reign of Augustus, and the transition to his successor, Tiberius.

Book II (16–19).   The military activities of Germanicus, Tiberius's adopted son.

Book III (20–22).   The trial of Gnaeus Calpurnius Piso, the alleged murderer of Germanicus.

Book IV (23–28).   The activities of Tiberius's flamboyant and arrogant associate Aelius Sejanus; and the decision of Tiberius to leave Rome and move to the island of Capri.

Book V (29).   The death of Tiberius's mother, Livia.

Book VI (31–37).   The final years of Tiberius, years filled with brutality and licentious behavior.

Book XI (47–49).	The seventh year of the emperor Claudius's reign.
Book XII (49–54).	The marriage of Claudius to Agrippina, whose son by a previous marriage would become the emperor Nero; Claudius's death; and Nero's accession (A.D. 54).
Book XIII (55–58).	The early years of Nero's reign, including the poisoning of Claudius's son, Britannicus, a deed allegedly ordered by Nero.
Book XIV (59–62).	The murder of Nero's mother; and military activities in Britain and Armenia.
Book XV (62–65).	Military activities in Armenia; and a description of the disastrous fire in Rome (A.D. 64) and its aftermath.
Book XVI (65–66).	Acts of brutality and extravagance committed by Nero.

Also surviving are four books, and parts of a fifth, of Tacitus's other notable work, *Histories* (which covers the years A.D. 69–70):

Book I.	An account of the deeds of three of the four emperors who reigned in A.D. 69 (Galba, Otho, and Vitellius).
Book II.	Vitellius's emperorship.
Book III.	The struggle for power between Vitellius and Vespasian.
Book IV.	Vespasian prevails, and assumes the purple; and the revolt of the Batavians.
Book V.	The foray into Jerusalem of Titus (Vespasian's son).

Tacitus also wrote a biography of his father-in-law (*Agricola*); a description of Germany (*Germania*); and a treatise on oratory (*Dialogue on Oratory*).

The Twelve Caesars

The Lives of the Twelve Caesars is the title popularly assigned to a collection of biographies by the Roman writer Suetonius (ca. A.D. 70–140). Included are biographies of Julius Caesar and the first Roman emperors:

1. Julius Caesar (d. 44 B.C.)
2. Augustus (reigned 27 B.C.–A.D. 14)
3. Tiberius (14–37)
4. Caligula (37–41)
5. Claudius (41–54)
6. Nero (54–68)
7. Galba (68–69)
8. Otho (69)
9. Vitellius (69)
10. Vespasian (69–79)
11. Titus (79–81)
12. Domitian (81–96)

The Twelve Carceres

The Circus Maximus, the great chariot racetrack in Rome, was equipped with 12 *carceres* (a word literally meaning "jail cells"), or starting gates, thus indicating that 12 chariots typically competed in a race.

Twelve Cities Destroyed in an Earthquake

In Book II of his *Annals* the historian Tacitus describes the destruction of 12 Asian cities (A.D. 17) in a devastating earthquake. The 12 cities, in Tacitean order were

1. Sardis
2. Magnesia (Sipylus)
3. Temnos
4. Philadelphia
5. Aegeae
6. Apollonia
7. Mosteni
8. Hyrcani
9. Hierocaesarea
10. Myrina
11. Cyme
12. Tmolus

Tacitus adds that Sardis suffered the most severely of the 12, and hence received a rebuilding grant of 10 million sesterces from the emperor Tiberius. At least some of the other cities on the list also obtained largesses, but Tacitus does not specify the amounts.

The Twelve Cities of the Achaean League

The Achaean League, formed in 280 B.C., consisted of cities on the Peloponnesus; its purpose was to serve as a counterpoint to the dominance of, first, Macedonian and, later, Spartan rule. Polybius (2.41) lists the original 12 cities:

1. Aegira
2. Aegium
3. Bura
4. Caryneia
5. Dyme
6. Helice
7. Leontium
8. Olenus
9. Patrae
10. Pellene
11. Pharae
12. Tritaea

Several other cities in the region eventually joined, including Sicyon, Corinth, Megara, and Argos.

The Achaean League remained a viable entity until 146 B.C., when it was defeated and disbanded by the Romans.

The Twelve Cities of the Ionian League

The cities of Ionia (modern western Turkey) were organized into a league, perhaps as early as the ninth century B.C. The following were the 12 member cities of the Ionian League:

1. Chios
2. Clazomenae
3. Colophon
4. Ephesus
5. Erythrae
6. Lebedos
7. Miletus
8. Myus
9. Phocaea
10. Priene
11. Samos
12. Teos

The Twelve Fratres Arvales

The 12 *Fratres Arvales* (Arval brothers) were priests whose prime responsibility involved the offering of sacrifices in May to Dea Dia, the Roman goddess of the harvest.

The Twelve Holidays of Rome

The Roman year was liberally sprinkled with a variety of holidays, festivals, and celebrations. The list that appears below is not inclusive, but presents the name of one holiday period in each month of the year. (The Parilian festival, originally celebrated in honor of the rural deity Pales, was later associated with the calendar date of the founding of Rome by Romulus in 753 B.C. By Cicero's time [in the first century B.C.], the Parilian festival—April 21—had become a Roman equivalent to the Fourth of July.)

Name of festival	Deity/ies honored (if any)	Date(s)
1. Festival of Janus	Janus	January 1
2. Lupercalian festival	Pan	February 15
3. Quinquatrian festival	Minerva	March 19–23
4. Parilian festival	Pales	April 21
5. Bona Dea festival	Fauna	May 1
6. Vestalian festival	Vesta	June 9
7. *Ludi Apollinares* (games in honor of Apollo	Apollo	July 5
8. Consualian festival	Neptune	August 18
9. *Ludi Romani* (Roman games)	Jupiter, Juno, Minerva	September 4–13
10. Fontinalian festival	—	October 13
11. *Ludi plebeii*	—	November 15
12. Saturnalian festival	Saturn	December 17–24

The Twelve Hours of the Day and the Night

As in the modern era, the ancient Romans divided each day into 24 hours, but with these differences: daylight and darkness were assigned 12 hours each. The length of the hours was determined by the amount of the daylight and darkness on any given day in the year; hence, a daylight hour was much shorter in midwinter than it was in the summer. (According to J. P. V. D. Balsdon, *Life and Leisure in Ancient Rome*, a midsummer hour lasted about 75 minutes, whereas its midwinter counterpart was only about 45 minutes in length.)

The Twelve Labors of Hercules

The famous hero Hercules was assigned 12 seemingly impossible tasks. The reason given for the imposition of these tasks varies among the ancient authorities; some say the labors served as Hercules' penance for the slaying of his wife and

children. The Twelve Labors (all of which Hercules completed successfully) were
as follows:

      1. Slaying the Nemean lion, a beast with a hide impervious to arrows
or spears;
      2. Killing the Lernaean hydra, a creature with nine heads;
      3. Capturing the Cerynean stag, sacred to the goddess Artemis;
      4. Capturing the Erymanthian boar, a vicious animal that had been
terrorizing the people who lived on Mount Erymanthus;
      5. Cleansing the Augean stables, which had gone 30 years without a
cleaning;
      6. Slaying the Stymphalian birds, storklike man-eaters with bronze
claws;
      7. Capturing the man-eating mares of Diomedes;
      8. Capturing the Cretan bull, another man-killer;
      9. Stealing the girdle of Hippolyta, queen of the Amazons;
      10. Capturing the cattle of Geryon;
      11. Obtaining and absconding with three golden apples from a tree in
the garden of the Hesperides; and
      12. Transporting to earth Cerberus, a three-headed dog and guardian
of the entrance to the Underworld.

An amusing story is told about Hercules' interview with Augeas, king of
Elis, prior to the cleansing of the stables. He wanted to know how many herds
of cattle Augeas owned. The king's reply:

> One-half pasture near the Alpheus River;
> One-eighth near the Hill of Cronus;
> One-twelfth are at Taraxippus;
> One-twentieth graze in Elis;
> One-thirtieth I left in Arcadia;
> You see the remaining 50 before you.

The epigrammatist who recounts this tale does not indicate whether Hercules possessed the mental acuity to calculate the total: 240 herds (120 + 30 +
20 + 12 + 8 + 50). Other sources suggest that the 240 herds contained a grand
total of 3,000 cattle.

Augeas purportedly promised to give one-tenth of his herds to Hercules
upon completion of the cleansing of the stables. However, when Hercules had
finished the foul task, the king reneged.

The Twelve Lictors

When a Roman consul appeared in public, he was preceded by 12 officials
called lictors. The lictors carried the *fasces*, a bundle of sticks tied together with
an ax head protruding from one end, a symbol of the power of the consul and
the government that he represented. Other magistrates were also attended by
lictors (lictors also attended certain priests and priestesses and assisted in various
public ceremonies and sacrifices):

Office	Number of lictors
Dictator	24
Magister equitum, a phrase literally meaning "master of the horse"; the *magister equitum* was a dictator's second-in-command	6
Praetor (in Rome)	2
Provincial praetor	6
Provincial proconsul	12
Quaestor	5

Twelve Lines / Duodecim Scripta

The Romans enjoyed a variety of board games; one of the most popular was *Duodecim Scripta*. Play proceeded as follows:

> *Duodecim Scripta* was played on a board marked out in twenty-four squares, marked successively one to twelve in the first row and then backwards from thirteen to twenty-four in the second, square 24 being directly above square 1 ... Each player had fifteen pieces, and moves were determined by the throwing of three dice. At the start of the game the white pieces were on square 1 and moved forward, the black on square 24, moving backwards. The winner was the player who first succeeded in moving all his pieces from square 1 to square 24, or from square 24 to square 1, or was perhaps the player with the highest score on points. If one enemy piece was on the square to which your throw took you, it was driven back to base; if two or more enemy pieces held the square, then you yourself could not occupy it [quoted from Balsdon, *Life and Leisure in Ancient Rome*, p. 156].

The Twelve Months of the Athenian Year

The Athenian year was divided into 12 months. The month names appear below, with the modern month to which each corresponds in parentheses.

1. Gamelion (January)
2. Anthesterion (February)
3. Elaphebolion (March)
4. Munychion (April)
5. Thargelion (May)
6. Scirophorion (June)
7. Hecatombeon (July)
8. Metageitnion (August)
9. Boedromion (September)
10. Pyanopsion (October)
11. Memacterion (November)
12. Poseideon (December)

The Twelve Months of the Roman Year

The Roman calendar (in the manner of the Athenian and modern calendars) was divided into 12 months (where *mensis* means month) as follows:

1. Mensis Januarius
2. Mensis Februarius
3. Mensis Martius
4. Mensis Aprilis
5. Mensis Maius
6. Mensis Junius

7. Mensis Quintilis
8. Mensis Sextilis
9. Mensis September

10. Mensis October
11. Mensis November
12. Mensis December

Quintilis and Sextilis were subsequently renamed Mensis Julius and Mensis Augustus in honor of Julius Caesar and Augustus, respectively. The words Quintilis, Sextilis, September, October, November, and December mean fifth, sixth, seventh, eighth, ninth, and tenth. In Rome's earliest years, March (not January) was the first month of the year; this accounts for the numbering sequence which has the seventh month labelled "fifth." In the mid–second century B.C. the reckoning of the months was changed, with January recognized as the first month.

The Twelve Olympians

The tales of Greek mythology are replete with the names of hundreds of gods, goddesses, demigods, and heroes. However, only 12 of these were permitted the honor of dwelling on Mount Olympus; the select few (sometimes called the Twelve Great Olympians) were as follows:

1. Zeus
2. Hera
3. Poseidon
4. Demeter

5. Apollo
6. Artemis
7. Hephaestus
8. Athena

9. Ares
10. Aphrodite
11. Hermes
12. Hestia

The Twelve Sempronii Gracchi

The two famed Roman land reformers of the second century B.C., the brothers Tiberius and Gaius Sempronius Gracchus, had nine siblings. However, only one of these, their sister Sempronia, survived to adulthood.

The Twelve Ships of Odysseus

Odysseus set out from Troy with 12 ships for the return trip to Ithaca. The Laestrygonians, fierce and ruthless cannibals encountered by Odysseus en route, destroyed 11 of his 12 ships.

The Twelve Tables

The Twelve Tables was the earliest (ca. 450 B.C.) codification of Roman law, and as such, it is an important source of information about Roman legal and social history. The Twelve Tables and a summary of their provisions (following Naphtali Lewis and Meyer Reinhold's *Roman Civilization*, vol. I: *The Republic*) are as follows:

Table I.　　Preliminaries to and rules for a trial.
Table II.　　Further enactments on trials.

Table III.	Execution; Law of debt.
Table IV.	Rights of the head of the family.
Table V.	Guardianship and succession.
Table VI.	Acquisition and possession.
Table VII.	Rights concerning land.
Table VIII.	Torts or delicts.
Table IX.	Public law.
Table X.	Sacred law.
Table XI.	Supplementary laws.
Table XII.	Supplementary laws.

The Twelve Titans

The Titans, the 12 children of Uranus (Heaven) and Ge (Earth) were named

1. Oceanus	5. Iapetus	9. Themis
2. Hyperion	6. Rhea	10. Mnemosyne
3. Coeus	7. Tethys	11. Phoebe
4. Crius	8. Theia	12. Cronus

The Twelve Tribes of the Amphictyonic Council

An Amphictyonic (literally meaning "those who live around") Council was responsible for maintaining the temple and cult of a Greek deity. Prominent among these councils was the one associated with the temple of Apollo at Delphi. It was composed of the following 12 tribes:

1. Thessalians	5. Perrhaebians	9. Aenianes
2. Boeotians	6. Dolopians	10. Phthiotic Achaeans
3. Dorians	7. Magnetes	11. Malians
4. Ionians	8. Locrians	12. Phocians

The Twelve Vultures and the Founding of Rome

Although Aeneas is generally regarded as the founder of the Roman race, the city itself was laid out and constructed by Romulus. He and his brother Remus initially cooperated in the great undertaking, but they could not agree which hill to use as the city's center. So each chose a separate hill, climbed to the summit, and awaited a sign from the gods. Six vultures appeared first to Remus; shortly thereafter, Romulus observed 12. Romulus claimed that quantity should supersede priority in such affairs; accordingly, he proceeded with the city's construction.

The Twelve Works Extant of Ovid

The Roman writer Ovid (43 B.C.–A.D. 17) wrote poems on a wide variety of subjects. Some of his erotic poems apparently roused the ire of the emperor Augustus; the publication of these poems was the probable cause of the poet's banishment from Rome to Tomis on the Black Sea (in A.D. 8). Ovid's 12 extant works are as follows:

1. *Amores*: 49 love poems.

2. *Ars Amatoria*: Poems containing instructions for men on the acquisition of a mistress, and similar instructions for women.

3. *Epistulae ex Ponto*: Letters from Pontus, written during the poet's period of exile.

4. *Fasti*: A poem devoted to the Roman calendar and the historical and religious importance of specific days.

5. *Halieutica*: A fragmentary poem on fish and fishing.

6. *Heroides*: Fictionalized letters written by legendary women to their paramours.

7. *Ibis*: A curse poem directed against a former friend who had caused trouble for Ovid and his wife.

8. *Medicamina Faciei Femineae*: A fragmentary poem on facial lotions and cosmetics for women.

9. *Metamorphoses*: Perhaps Ovid's most famous work, contains mythological stories that have as their common theme some sort of transformation (hence the title).

10. *Nux*: A poem about a nut tree and the sufferings it incurs from people who throw rocks at it.

11. *Remedia Amoris*: Remedies for extricating oneself from an unfulfilling love affair.

12. *Tristia*: Poems written in Tomis in which Ovid pleads for a revocation of his banishment.

Ovidian authorship of *Halieutica* and *Nux* has been questioned.

The THIRTEENS through the TWENTYS

The Thirteen Books of Euclid's Elements

The mathematician Euclid (third century B.C.) wrote the noted treatise *Elements* in 13 books:

Books I–IV.	Plane geometry
Book V.	Proportions
Book VI.	Plane geometry
Books VII–X.	Number theories
Books XI–XIII.	Solid geometry

It is said that Ptolemy I (king of Egypt 323–283 B.C.) once asked Euclid if there were any easier method of learning geometry than by studying the *Elements*. Euclid's terse reply that there was "no royal road to geometry" has achieved lasting fame.

The Thirteen Thermae of Rome

Ancient Rome was adorned with 13 immense public bathing establishments (*thermae*), some accommodating several thousand patrons at once. The 13 baths were built by the following:

1. Agrippa	6. Decius	10. Severus
2. Alexander	7. Diocletian	11. Sura
3. Caracalla	8. Helena	12. Titus
4. Commodus	9. Nero	13. Trajan
5. Constantine		

Nero's baths were built in A.D. 64; they were rebuilt around 228 by the emperor Severus Alexander, and renamed for him (number 2 on the above list).

Of these establishments, the largest were Diocletian's baths, constructed early in the fourth century A.D. The building housing the baths of Diocletian measured over 1,000 yards in both length and width; it could accommodate over 3,000 bathers.

The Fourteen Books of Aelian's Various Histories

The rhetorician Claudius Aelianus (Aelian, ca. A.D. 170–235) wrote a treatise called *Various Histories* in 14 books; in this work he described the deeds, character traits, and idiosyncrasies of various noteworthy people. He also authored a quasi-companion volume called the *Characteristics of Animals*, in 17 books, as well as 20 *Rustic Epistles* (brief essays on literary styles).

The Fourteen * Children of Niobe

In Greek mythology Niobe, a woman blessed with seven sons and seven daughters, was obsessed with jealousy over the homage paid to the goddess Leto, whose only offspring were Apollo and Artemis. Niobe believed that she, not Leto, was deserving of greater respect because of her much larger brood. Leto, insulted by such arrogance, ordered Apollo and Artemis to kill Niobe's children, which they did (except for one daughter, Chloris), and Niobe was subsequently turned to stone. In Book VI of the *Metamorphoses*, Ovid mentions the names of the seven sons, as follows:

1. Ismenus	5. Alphenor
2. Sipylus	6. Damasichthon
3. Phaedimus	7. Ilioneus
4. Tantalus	

The Fourteen Comic Poets of the Canon

The Alexandrian scholars rated as the best the following 14 comic poets:

1. Alexis (ca.372–270 B.C.)	8. Epicharmus (fifth century B.C.)
2. Antiphanes (ca.388–311 B.C.)	9. Eupolis (430–410 B.C.)
3. Apollodorus (third century B.C.)	10. Menander (342–292 B.C.)
4. Aristophanes (ca.445–385 B.C.)	11. Pherecrates (430–410 B.C.)
5. Crates (fifth century B.C.)	12. Philemon (ca.361–262 B.C.)
6. Cratinus (ca.484–419 B.C.)	13. Philippides (fourth century B.C.)
7. Diphilus (b. ca.340 B.C.)	14. Plato (428–389 B.C.)

The number of Niobe's children seems to have been a matter of some controversy among the ancient authors. Aulus Gellius (20.7) notes the differences in the numbers and gender for the following authors:

> Homer: 12; 6 boys; 6 girls
> Euripides: 14; 7 boys, 7 girls
> Sappho: 18; 9 boys, 9 girls
> Bacchylides: 20; 10 boys, 10 girls
> Pindar: 20; 10 boys, 10 girls
> Quidam alii scriptores *(certain other writers):* 6; 3 boys, 3 girls

According to Ovid, Niobe had 14 children, while Hesiod put the number at 20.

The Fourteen Districts of Rome

During the reign of Augustus, the city of Rome was divided into 14 administrative districts. The names of the districts were as follows:

1. Porta Capena
2. Caelimontium
3. Isis and Serapis
4. Templum Pacis
5. Esquiliae
6. Alta Semita
7. Via Lata

8. Forum Romanum
9. Circus Flaminius
10. Palatium
11. Circus Maximus
12. Piscina Publica
13. Aventinus
14. Trans Tiberim

The Fourteen Epinician Odes Extant of Bacchylides

Bacchylides (fifth century B.C.), an epinician poet and presumed rival of Pindar, the greatest practitioner of the genre, wrote 14 surviving poems, most in fragmentary form:

Poem number	In honor of	Event/festival/date (if known)
1	Argeius of Ceos	Boy's boxing/Isthmian games
2	Argeius of Ceos	Boy's boxing/Isthmian games
3	Hieron of Syracuse	Chariot racing/Olympian games of 468 B.C.
4	Hieron of Syracuse	Chariot racing/Pythian games
5	Hieron of Syracuse	Chariot racing/Olympian games of 476 B.C.
6	Lachon of Ceos	Boy's stade race/Olympian games of 452 B.C.
7	Lachon of Ceos	Boy's stade race/Olympian games of 452 B.C.
8	Liparion(?) of Ceos(?)	Uncertain
9	Automedes of Phlius	Pentathlon/Nemean games
10	Unknown Athenian athlete	Stade race(?)/Isthmian games
11	Alexidamus of Metapontion	Boy's wrestling/Pythian games
12	Tisias of Aegina	Wrestling/Nemean games
13	Pytheas of Aegina	Pankration/Nemean games
14	Cleoptolemus of Thessaly	Chariot racing/Petraean games

Fragments of six dithyrambs ascribed to Bacchylides also survive.

The Fourteen Legendary Kings of Rome

The Romans regarded Aeneas (d. ca.1180 B.C.) as the founder of their race, whereas Romulus was considered to be the founder-builder of the city of Rome. However, over 400 years separated the two; there was reputedly a line of 14 legendary kings bridging the chronological gap. According to Dionysius of Halicarnassus (1.71) the 14 kings were:

Name	Number of years he ruled
1. Ascanius	38
2. Silvius	29
3. Aeneas Silvius	30 +
4. Latinus	51
5. Alba	39
6. Capetus	26
7. Capys	28
8. Calpetus	13
9. Tiberinus	8 (the Tiber River is supposedly named for this king)
10. Agrippa	41
11. Allodius	19
12. Aventinus	37 (the Aventine Hill is supposedly named for this king)
13. Proca	23
14. Amulius	42

The Fourteen Poems of Tibullus

The poet Albius Tibullus (ca.55–19 B.C.) wrote two books of elegaic love poems; eight entries are included in the first book, six in the second. Most of his poems recount his love for various paramours.

Fourteen Purchase Prices for Roman Slaves

Skilled, educated slaves were valuable commodities in ancient Rome, as the following list (adapted from Richard Duncan-Jones's *The Economy of the Roman Empire*) indicates:

Purchase price (expressed in sesterces)	Transaction details
1. 700,000	The purchase price for a slave called Daphnis, a *grammaticus*, or literary expert.
2. 100,000	The emperor Elagabalus (reigned A.D. 218–222) paid this amount for a prostitute.
3. 100,000	Each of 11 slaves who had memorized the works of a Greek poet commanded this purchase price.
4. 50,000	P. Decimus Merula, a (slave) doctor, paid this sum to obtain his freedom.

5.	10,000	The first century A.D. (slave) actor Paris paid this amount for his freedom.
6.	6,000–8,000	A skilled vine-dresser might command a purchase price in this range.
7.	4,050	The price paid for a male slave in the town of Herculaneum (near Pompeii).
8.	2,700	The purchase price for a cook.
9.	2,650	Each of two *mancipia veterana* (skilled slaves) were obtained for this price.
10.	2,500	The price paid for a female slave in the town of Ravenna.
11.	1,400	A young female slave was obtained at Herculaneum for this price.
12.	900	Another purchase price at Herculaneum, for a male slave.
13.	725	Each of two slave boys were procured in Pompeii for this price.
14.	600	Another purchase price for a female slave at Herculaneum.

The poet Horace (*Satires* 2.7) suggests that a slave with no special skills could be purchased for 2,000 sesterces.

The Fourteen Rows

In 67 B.C. a tribune by the name of Lucius Roscius Otho proposed a law, subsequently approved, granting special seating privileges in theaters and amphitheaters to members of Rome's equestrian class. Specifically, the so-called *Lex Roscia* reserved the first 14 rows for them. An unpopular measure, it was defended by Cicero.

The Fourteen Works of Xenophon

Xenophon (ca.430–354 B.C.), one of the ten historians of the canon, produced 14 books and treatises on a variety of subjects.

1. *Agesilaus*: A laudatory treatise on the Spartan king, thought to have been written shortly after the king's death in 360 B.C.

2. *Anabasis* (*The Expedition*): Perhaps Xenophon's most famous work, it describes the military activities, adventures, and hardships of Cyrus the Younger and the Ten Thousand, a mercenary army of Greeks recruited to assist the Persian Cyrus in warfare against his brother Artaxerxes (401 B.C.; see below for a fuller description). Xenophon himself participated in the march, and so writes as an eye-witness to the events he describes.

3. *Apology*: A recounting and a critique of Socrates' defense during his trial (in 399 B.C.) for impiety and corrupting the youth of Athens.

4. *Constitution of the Lacedaemonians*: A description of Spartan customs.

   5. *Cynegeticus* (*On Hunting*): As the title suggests, a manual on hunting.
   6. *Cyropaedia* (*The Education of Cyrus*): A biography of King Cyrus the Elder (sixth century B.C.), which portrays him as the ideal ruler. (According to Albin Lesky, this treatise contains more fiction than fact and, as such, it may be considered to be the earliest historical novel.)
   7. *Hellenica*: An account of Greek history from 411–362 B.C.
   8. *Hieron*: A philosophical dialogue between Hieron of Syracuse (ruler of Syracuse ca.478–467 B.C.) and the poet Simonides.
   9. *Hipparchicus* (*Concerning the Cavalry Commander*): A manual detailing the responsibilities of a cavalry commander.
   10. *On Horsemanship*: A manual for individual cavalrymen, including information on the care of horses. Factual and detailed, it is the oldest extant work on the subject.
   11. *Memorabilia*: In four books, devoted to Socratic dialogues and discussions.
   12. *Oeconomicus*: A narrative about the organization of an upscale Athenian household, including useful information on the duties of servants and the role of women in Athens.
   13. *On Revenues*: A treatise about the Athenian economy, including suggestions for revenue enhancement.
   14. *Symposium*: An account of the conversations at a dinner party given by Callias, a wealthy Athenian nobleman.

The following is a synopsis of the seven books of *Anabasis*:

Book I.   Cyrus organizes his forces; the beginning of the march; and character delineation of Cyrus.
Book II.   The Greek mercenaries join with Cyrus; and after the Battle of Cunaxa (in Babylon, 401 B.C.), in which Cyrus was killed, five Greek generals were executed:
             1. Clearchus of Sparta
             2. Proxenus of Boeotia
             3. Menon of Thessaly
             4. Agias of Arcadia
             5. Socrates of Achaea
Book III.   The Greeks begin to withdraw from Babylon.
Book IV.   The Greeks cross mountains and brave snowstorms, finally reaching Trapezus, on the Black Sea.
Book V.   Xenophon, having succeeded Proxenus as one of the generals, expounds upon various pertinent military matters.
Book VI.   The march continues to the Bosporus.
Book VII.   The march continues to Byzantium and ultimately to Lampsacus, where Xenophon resigns from the army, leaving Thibron the Spartan in charge.

The Fourteen Youths for the Labyrinth
   Daedalus, Greek mythology's most famous architect, constructed a maze

for the Cretan king Minos; so intricate was this maze — known as the Labyrinth — that no one, once imprisoned in it, could escape. To make matters worse, it was patroled by the Minotaur ("Minos's bull"), a fearsome, man-eating beast, half man and half bull.

Because one of King Minos's ambassadors was slain in Athenian territory, Minos demanded as retribution a bizarre sacrifice: every nine years Athens would be required to send seven of its strongest young men and seven of its noblest young women to Crete to die in the Labyrinth. This macabre custom continued until the Athenian hero Theseus (who was one of the 14) killed the Minotaur, and escaped from the Labyrinth with the assistance of Ariadne, daughter of Minos.

The Fifteen Books of Athenaeus's Deipnosophistae (Witty Dinner Conversationalists)

Athenaeus's (ca. A.D. 200) *Deipnosophistae* is a vast compendium of all kinds of information that one might reasonably expect to be discussed over the dinner table by knowledgeable and clever dinner guests. The 15 books are organized as dialogues; the epitomizer (Books I and II survive as epitomes) of Book I lists 14 diners/conversationalists (and, of course, Athenaeus himself was present), in the following order:

1. Masurius, a jurist, poet and scholar
2. Plutarch, a philologist
3. Leonides of Elis, a philologist
4. Aemilianus Maurus, a philologist
5. Zoilus, a philologist
6. Pontianus of Nicomedia, a philosopher
7. Democritus of Nicomedia, a philosopher
8. Philadelphus of Ptolemais, a philosopher
9. Cynulcus, a philosopher
10. Ulpian of Tyre, the well-known jurist
11. Daphnus of Ephesus, a physician
12. Galen of Pergamum, a physician and prolific author
13. Rufinus of Nicaea, a physician
14. Alcides, a musician

The following list contains one example from each of the 15 books of a topic discussed at the dinner party.

Book I.   A story is related about a particularly voracious diner who trained himself to eat extremely hot food, thus enabling him to consume more than his share at dinners (since the other diners could not tolerate food fresh from the oven).

Book II.   A tale is told about a house in Agrigentum, in Sicily, called "Trireme," so named because it was the scene of a drinking party in which the guests became so inebriated that

they imagined they were on a ship at sea during a raging
storm. Hence, they began tossing furniture out of the
windows in an effort to lighten the ship's load to prevent
it from sinking.

Book III.   Here appears a long discussion about the properties and
characteristics of certain mollusks: oysters, scallops, bar-
nacles, urchins, and clams.

Book IV.   This book relates a conversation on the merits of lentils and
lentil soup.

Book V.   In this book the diners discuss a lavish parade organized by
King Antiochus IV of Syria, a parade that featured

> 5,000 armored youth
> 5,000 Mysians
> 3,000 armored Cilicians, wearing gold crowns
> 3,000 Thracians
> 5,000 Celts
> 20,000 Macedonians (10,000 equipped with gold
>   shields, 5,000 with silver shields, and 5,000
>   with bronze)
> 240 pairs of gladiators
> 1,000 Nisaean horsemen
> 3,000 armored citizens, many wearing gold crowns
> 1,000 horsemen
> An unnumbered contingent of the king's friends
> 1,000 members of an elite military unit
> 1,500 armored cavalrymen
> 100 six-horse chariots, 40 four-horse chariots, 1
>   chariot pulled by 4 elephants; 1 pulled by 2 ele-
>   phants; and a line of 36 elephants with lavish
>   headdresses
> 800 golden-crowned young men
> 1,000 fatted oxen
> Almost 300 tables for sacrifices
> 800 elephant's tusks
> Innumerable statues of gods and goddesses
> 1,600 slaves
> 200 perfumed women
> 580 women in litters

The celebrations that followed included 30 days of
gladiatorial shows and mock beast hunts and 2 magnificent dinners, one for 1,000 guests, the other for 1,500.

Book VI.   A discussion is related about the use of silver utensils at dinner parties, which leads to a more general consideration of
money and other items fabricated of gold and silver.

Book VII.   In this book occurs a long and lively exchange about various
kinds of fish: their unusual anatomical features; their
color; their taste; the best eating fish; and sacred fish.

Book VIII.   One of the diners engages in a sarcastic lambasting of
              Aristotle's biological dicta; the diner wonders how Aris-
              totle knew, for example, that a fly could live for seven
              years, or that fish sleep, or that lions' bones are so hard
              that sparks could be struck from them.

Book IX.   There appears in this book a lengthy description of the at-
              tributes of birds, including a reference to the purple coot,
              which, when tamed and trained, will strangle itself if it
              observes the wife of a household committing adultery.

Book X.   This book contains a discussion of riddles and enigmas,
              replete with many examples.

Book XI.   The diners consider the themes and scenes embossed onto
              drinking cups.

Book XII.   In this book there ensues a discussion of a mass wedding ar-
              ranged by Alexander the Great after his conquest of King
              Darius III of Persia (330 B.C.). This wedding featured a
              structure containing 92 bridal chambers, large enough to
              accommodate 100 couches, each one worth one-third of a
              talent. Supporting the roof were jewelry-studded, 30-feet-
              tall columns; and the perimeter measured about one-half
              mile. The wedding celebrations spanned five days, and
              noted entertainers, including jugglers, singers, dancers,
              actors, comedians, harpists, and flautists, were in at-
              tendance.

Book XIII.   In this book there is an interesting discussion of famous
              courtesans, including Mania, Thais, Aspasia, and Lais.
              Also mentioned is the story that Themistocles once drove
              into the Athenian agora a chariot drawn by four pros-
              titutes: Lamia, Scione, Satyra, and Nannion.

Book XIV: The diners turn their attention to music, musical in-
              struments, and essays on music.

Book XV.   The concluding book contains a discussion of various kinds
              of wreaths, including their composition and purpose.

The Fifteen Books of Ovid's Metamorphoses

Perhaps the best known of Ovid's (43 B.C.–A.D. 17) many literary efforts,
the *Metamorphoses* recounts about 250 tales of Greek and Roman mythology
that have as their common theme some sort of transformation (hence, the title
of the work).

The 15 books are listed below, together with a transformation example
from each.

Book I.   Apollo pursues the unwilling Daphne, who is transformed
              into a laurel tree in order to avoid the god's advances.

Book II.   Zeus transforms himself into a bull to pursue the beautiful
              Europa, daughter of King Agenor of Phoenicia.

Book III.   Narcissus is so enamored of his own reflection in a pool of water that he is transformed into a flower (possibly the daffodil; compare its scientific name, *Narcissus pseudo-narcissus*).

Book IV.   Relates the tales of Perseus, killer of Medusa (whose eyes could transform an onlooker to stone).

Book V.   The unwilling Arethusa is pursued by the river god Alpheus; and the goddess Artemis transforms Arethusa into a stream.

Book VI.   Arachne unwisely challenges the goddess Athena to a weaving contest. When Athena rips her handiwork, Arachne commits suicide and is transformed into a spider.

Book VII.   Swarms of ants are turned into soldiers—the Myrmidons—to assist Achilles during the Trojan War.

Book VIII. The clever and inventive Daedalus constructs a pair of wax-and-feather wings for himself and his son, Icarus—thus endowing them with birdlike qualities—in order that they may fly away from Crete and King Minos.

Book IX.   The maiden Dryope is transformed into a lotus tree.

Book X.   The sculptor Pygmalion creates a statue of a beautiful woman. He falls in love with his creation, and prays to Aphrodite to transform it into a living woman. The goddess complies, and Pygmalion marries his erstwhile statue, now named Galatea.

Book XI.   King Midas is given the ability to transform ordinary objects into gold merely by his touch.

Book XII.   Caenis is transformed from a woman into a man and renamed Caeneus.

Book XIII. The fisherman Glaucus becomes a fish.

Book XIV.   Circe turns Odysseus's men into pigs.

Book XV.   Julius Caesar is assassinated and transformed into a comet.

The Fifteen Conspirators Against Caesar

Appian (*Civil Wars* 2.113) lists 15 men who were actively involved in the plot to assassinate Julius Caesar. These 15 are listed in the order given by Appian:

1. Marcus Brutus Caepio
2. Gaius Cassius Longinus
3. Decimus Brutus Alpinus
4. Caecilius
5. Bucolianus
6. Rubrius Ruga
7. Quintus Ligarius
8. Marcus Spurius
9. Servilius Galba
10. Sextius Naso
11. Pontius Aquila
12. Publius Servilius Casca
13. Gaius Trebonius
14. Tillius Cimber
15. Minucius Basilus

According to Suetonius (*Julius Caesar* 80) there were more than 60 conspirators, although he does not name them.

The Fifteen-Day March Over the Alps

In the Second Punic War (Romans against Carthaginians, 218–201 B.C.), the Carthaginian general Hannibal attempted one of ancient history's more amazing feats: a march over the intractable Alps in the autumn of 218 B.C. Hannibal commenced the arduous journey with 50,000 men; up to half of these may have perished en route. Despite hostile natives, unfamiliar terrain, and blinding snow, the survivors completed the trek in only 15 days.

The Fifteen Flamines

A Roman priest associated with the worship of a particular deity was called a *flamen*. There were 15 such *flamines* in ancient Roman religious practice; and 13 are known by name. Of these 13, the most important ones were the priests connected with Jupiter (*flamen Dialis*); Mars (*flamen Martialis*); and Romulus (*flamen Quirinalis*).

The 13 known *flamines* were as follows:

Title	Deity
1. *flamen Carmentalis*	Carmenta, or Carmentis
2. *flamen Cerialis*	Ceres
3. *flamen Dialis*	Jupiter
4. *flamen Falacer*	Falacer
5. *flamen Floralis*	Flora
6. *flamen Furrinalis*	Furria
7. *flamen Martialis*	Mars
8. *flamen Palatualis*	Pales
9. *flamen Pomonalis*	Pomona
10. *flamen Portunalis*	Portunus
11. *flamen Quirinalis*	Romulus
12. *flamen Volcanalis*	Vulcan
13. *flamen Volturnalis*	Volturnus

The Fifteen Terms of Pericles as General

In the fifth century B.C. the most powerful elected entity in Athens was the Board of the Ten Generals. Although ten were elected annually, one of the ten often emerged as the most influential, and such was the case with the noted statesman Pericles. He served 15 consecutive one-year terms on this board, 443–429.

The Fifteen Trojan Allies

In Book II of the *Iliad* Homer lists the 15 contingents of people who fought for Troy against the Greeks in the Trojan War. While this list is not nearly as comprehensive or detailed as his preceding Catalogue of the (Greek) Ships it does offer a useful overview of the participants on the Trojan side.

Contingent	Leader(s)
1. Trojans	Hector
2. Dardanians	Aeneas

Contingent	Leader(s)
3. Zeleians	Pandarus
4. Adresteians et al.	Adrestus, Amphius
5. Arisbeans et al.	Asius
6. Pelasgians	Hippothous, Pylaeus
7. Thracians	Acamas
8. Cicones	Euphemus
9. Paeonians	Pyraechmes
10. Paphlagonians	Pylaemenes
11. Alizones	Odius, Epistrophus
12. Mysians	Chromis, Ennomus
13. Phrygians	Phorcys, Ascanius
14. Carians	Nastes, Amphimachus
15. Lycians	Sarpedon, Glaucus

The Sixteen Books of the Greek Anthology

Around A.D. 900 a Byzantine scholar named Constantine Cephalus compiled an anthology of short poems, inscriptions, and epigrams, written by a wide variety of Greek authors from the seventh century B.C. up to Cephalus's own time. This collection, with some subsequent additions by the thirteenth-century monk Planudes, is now known as the *Greek Anthology*.

Book number/title	Number of Entries
I/Christian epigrams	123
II/Christodorus of Thebes (Egypt)	65
III/Epigrams from Cyzicus	19
IV/Various poems	4
V/Love poems and epigrams	309
VI/Dedicatory epigrams	358
VII/Epitaphs	748
VIII/Epigrams of St. Gregory of Nazianzus (fourth century A.D.)	254
IX/Declamatory and descriptive epigrams (including inscriptions on statues, paintings, and public buildings	827
X/Proverbs and aphorisms	126
XI/More proverbs; humorous epigrams on human idiosyncrasies	442
XII/Amatory epigrams	258
XIII/Epigrams with various metrical patterns	31
XIV/Riddles and mathematical problems	150
XV/Miscellaneous epigrams	51
XVI/Epigrams collected and added by Planudes	388

The total number of entries in the *Greek Anthology*: 4,153. All 65 entries of Book II pertain to descriptions of statues in the gymnasium called Zeuxippos, in Byzantium.

A Sixteen-Day Dictatorship

As originally conceived by the Romans, the office of dictator was to be conferred only in times of extreme emergency and was to be held for six months at the most, and for a lesser period if the crisis abated before the six months had elapsed. Touted as the exemplar of proper dictatorial behavior was Lucius Quinctius Cincinnatus, who was appointed to the office about 458 B.C. He organized a relief force, rescued a surrounded Roman army, and returned to the city 16 days later, according to Livy (3.29) and Dionysius of Halicarnassus (10.25), whereupon he summarily resigned his dictatorship and returned to his farm.

The Sixteen Gates of Rome

Rome was a walled city, but its walls were punctuated by numerous gates (*portae*). The 16 identifiable gates were

1. Porta Caelemontana
2. Porta Capena
3. Porta Carmentalis
4. Porta Collina
5. Porta Esquilina
6. Porta Fontinalis
7. Porta Flumentana
8. Porta Lavernalis
9. Porta Naevia
10. Porta Querquetulana
11. Porta Quirinalis
12. Porta Raudusculana
13. Porta Salutaris
14. Porta Sanqualis
15. Porta Trigemina
16. Porta Viminalis

The Sixteen Gladiatorial Classifications

Newly recruited Roman gladiators were generally assigned to one of 16 classifications. The classifications were differentiated primarily by means of the armor and equipment worn by the gladiators. Some of these gladiatorial categories are quite well documented; for others, however, almost nothing is known. The 16 classifications were

1. Andabatae
2. Dimachaeri
3. Equites
4. Essedarii
5. Galli
6. Hoplomachi
7. Laquearii
8. Murmillones
9. Paegniarii
10. Provocatores
11. Retiarii
12. Sagittarii
13. Secutores (sometimes called Samnites)
14. Scissores
15. Thracians
16. Veletes

Of these 16 categories, the best known were probably the *retiarii* (literally meaning "net men"). These gladiators were distinctively equipped and costumed with a net, a trident, and very little armor. A *retiarius* apparently endeavored to win his match by entangling an opponent in the net, and then using the trident as the primary offensive weapon. Adversaries for the *retiarii* were generally drawn from the ranks of the heavily armed gladiators, such as the *secutores* and *murmillones*.

Equites ("horsemen") fought from horseback, evidently in the manner of medieval knights at a jousting tournament. *Essedarii* contested in pairs while riding in chariots: one man apparently drove the chariot, while his partner engaged in the actual fighting.

The Sixteen Praenomina

Roman parents had little choice when selecting a *praenomen* ("first name") for a newborn son. There were only about 16 possibilities:

1. Aulus	7. Marcus	12. Servius
2. Appius	8. Manius	13. Sextus
3. Gaius	9. Numerius	14. Spurius
4. Gnaeus	10. Publius	15. Titus
5. Decimus	11. Quintus	16. Tiberius
6. Lucius		

Female babies usually (although not always) received the feminized form of the parents' family name. For example, the daughter of Gaius Julius Caesar was named Julia. Subsequent daughters might also be called Julia.

Sixteen Roads of Rome

The famous dictum "all roads lead to Rome" clearly has a factual basis. Ancient Rome was the hub, with many paved roads — ancient superhighways — emanating from it. The 16 main roads (*viae*) were

1. Via Appia	7. Via Flaminia	12. Via Portuensis
2. Via Ardeatina	8. Via Labicana	13. Via Praenestina
3. Via Asinaria	9. Via Latina	14. Via Salaria
4. Via Aurelia	10. Via Nomentana	15. Via Tiburtina
5. Via Collatina	11. Via Ostiensis	16. Via Triumphalis
6. Via Cornelia		

Of these, the Via Appia (Appian Way) was Rome's oldest paved road; construction on it began in 312 B.C. The Via Appia originally connected Rome with the city of Capua, about 70 miles to the southeast. Eventually, however, the road was extended to the port city of Brundisium, at the southern tip of Italy, giving it a total length of 360 miles.

Sixteen Satires *of Juvenal*

The Roman poet Decimus Junius Juvenalis (Juvenal; ca. A.D. 50–127) wrote 16 satirical poems; many contain bitter comments about Roman culture and society.

Satire I. In an introductory satire Juvenal explains that he intends to write about the human vices that he encounters daily in Rome. This satire is the source of one of the more famous lines in Latin literature: *difficile est non scribere saturam*, "it is difficult not to write satire."

Satire II. In this satire Juvenal excoriates homosexual practices, which he sees as evidence of the moral decline and degradation of contemporary Rome.

Satire III. The themes of this satire revolve around the dangers of living in Rome, and the favoritism shown to the wealthy citizens at the expense of the middle class and poor.

Satire IV. In the fourth satire Juvenal ridicules the profligacy and waste of the emperor Domitian and his close advisers.

Satire V. Juvenal bitterly attacks Rome's long-standing patron/client system by showing the manner in which a wealthy patron takes advantage of one of his powerless clients.

Satire VI. In this satire Juvenal warns a friend contemplating matrimony of the evils of women.

Satire VII. Juvenal laments the mistreatment and lack of appreciation suffered by poets, historians, teachers, and orators, and expresses the hope that the situation might improve with the advent of the new emperor (thought to be Hadrian [reigned A.D. 117–138]).

Satire VIII. The eighth satire is an encomium of sorts on the virtuous and noble men of Rome who have sprung from humble backgrounds.

Satire IX. In the ninth satire Juvenal decries the lot of a certain Naevolus, a man whose base lifestyle has left him penniless and desperate.

Satire X. Often considered Juvenal's masterpiece, the tenth satire explores the futility of praying to the gods for ephemeral or even harmful gifts such as power, eloquence, military glory, or wealth. The best gift is that which can fortify a person against all the travails that life has to offer: *mens sana in sano corpore*, "a sound mind in a sound body," one of Juvenal's most memorable lines.

This satire is the source of another well-known Juvenalian phrase: *panem et circenses*, "bread and circuses," a phrase springing from Juvenal's cynical belief that in his day the common people of Rome cared only for food and entertainments.

Satire XI. In the eleventh satire Juvenal criticizes those who are too fond of expensive food.

Satire XII. Juvenal mocks legacy hunters in this satire.

Satire XIII. The thireenth satire is addressed to Juvenal's friend Calvinus, who has been swindled out of a large sum of money. Juvenal reminds his friend that many such thefts take place daily in Rome; he should be comforted by the knowledge that the perpetrator will be tortured by his own guilty conscience.

Satire XIV. In his fourteenth satire Juvenal returns to one of his favorite themes: the evil that lust for money can bring about.

Satire XV. The subject of this satire is the quality that distinguishes human beings from animals: the ability to feel compassion for one another.

Satire XVI. In this fragmentary satire Juvenal expresses envy for the perquisites of the soldiering profession.

The Seventeen Books of Silius Italicus's Punica

Tiberius Catius Asconius Silius Italicus (A.D. 26–101) authored the longest extant Latin poem, an epic about the Second Punic War. The 17 books of his *Punica*, along with a summary of contents are listed below:

Book I.   Introduction; Hannibal's background; his siege of
            Saguntum; and the Roman response.

Book II.   Rome declares war; and Saguntum capitulates.

Book III.   Hannibal moves overland toward Rome, a journey that
            included his celebrated trek over the Alps. This book
            contains a lengthy catalogue (almost 200 lines) of
            Hannibal's forces. Ten of the major cities or regions
            that supplied troops, according to Silius Italicus were

1. Carthage	6. Numidia
2. Utica	7. Gaetulia
3. Cyrene	8. Asturia
4. Tyre	9. Gallicia
5. Ethiopia	10. Lusitania

Book IV.   Initial skirmishes in Italy; and the first decisive battle (of
            the Trebia River, in December of 218 B.C.).

Book V.   The Battle of Lake Trasimene (May 217 B.C.).

Book VI.   Aftermath of Trasimene; Hannibal moves to south cen-
            tral Italy; and Fabius Maximus is appointed dictator.

Book VII.   Fabius Maximus's strategy of delaying and harassing
            Hannibal.

Book VIII. Background to the Battle of Cannae. Included in this
            book is a catalogue of the Roman forces assembled to
            oppose Hannibal at Cannae. Ten of the major cities
            that supplied troops were

1. Rome	6. Picenum
2. Tibur	7. Paestum
3. Praeneste	8. Clusium
4. Velitrae	9. Capua
5. Arpinum	10. Brundisium

Book IX.   The Battle of Cannae (August 216 B.C.).

Book X.   Conclusion of the Battle of Cannae; and its aftermath.

Book XI.   Capua defects to the Carthaginian cause; and dissension
            in Carthage over the post–Cannae course to be pursued.

Book XII.   Hannibal's maneuvers in southern and central Italy, in-
            cluding an abortive attack on Rome itself.

Book XIII. Capua retaken by Rome; Scipio descends to the Under-
            world (in the manner of Odysseus and Aeneas in
            earlier epics).

Book XIV.   The Sicilian theater; and the siege of Syracuse, including
            a description of the celebrated defenses of the city,
            designed by Archimedes.

Book XV.	Accounts of the war in Spain and southern Italy.
Book XVI.	Rome pacifies Spain; and Scipio, the newly elected consul, crosses into Africa with the army.
Book XVII.	Hannibal returns to Africa, where Scipio defeats him at the decisive Battle of Zama (202 B.C.); and Scipio returns triumphantly to Rome.

The Seventeen Books of Strabo's Geography

The erudite and widely traveled historian Strabo (ca.64 B.C.–A.D. 21) wrote a *Geography*, divided into 17 books, each listed below with a summary of contents:

Book I.	A consideration and critique of the theories and beliefs of Homer and Eratosthenes; and a survey of the areas of knowledge essential for geographers, especially mathematics, astronomy, and climatology.
Book II.	Additional critiques, especially of Eratosthenes, Polybius, Hipparchus and Posidonius; distances between various locations; and the earth's zones (especially arctic, temperate, and tropic).
Book III.	A description of Spain—size; rivers; mountains; cities; mineral resources; the inhabitants; and the islands lying off the coast of Spain.
Book IV.	A description of Gaul, including a short essay on Massilia (modern Marseilles—its government [600 assemblymen, of whom 15 preside over the assembly], laws, shipping, and military victories); islands near Gaul; a description of Britain; nearby islands; a description of the Alps—inhabitants; topography; roads; and mineral resources, especially gold—Strabo mentions one mine so rich in pure gold that one need dig down only two feet to find the metal.
Book V.	A description of Italy; islands (especially Sardinia and Corsica); accounts of the founding of Rome; and a description of Mount Vesuvius (destined to erupt in volcanic fury 50 years after Strabo's death), in which Strabo states that the mountain's appearance suggests that it had been on fire at one time, and that its ashes account in part for the agricultural fertility of the surrounding regions.
Book VI.	A continuation of the description of Italy. Cities described include Rhegium, Thurii, Sybaris, Brundisium, and Croton (well known for its champion athletes and also for its colony of Pythagorean philosophers); and a description of Sicily. Book VI concludes with an essay about the rise to power of the Romans, and how the topography of Italy contributed to this.

Book VII.   A description of northern and eastern Europe. (An anec-
dote about one of the region's tribes, the Getae,
relates that most of their men had 10 or 12 wives, and
that a man who died having married fewer than six
times was viewed as a pitiable wretch.)

Book VIII.   A description of southern Greece, and specifically the
Peloponnesus; and a history of Olympia and the
founding of the Olympic games.

Book IX.   A description of central Greece: geographical divisions;
descriptions of Attica, Boeotia, Phocis, Locris, and
Thessaly; chief cities, including a lengthy enumeration
of the demes, or local governments, of Athens; and
the island of Salamis.

Book X.   A description of the rest of Greece, especially Aetolia
and the island of Euboea; a description of Crete; and
islands near Crete, including the Cyclades.

Book XI.   A description of Northern and Western Asia; a description of the Amazons; lands and people surrounding
the Caspian Sea; a consideration of the Parthians,
longtime nemesis of the Romans; and a description of
Taurus and Armenia.

Book XII.   A description of the northern and eastern coastal areas
of Asia Minor (modern Turkey): Cappadocia; Pontus;
Bithynia; Phrygia; Galatia; Pisidia; cities, including a
description of Comana, so well noted for the lascivious ways of its citizens that it was dubbed "Little Corinth."

Book XIII.   A description of the northwestern coastal areas of Asia
Minor—Mysia; the Propontis; Troy, the Trojan Plain,
and the background to the Trojan War; a description
of the island of Lesbos, whose chief city, Mitylene,
produced several individuals of note, including Pittacus (one of the Seven Sages) and the poets Alcaeus
and Sappho; islands near Lesbos; and a description of
the cities of Pergamum and Sardis.

Book XIV.   A description of the southern and southwestern areas of
Asia Minor: Lydia, Caria, Lycia, Pamphylia, and
Cilicia; a description of the city of Ephesus, including
the Temple of Artemis, one of the Seven Wonders of
the Ancient World; a discussion of the island of
Rhodes, whose chief city (also called Rhodes) Strabo
felt was unequalled in terms of its city plan, its
buildings, and its government.

Book XV.   A description of India, including bizarre native
creatures, such as ants that mine gold, flying reptiles,
winged scorpions, and dogs that bite so fiercely that
their eyes fall from their sockets. A list of the seven
castes of India is included (rank-ordered):

1. Philosophers
2. Farmers
3. Shepherds and hunters (including a long discussion of the nature and habits of elephants
4. Craftsmen and laborers
5. Soldiers
6. Government inspectors
7. The king's advisers

Also included in Book XV are discussions of Indian and Persian lifestyles and customs.

Book XVI.   Descriptions of Assyria, Mesopotamia, Syria, Judaea, and Arabia. The account of Assyria contains a description of the city of Babylonia, including the Hanging Gardens, one of the Seven Ancient Wonders.

Book XVII.   A description of Egypt — the course of length of the Nile River; a long discussion of Alexandria; the pyramids; animal veneration and worship; and temples and oracles; descriptions of Ethiopia and Libya; a lengthy discussion of Carthage — Strabo records that prior to the First Punic War (began 264 B.C.), Carthage controlled 300 Libyan cities and had a population of 700,000; when the Carthaginians capitulated to the Romans at the close of the Third Punic War (146 B.C.), they surrendered 200,000 suits of armor and 3,000 catapults.

Strabo also notes the following statistics regarding Carthaginian activity between the end of the Second Punic War (201 B.C.) and the beginning of the Third (149 B.C.): the daily armament production was 140 shields, 300 swords, 500 spears, and 1,000 missiles for catapults. In addition, they also constructed 120 ships during that time. Book XVII concludes with a discussion of Roman provincial organization. Strabo lists 12 Roman provinces:

1. Libya
2. Western Asia
3. Iberia
4. Narbonitis
5. Sardinia-Corsica
6. Sicily
7. Macedonia
8. Illyria
9. Achaea
10. Crete
11. Cyprus
12. Bithynia-Pontus

Eighteen Cities Founded by Alexander the Great

According to Plutarch, Alexander the Great founded some 70 cities, although this figure is generally viewed with skepticism by modern scholars. Alexander was, however, a city founder of the first rank; the Byzantine writer Stephanus lists 18 cities established by Alexander — all named Alexandria. The 18 cities were

1. Alexandria in Arachotia
2. Alexandria in Aria
3. Alexandria in Babylonia
4. Alexandria in Bactria
5. Alexandria Bucephala
6. Alexandria in Carmania
7. Alexandria of the Caucasus
8. Alexandria in Egypt
9. Alexandria Eschate
10. Alexandria Iomousa
11. Alexandria near Issus
12. Alexandria in Makarene
13. Alexandria in Margiana
14. Alexandria Nicaea
15. Alexandria Prophthasia
16. Alexandria in Sogdiana
17. Alexandria in Susiana
18. Alexandria Troas

The Eighteen Cities of Ancient Italy

According to Diodorus Siculus (7.5), the legendary King Latinus Silvius (eleventh century B.C.?) founded 18 ancient Italian cities:

1. Aricia
2. Boilum (Bola)
3. Caenina
4. Cameria
5. Cora
6. Crustumerium
7. Fregellae
8. Gabii
9. Labici
10. Lanuvium
11. Medullia
12. Pometia
13. Praeneste
14. Satricum
15. Scaptia
16. Tellenae
17. Tibur
18. Tusculum

The Eighteen-Month Censorship

Every five years the Romans elected two officials called censors. During their 18-month terms of office, they were charged with many important responsibilities, including revising the roll of the Roman Senate; initiating and contracting for the maintenance and construction of roads, aqueducts, and temples; and compiling citizen registries, for taxation and conscription purposes.

The Eighteen Satires of Horace

The Roman poet Horace wrote 18 *Sermones* (*Satires*) ("conversational poems"), divided into two books, of ten and eight, respectively. These were written between 35 and 30 B.C. The 18 satires are as follows:

Book I

Satire 1. Human beings would be much happier if they simply enjoyed their own lives and possessions, rather than envying what others have. To live life within the bounds of moderation is the best course.

Satire 2. A continuation of the theme of the first satire, with particular reference to the folly of envying adulterers. In this satire Horace lists the seven impediments to seducing a *matrona* (a married woman of nobility):

1. Her bodyguards
2. Her litter bearers
3. Her hairdressers
4. Her hangers-on
5. The long dress that covers her legs all the way to the ankles
6. The cloak that hides her other endowments
7. *Plurima*, "many other things."

Satire 3. One should not be overly critical of a friend's faults or mistakes, especially if the critic has flaws of similar or greater magnitude.

Satire 4. A philosophical defense of the satiric genre, and its expression as found in Horace's satires.

Satire 5. A pleasant description of a trip Horace made down the Appian Way, from Rome to Brundisium. The satire is filled with humorous portrayals of typical tourist complaints: tainted water; diarrhea; difficulty in sleeping; inconsistent quality of accommodations; and bad weather and equally bad stretches of highway. The 360-mile journey required about three weeks for the slow-traveling Horace to complete.

Satire 6. In this satire Horace reflects upon and defends his station in life in Rome; the fact that he was born into a relatively obscure family cannot prevent him from enjoying life or developing his creative powers.

Satire 7. A satire on a lawsuit brought before Brutus (Caesar's assassin).

Satire 8. Horace describes the bewitching incantations of two old women.

Satire 9. In this satire Horace recounts an amusing incident in which he is pestered with mindless questions by a boring acquaintance.

Satire 10. Horace defends his gentle criticisms of one of his predecessors in the satiric art, Lucilius.

Book II

Satire 1. Another satire in which Horace defends the tone and content of his satirical writing.

Satire 2. One of Horace's favorite themes—living a simple, moderate lifestyle is preferable to conspicuous consumption.

Satire 3. A satire of Stoic doctrine and teachings. The four forms of a fool's insanity are listed in this satire—ambition, greed, luxuriousness, and superstition.

Satire 4. A satire on the fastidiousness of gourmets; this satire contains a good deal of information about the kinds of food served at a formal dinner party.

Satire 5. This satire on legacy hunting is cast in the form of a conversation between Odysseus and Tiresias.

Satire 6. The theme of this satire—plain and simple living, a lifestyle more easily achieved in a rural setting—is expressed in a dialogue between a city mouse and a country mouse.

Satire 7. This satire on Stoic paradoxes takes the form of a discussion between Horace and his slave, Davus. (At the very end of this satire Horace threatens to exile Davus to the country, to labor on Horace's

Sabine farm; Davus would become Horace's ninth farmhand, should such an eventuality come to pass.)

Satire 8. A satirical sketch of a luxurious dinner party. As with the fourth satire of Book II, this one describes in some detail the various kinds of food served. Horace lists the five ingredients of a good fish sauce — olive oil, mackerel roe, five-year-old wine, pepper, and vinegar.

Horace also composed four books of *Odes* on various themes, including the shortness of life; the pleasures of country living; the poetic art; unrequited love; and patriotism.

The collection contains 103 poems, organized as follows:

Book I: 38 poems   Book III: 30 poems
Book II: 20 poems   Book IV: 15 poems

Additionally, Horace authored 23 poetic *Epistles*, and 17 *Epodes*.

Eighteen Votes for Impeachment

In the tumultuous year of 133 B.C. the tribune Tiberius Sempronius Gracchus moved to depose a fellow tribune by the name of Marcus Octavius. A simple majority of the 35 Roman tribes (voting en bloc) would be required to remove Octavius. After the first 17 tribes had all declared in favor of the impeachment resolution, Gracchus appealed to Octavius to resign, thus to be spared the ignominy of an all but certain formal deposition. Octavius refused; the eighteenth tribe voted as the others had, and Octavius was deprived of his office.

The Nineteen Books Extant of Dio's Roman History

Dio Cassius (name sometimes appears as Cassius Dio, or Cassius Dio Cocceianus) wrote a history of Rome (in Greek), from its earliest beginnings up to A.D. 229. Of the 80 books in this treatise, only numbers 36 to 54 survive intact, although fragments and detailed summaries of many of the others are also extant.

Dio spent 22 years researching and writing his Roman history. The following is a summary of the contents of Books 36–54:

Book *number* / *years covered*	*Content summary*
1. Book 36 / 69–66	The career of Pompey the Great, and particularly the debate over a measure giving him a military command against Mediterranean pirates.
2. Book 37 / 65–60	Pompey's activities in the east; the Catilinarian conspiracy; and the First Triumvirate.
3. Book 38 / 59–58	Cicero's exile; and Caesar's early battles in Gaul.
4. Book 39 / 57–54	Cicero's return from exile; activities of Pompey and Crassus; and further accounts of Caesar's war in Gaul.

Book number / years covered	Content summary
5. Book 40 / 54–50	Additional accounts of Caesar's Gallic War; and Crassus's defeat and death at the hands of the Parthians.
6. Book 41 / 49–48	The beginnings of the civil war between Pompey and Caesar; and the decisive Battle of Pharsalus.
7. Book 42 / 48–47	Caesar's military exploits in Egypt, Asia, and North Africa.
8. Book 43 / 46–44	The final events of the civil war; and Caesar's reforms.
9. Book 44 / 44	The conspiracy against Caesar, his assassination, and his funeral.
10. Book 45 / 44–43	The machinations of Octavian and Mark Antony; and a Ciceronian speech against Antony.
11. Book 46 / 43	A defender of Mark Antony has his say; conflicts between Antony and Octavian; and the formation of the Second Triumvirate.
12. Book 47 / 43–42	The proscriptions of the Second Triumvirate; the demise of the conspirators Brutus and Cassius at the Battle of Philippi (42 B.C.).
13. Book 48 / 42–37	Battles with Sextus Pompey (son of Pompey the Great); and conflicts and battles with the Parthians.
14. Book 49 / 36–33	Octavian's subjugation of Pompey; and continuing conflicts with the Parthians.
15. Book 50 / 33–31	Open hostility and warfare between Antony and Octavian; and the Battle of Actium (31 B.C.).
16. Book 51 / 31–29	Immediate aftermath of the Battle of Actium; and death of Mark Antony.
17. Book 52 / 29	Octavian maintains and strengthens his hold on the Roman government.
18. Book 53 / 28–23	The granting of the title "Augustus" to Octavian; and dedications of various temples and other structures.
19. Book 54 / 22–10	Government appointments; theater dedications; and foreign wars and adventurism.

The Nineteen Plays Extant of Euripides

One of fifth-century B.C. Athens's greatest tragedians, Euripides (ca.480– 405) wrote about 90 plays. Of these, 19 survive.

1. *Alcestis* (438): Hercules successfully wrestles Hades for the right to return the deceased Alcestis, queen of Thessaly, to the land of the living.

2. *Andromache* (ca.426): The post–Trojan War sufferings of Hector's widow, Andromache.

3. *Bacchae* (ca.405): The wine god Dionysus and his frenzied followers, the Bacchantes, wreak havoc in Thebes.

4. *Children of Hercules* (ca.427): After Hercules' death, King

Eurystheus, who supervised Hercules' performing of the Twelve Labors, persecutes his children.

5. *Cyclops* (423): A humorous look at Odysseus's encounter with the Cyclops Polyphemus.

6. *Electra* (413): Electra persuades her brother Orestes to kill their mother Clytemnestra for her part in the murder of their father, Agamemnon.

7. *Hecuba* (ca.425): Hecuba, widow of Troy's King Priam, is captured by Agamemnon and taken from Troy.

8. *Helen* (412): An alternate version of the abduction of Helen by Paris suggests that Paris took a phantom of Helen to Troy, while Hermes conveyed the real Helen to Egypt, where she remained for the duration of the Trojan War. The play *Helen* deals with her difficulties in Egypt.

9. *Hippolytus* (428): Phaedra, wife of Theseus of Athens, falls in love with her stepson Hippolytus. Both are brought to ruin by this unnatural passion.

10. *Ion* (ca.417): Ion, son of Apollo and Creusa, is taken to Athens, where he becomes a king and founder of the Ionian people.

11. *Iphigenia in Aulis* (ca.405): The plans of the Greek fleet to sail to Troy are stymied by contrary winds at Aulis, a situation that can be remedied only by the sacrifice of Iphigenia, the daughter of Agamemnon, leader of the fleet.

12. *Iphigenia in Tauris* (ca.414–412): In this version of the myth, a stag is secretly sacrificed in place of Iphigenia, who is transported to Tauris. There she is visited by her brother, Orestes, who has been commanded to retrieve an image of the goddess Artemis and convey it to Athens.

13. *Madness of Hercules* (ca.422): Hercules is driven insane at the behest of the goddess Hera, and murders his wife and children.

14. *Medea* (431): Jason deserts Medea in Corinth; as an act of vengeance, she kills their two children.

15. *Orestes* (408): The Argives are about to execute Orestes for matricide, until Apollo intervenes and explains that they must let him stand trial in Athens for his crime.

16. *Phoenician Women* (409): A Euripidean version of the Oedipus story.

17. *Rhesus* (date uncertain; some authorities doubt that Euripides authored this play): Rhesus, a king of Thrace and an ally of the Trojans, dies in the Trojan War at the hands of Odysseus and Diomedes.

18. *Suppliants* (420): The women of Argos journey to Athens to seek Athenian aid in persuading the Thebans to permit the burial of the Argive warriors who died fighting against Thebes.

19. *Trojan Women* (415): The hardships suffered by the women and children of Troy as a consequence of the Trojan War.

The Twenty Books of Aulus Gellius's Attic Nights

Aulus Gellius (ca. A.D. 123–165), jurist, rhetorician, and man of letters, gained fame for his *Attic Nights*, a 20-book collection of information and anecdotes on a wide variety of topics. (The title is derived from the period of time he spent in Athens, where he began writing the treatise *longuinguis per hiemem noctibus*, "during winter, with its long nights.")

The number of chapters per book ranges from 8 in Book XIV, to 31, in Books XIII and XV. Listed below are the books of *Attic Nights*, along with a sample of topics and the chapter in which they are located.

Book I.   The use of musical instruments as accoutrements for warfare and oratory (chapter 11).

Book II.   Whether children should always obey a parent's command (chapter 7).

Book III.   The story of the miraculous horse of Gnaeus Seius, a magnificent animal, but whose owners all suffered cruel fates or ignominious deaths (chapter 9):

> 1. Seius himself, who died in the proscriptions of 43 B.C.;
>
> 2. Cornelius Dolabella, who paid 100,000 sesterces for the horse, and who was soon after killed in battle;
>
> 3. Gaius Cassius, who took the horse as a war prize, but then soon met his end; and
>
> 4. Mark Antony, whose decline in power and influence coincided with his acquisition of the horse.

Book IV.   A lawsuit against a prostitute named Manilia, brought by Aulus Hostilius Mancinus, an aedile; he claimed that Manilia threw a rock at him (and hit him with it) when he tried to enter her place of business (chapter 14).

Book V.   Some anecdotes about Bucephalus, the noted warhorse that belonged to Alexander the Great (chapter 2).

Book VI.   A story about the affection of a dolphin for a boy (chapter 8).

Book VII.   An encounter in Africa between the consul Atilius Regulus (256 B.C.) and a huge snake; when it was with some difficulty killed, its 120-feet-long skin was sent to Rome (chapter 3).

Book VIII.   Book VIII is fragmentary; summaries of its entries— many on grammatical and literary matters—survive.

Book IX.   On some old and dust-covered books that Gellius bought for a remarkably low price—books that detailed some miraculous stories about foreign peoples (chapter 4).

Book X.   The three age classifications recognized by the Romans (chapter 28) were

> 1. *pueri* (boys), under age 17;
>
> 2. *juniores* (young men), ages 17 to 46; and
>
> 3. *seniores* (older men), over age 46.

Book XI.   Reflections on various law codes, including those of
                 Draco and Solon, as well as the Twelve Tables
                 (chapter 18).
Book XII.   Two examples of reconciliations of noblemen who were
                 at one time enemies (chapter 8) are

> 1. Publius Cornelius Scipio Africanus and
> Tiberius Sempronius Gracchus, who often
> disagreed over politics, but whose reconciliation
> was effected by the marriage of Scipio's
> daughter Cornelia to Gracchus (in the early sec-
> ond century B.C.); and
> 2. Marcus Aemilius Lepidus and Marcus
> Fulvius, whose mutual hatred ended when both
> were elected censors for 179 B.C.

Book XIII.   Several of Cato the Elder's aphorisms on wealth and
                 possessions (chapter 24).
Book XIV.   Chaldean astrologers (chapter 1).
Book XV.   The strange death of the famous wrestler Milo of Croton
                 (chapter 16).
Book XVI.   The lyre player Arion, and how he was rescued from
                 drowning by a dolphin (chapter 19).
Book XVII.   The story that King Mithridates VI could speak 25
                 languages, and never required an interpreter (chapter
                 17).
Book XVIII.   The kinds of questions Aulus Gellius and his Roman
                 friends discussed when celebrating the Saturnalian
                 festival in Athens (chapter 2).
Book XIX.   Why an embarrassed person blushes, but a fearful one
                 grows pale (chapter 6).
Book XX.   The low esteem in which actors are — and should be —
                 held (chapter 4).

The following is a list of the 20 books, followed by the number of chapters
in each:

Book I:	26	Book XI:	18
Book II:	30	Book XII:	15
Book III:	19	Book XIII:	31
Book IV:	20	Book XIV:	8
Book V:	21	Book XV:	31
Book VI:	22	Book XVI:	19
Book VII:	17	Book XVII:	21
Book VIII:	15	Book XVIII:	15
Book IX:	16	Book XIX:	14
Book X:	29	Book XX:	11

The total number of chapters for all 20 books is 398.

The Twenty Books of Dionysius's Roman Antiquities

The first-century B.C. historian Dionysius of Halicarnassus was a man of wide-ranging literary interests. In addition to his 20-book history of Rome, he also wrote essays on topics such as oratory, literary criticism, and prose style in general, and the style of Thucydides in particular.

His reputation today, however, rests largely upon his *Roman Antiquities*, a history of Rome down to the First Punic War (ca. mid–third century B.C.). Dionysius was fond of quoting speeches at great length, which, in their totality, offer an interesting picture of political debate in Rome, especially in the sixth and fifth centuries.

The first ten books are intact; the final ten are fragmentary or survive only in an abridged form. The following is a list of these, along with a summary of their contents:

Book I.	Introduction; prehistory; Trojan War; Aeneas's wanderings and arrival in Italy; Aeneas's regal successors; and Romulus and Remus.
Book II.	Kingship of Romulus; his acts, policies, and decrees; reign of the second king, Numa Pompilius; and the various priestly colleges established by Numa.
Book III.	Reign of Rome's third king, Tullus Hostilius; the Horatii versus the Curiatii; and the reigns and accomplishments of the fourth king, Ancus Marcius, and the fifth king, Lucius Tarquinius Priscus.
Book IV.	Reign and accomplishments of the sixth king, Servius Tullius, and the seventh (and final) king, Lucius Tarquinius Superbus; and the eviction of Tarquinius and the establishment of the Roman Republic.
Book V.	Acts and accomplishments of the first consul, Junius Brutus, and subsequent consuls, to 496 B.C. Famous legends, including the stories of Horatius at the bridge and the burning of Mucius Scaevola's right hand.
Book VI.	Events from 495 to 493 B.C., including wars against the Sabines and the Volscians, and civil struggles between the plebeians and the patricians; and the first plebeian secession (ca.494) and the creation of the tribunate.
Book VII.	Events from 492 to 488. More conflicts between plebeians and patricians, especially as exemplified by the enmity between the hard-line patrician Gaius Marcius Coriolanus and the plebeian tribunes; and Coriolanus's trial and banishment.
Book VIII.	Events from 487 to 480. Coriolanus's desertion to the Volscians; Rome's battles with the Volscians and the Hernicans; and more plebeian-patrician disputes.
Book IX.	Events from 479 to 460. Rome's wars against the Tyrrhenians and the Aequians, including a defeat suffered at

the hands of the former and a victory over the latter;
and disputes between plebeians and patricians over
land distribution.

Book X.   Events from 459 to 448. More plebeian pressure for
equality with patricians; Cincinnatus's dictatorship;
wars against the Sabines and the Aequians; and enactment of the Twelve Tables.

Book XI.   Events from 447 to 439. Continuing conflicts with the
Sabines and the Aequians; and civil intrigue and
debates over the continued existence of the decem-
virate.

Book XII.   Events from 435 to 395. The conspiracy of Spurius
Maelius (who attempted to gain political influence by
arranging for largesses of grain to the plebeians).

Book XIII.   Events from 394 to 391. The exploits of the dictator
Camillus; and the Gallic attack on Rome.

Book XIV.   Events from 390 to 357. The activities of various consuls, dictators, and tribunes.

Book XV.   Events from 348 to 326. The first Samnite War; and
negotiations with the Samnites.

Book XVI.   Events from 321 to 314. The second Samnite War.

Book XVII.   Events from 298 to 293. The third Samnite War, and
other hostilities with the Samnites.

Book XVIII. A continuation of Book XVII.

Book XIX.   Events from 292(?) to 280. First Roman contacts and
negotiations with King Pyrrhus, the noted Epirote
mercenary general.

Book XX.   Events ca.280 to 275. The Battle of Asculum and other
confrontations with Pyrrhus.

Twenty Cauldrons and Twenty Women

In the ninth book of the *Iliad*, Homer records Agamemnon's desperate attempt to smooth over his differences with the sulking Achilles, and to lure
Achilles back into active combat against the Trojans. In a council with the other
Greek chieftains, Agamemnon suggested that the following list of gifts might
persuade Achilles to return:

20 bright cauldrons;
20 Trojan women, should the Greeks sack Troy;
12 fleet race horses, all of which had won racing victories;
10 talents of gold
7 beautiful women, captured on the island of Lesbos, and with them
Briseis, whose expropriation from Achilles by Agamemnon started their
feud in the first place; and
7 tripods that had never been placed over a fire.

Additionally, Agamemnon vowed that if the Greeks returned home safely
after the war, he would give Achilles his choice of his (Agamemnon's) three

daughters: Chrysothemis, Laodice, or Iphianassa. Finally, Agamemnon proposed giving Achilles sway over seven strong citadels:

1. Cardamyle   5. Antheia
2. Enope   6. Aepeia
3. Hire   7. Pedasus
4. Pherae

The crafty Odysseus conveyed this generous offer to Achilles, who categorically refused to accept it.

The Twenty Plays Extant of Plautus

Titus Maccius Plautus (255–184 B.C.), a Roman comic playwright, is thought to have written about 130 plays. Some of the most common themes include parents searching for long lost children; love triangles and other romantic "situation comedies," often involving complicated disguises and deceptions; and clever, scheming slaves who frequently outwit their masters. Twenty Plautine plays survive; most are undatable.

1. *Amphitryon*: Jupiter disguises himself as Amphitryon, husband of Alcmena, in order to spend a night with her (the exertions of which later resulted in Alcmena giving birth to Hercules).
2. *The Bragging Soldier*: The vain and inept Pyrgopolynices foolishly attempts to duplicate his battlefield conquests with romantic conquests. (The popular film *A Funny Thing Happened on the Way to the Forum* is loosely based on this play.)
3. *The Captives*: The aged Hegio endeavors to locate his two long lost sons, one of whom is a prisoner of war.
4. *The Little Carthaginian*: Hanno, a Carthaginian, attempts to rescue his kidnapped daughters from a life of prostitution.
5. *Casina*: A father (Lysidamus) and his son (Euthynicus) are both enamored of the slave girl, Casina, who eventually marries the son.
6. *The Casket*: The contents of a box reveal that the courtesan Selenium is in fact the daughter of a freeborn Athenian citizen.
7. *The Comedy of Asses*: The attempts of the aged Demaenetus to arrange a marriage for his son are foiled by his disapproving wife, Artemona.
8. *Curculio*: Phaedromus falls in love with the slave girl Planaesium. With the help of the parasite Curculio, he devises a plan to obtain the money to buy Planaesium.
9. *Epidicus*: The slave Epidicus attempts to help his young master Stratippocles in matters of love and money.
10. *The Girl from Persia*: The romantic adventures of a slave named Toxilus are chronicled in this play.
11. *The Haunted House*: In his father's absence, a young Athenian, Philolaches, purchases and lives with the slave girl he loves, Philematium. When his father returns, Philolaches—knowing that the old man will be

upset over the marriage—attempts to deceive him by convincing him that his house is haunted by the ghost of a man murdered by the house's previous owner.

12. *The Menaechmi Twins*: A tale of twin boys from the city of Syracuse, Menaechmus and Sosicles, and the confusion that arises when Menaechmus is kidnapped at age seven, survives the ordeal, and becomes the object of his brother's six-year search.

13. *The Merchant*: An Athenian merchant, Demipho, and his son, Charinus, fall in love with the same girl.

14. *Pot of Gold*: A suspicious and miserly old Athenian, Euclio, discovers a pot of gold buried under his house.

15. *Pseudolus*: The slave Pseudolus helps his young master, Calidorus, purchase the courtesan he loves, Phoenicium.

16. *The Rope*: An aged Athenian, Daemones, loses his property and his daughter, only to regain them after a series of misadventures.

17. *Stichus*: The sons-in-law of the aged Athenian Antipho both achieve unexpected wealth, thereby gaining the acceptance of their previously disapproving father-in-law.

18. *The Three-Penny Day*: The profligate Lesbonicus, having wasted the family fortune, finds himself in need of money to fund his daughter's dowry.

19. *Truculentus*: The prostitute Phronesium attempts to profit from her relationships with three lovers.

20. *The Two Bacchises*: The romantic intrigues of two sisters, both named Bacchis and both courtesans, form the plot for this play.

Twenty Roman Laws

Roman politicians and legislative assemblies passed hundreds of laws (*lex*; plural, *leges*) over the course of Rome's long history. The following is a list of 20 of these laws:

Law/date of enactment	Chief provision(s)
1. Lex Aelia et Fufia/ ca.150 B.C.	Permitted consuls and praetors to disband legislative assemblies because of unfavorable signs from the heavens.
2. Lex Aelia Sentia/ A.D. 4	Placed restrictions on the freeing of slaves.
3. Lex Canuleia/ 445 B.C.	Legalized intermarriage between patricians and plebeians.
4. Lex Cassia/44 B.C.	Gave Julius Caesar the authority to create new patricians.
5. Lex Fannia/161 B.C.	Placed restrictions on the amount of money that could be spent on entertainments.
6. Lex Gabinia/67 B.C.	A special enactment granting Pompey the Great wide powers to rid the seas of pirates.

Law/date of enactment	Chief provision(s)
7. Lex Hirtia/46 B.C.(?)	A special enactment giving war- and peace-making powers to Julius Caesar.
8. Lex Icilia/fifth century B.C.	Permitted plebeians to farm and build houses on the Aventine Hill.
9. Lex Julia Papiria/430 B.C.	Hastened the demise of the barter system by specifying the payment of fines to be made in coins instead of farm animals.
10. Lex Junia de peregrinis/126 B.C.	Legalized the expulsion of noncitizens from Rome.
11. Lex Licinia Pompeia/55 B.C.	Authorized a second five-year term for Julius Caesar as governor in Gaul.
12. Lex Licinia Sextia/367 B.C.	Specified that no citizen could use more than 500 iugera (about 300 acres) of public land for grazing or tillage.
13. Lex Manilia/66 B.C.	A special enactment granting Pompey the command against Mithridates (one of Cicero's extant orations, *Pro Lege Manilia*, deals with this piece of legislation).
14. Lex Oppia/215 B.C.	A short-lived sumptuary law that regulated the amount of gold a woman could own; it also placed restrictions on women's clothing.
15. Lex Ovinia/ca.312 B.C.	Gave to the censors the right to select men to serve in the Roman Senate.
16. Lex Petronia/ca. A.D. 61	Prohibited slave owners from arbitrarily requiring their slaves to engage in mock beast hunts in the amphitheaters.
17. Lex Poetelia/ca.326 B.C.	Prohibited, or at least strictly regulated, the imprisonment of debtors.
18. Lex Titia/43 B.C.	Gave legal status to the Second Triumvirate (Octavian-Augustus, Mark Antony, and Lepidus).
19. Lex Valeria/449 B.C.	Reaffirmed the right of appeal for those sentenced in criminal courts.
20. Lex Voconia/169 B.C.	Limited the amount of real estate that could be willed to female heirs.

The Twenty Satrapies of King Darius

In Book III of his *Histories*, Herodotus compiled a list (or in many cases, a geographical description) of the 20 administrative units—satrapies—into which the Persian king Darius divided his empire in the sixth century B.C. Herodotus also provided the annual tributes required of the satrapies, as follows:

Satrapy or region	Tribute (in talents)
1. Far western Asia Minor	400
2. Western Asia Minor	500
3. Central Asia Minor	360
4. Cilicia	500 (and 360 white horses, 140 for the cavalry based in Cilicia, the rest for Darius's use)
5. Western Palestine and Cyprus	350
6. Egypt (including Libya and Cyrene)	700 (plus revenue from grain and from fish from Lake Moeris; 120,000 bushels of grain were earmarked for Persian troops stationed in the city of Memphis)
7. Eastern Persia	170
8. South-central Persia	300
9. Assyria and Babylon	1,000 (plus 500 eunuchs)
10. Media (central Persia)	450
11. Northern Persia	200
12. Bactria (east-central Persia)	360
13. Armenia	400
14. Central Persia	600
15. Northeastern Persia (Sacaeans and Caspians	250
16. Northeastern Persia (Parthians et al.)	300
17. Southeastern Persia	400
18. Eastern Black Sea area	200
19. Central Persia	300
20. India	360

In addition to the tributes listed above, several regions provided gifts to the Persian government:

Region	Gift	Frequency
Ethiopia	Two boxes of gold; 200 blocks of ebony; and 20 elephant's tusks	Biennial
Colchis	100 young men; and 100 young women	Quadrennial
Arabia	1,000 talents' worth of frankincense	Annual

The TWENTY-ONES
through
the THIRTYS

The Twenty-One Heroides

The Roman poet Ovid (43 B.C.–A.D. 17) composed a series of 21 fictional letters — *The Heroides* — in which the correspondents were famous figures from Greek and Roman mythology:

Letter number	Writer	Recipient
I	Penelope	Ulysses (Odysseus)
II	Phyllis	Demophoon
III	Briseis	Achilles
IV	Phaedra	Hippolytus
V	Oenone	Paris
VI	Hypsipyle	Jason
VII	Dido	Aeneas
VIII	Hermione	Orestes
IX	Deianira	Hercules
X	Ariadne	Theseus
XI	Canace	Macareus
XII	Medea	Jason
XIII	Laodamia	Protesilaus
XIV	Hypermnestra	Lynceus
XV	Sappho	Phaon
XVI	Paris	Helen
XVII	Helen	Paris
XVIII	Leander	Hero
XIX	Hero	Leander
XX	Acontius	Cydippe
XXI	Cydippe	Acontius

The Twenty-One Speeches Extant of Isocrates

The orator Isocrates (436–338 B.C.), founder of a noted school in Athens, ardent exponent of Panhellenism, and one of the finest oratorical stylists of his day, left 21 speeches, as well as nine letters. The 21 speeches, with their approximate dates, may be classified as follows:

Six law cases (forensic oratory):

1. *Aegineticus* (393)
2. *Against Callimachus* (402)
3. *Against Euthynus* (403)
4. *Against Lochites* (400)
5. *On the Four Race Horses* (397)
6. *Trapeziticus*, sometimes entitled *On the Banker* (393)

Four speeches for festivals or funerals (epideictic oratory):

1. *Busiris* (390)
2. *Evagoras* (365)
3. *Helen* (370)
4. *Panathenaicus* (342)

Three hortatory speeches, on ethical topics:

1. *Nicocles, or the Cyprians* (370)
2. *To Demonicus* (373)
3. *To Nicocles* (373)

Six political speeches:

1. *Archidamus* (366)
2. *Areopagiticus* (355)
3. *Panegyricus* (380)
4. *Peace* (355)
5. *To Philip* (346)
6. *Plataicus* (373)

Two treatises on education:

1. *Against the Sophists* (390)
2. *On the Antidosis* (353)

The speech on the racehorses is particularly interesting, not only because of the subject matter—a suit against the son of the famous Alcibiades, for five talents, on the grounds that his father (since deceased) had stolen the four prized horses from the plaintiff—but also because of its sympathetic treatment of Alcibiades' life and career.

Also of special interest is the David and Goliath theme of the speech against Lochites, in which the plaintiff, a poor and uninfluential citizen, brought suit against the wealthy and well-connected Lochites, on a charge of assault and battery.

Of all the orations, the *Panegyricus*, an expression of Isocrates' view on Panhellenism, is considered his masterpiece.

The Twenty-Two Biographies of Cornelius Nepos

The biographer Cornelius Nepos (ca.100–25 B.C.) authored numerous works on a variety of topics; the lone survivor of this literary output (apart from biographies of Cato the Elder and Atticus) is one book from a collection of sketches of the lives of famous men. Covered in this book are 22 noted foreign generals, most of them Greek:

1. Miltiades	12. Chabrias
2. Themistocles	13. Timotheus
3. Aristides	14. Datames
4. Pausanias	15. Epaminondas
5. Cimon	16. Pelopidas
6. Lysander	17. Agesilaus
7. Alcibiades	18. Eumenes
8. Thrasybulus	19. Phocion
9. Conon	20. Timoleon
10. Dion	21. Hamilcar
11. Iphicrates	22. Hannibal

The Twenty-Four Books of the Iliad

The *Iliad*, Homer's epic poem about the final days of the Trojan War, is divided into 24 books. The following is a summary of each of these:

Book I.　An explanation is offered for the plague that has beset the Greek army: Agamemnon, king of the Greeks, has offended Apollo by kidnapping the daughter of one of Apollo's priests. Agamemnon agrees to return the girl only if he may be compensated for the loss by taking one of Achilles' slave women, an action which fuels the "anger of Achilles." As a result, Achilles withdraws from the war.

Book II.　The Greek army, exhausted by ten years of warfare, makes plans to return to Greece. At the bidding of Athena, the crafty Odysseus persuades the army to reconsider.

Book III.　Menelaus, Agamemnon's brother, and Paris, abductor of Menelaus's beautiful wife Helen—the putative cause of the Trojan War—engage in single combat. Menelaus, on the verge of victory, is deprived of the triumph when Aphrodite envelops Paris in a mist and transports him to safety behind the walls of Troy.

Book IV.　A council of the gods decides that the Trojans are to break the truce that was declared prior to the battle between Paris and Menelaus.

Book V.　The fierce Greek warrior Diomedes enjoys success on the battlefield. He kills many enemy soldiers, including Pandarus, and wounds the most prominent of the Trojans, Aeneas. He even manages to inflict injury on two Olympian deities, Ares and Aphrodite.

Book VI.　Diomedes and the Trojan Glaucus conclude a personal truce based on the friendship between their grandfathers. Meanwhile, the most powerful Trojan warrior, Hector, once more prepares to do battle with the Greeks; and his brother Paris joins him.

Book VII.   The war resumes. After an inconclusive single combat
                   between Hector and Ajax, son of Telamon, a truce is
                   arranged so that the Greeks may cremate their fallen
                   soldiers.
Book VIII.   Another council of the gods. Zeus declares that divine
                   intervention in the war should cease, but he also in-
                   dicates that the Trojans will be temporarily successful.
Book IX.   A delegation of the Greeks, led by Odysseus, unsuc-
                   cessfully attempts to persuade Achilles to return to the
                   fighting.
Book X.   While on a reconnoitering mission, Diomedes and
                   Odysseus capture and kill a Trojan spy, Dolon, but
                   not before extracting information from him about the
                   Trojans' plans.
Book XI.   A heated battle scene in which many famous warriors
                   receive wounds, including Agamemnon, Diomedes,
                   and Odysseus.
Book XII.   The Trojans press the attack against the Greeks, driving
                   them toward their ships.
Book XIII.   The tide of battle seems to turn in favor of the Greeks,
                   but Hector continues to exhort the Trojans.
Book XIV.   Zeus is lulled to sleep, thus giving Poseidon an oppor-
                   tunity to rally the Greeks. In the course of the
                   fighting, Hector is wounded.
Book XV.   Despite Zeus's command to the contrary, many of the
                   gods and goddesses continue to intervene in the war,
                   some favoring the Greeks, others the Trojans. On the
                   battlefield the increasingly confident Trojans cause the
                   Greeks to flee to their ships.
Book XVI.   Patroclus dons the armor of Achilles, hoping that the
                   Greeks will mistakenly believe that Achilles himself
                   has returned to the fray. The plan works at first, but
                   Patroclus (contrary to Achilles' orders) carries the fight
                   all the way to the walls of Troy, where he is killed by
                   Hector.
Book XVII.   A fight over Patroclus's body is described, during the
                   course of which Hector strips it of the armor—
                   Achilles' armor.
Book XVIII.   Achilles learns of Patroclus's death. Overwhelmed by
                   grief and guilt, he decides to rejoin the war,
                   motivated by a desire to avenge Patroclus's death.
Book XIX.   The angry and defiant Achilles returns to the fighting.
Book XX.   In another council of the gods, Zeus retracts his earlier
                   prohibition against divine involvement in the war.
                   Achilles and Aeneas meet in single combat; Aeneas's
                   life is spared when the god Poseidon transports him
                   from the battlefield.

Book XXI.   Achilles pursues and kills many Trojans; and the sur-
               vivors flee to safety behind their city's walls.
Book XXII.   Achilles chases Hector three times around the walls of
               Troy before meeting him in single combat and bru-
               tally killing him.
Book XXIII.   Achilles sponsors funeral games in honor of Patroclus.
               The contests include chariot racing, boxing, wrestling,
               foot racing, sword fighting, discus throwing, and
               archery.
Book XXIV.   The aged Trojan king Priam, Hector's father, meets with
               Achilles and begs him to permit him to bury Hector.
               Achilles relents. The *Iliad* ends with a description of
               Hector's funeral.

The Twenty-Four Books of the Odyssey

The focus of Homer's epic poem *Odyssey*, in a sense a sequel to the *Iliad*, is centered upon the Greek hero Odysseus: the adventures he underwent during his ten-year return voyage to his island home of Ithaca, and the troubles that awaited him there. The *Odyssey*, like the *Iliad*, is divided into 24 books; the following is a summary of their contents:

Book I.   After a brief sketch of Odysseus's character and ex-
               periences, the poet notes that Odysseus alone of the
               surviving Greeks had yet to return home, having been
               held captive by the nymph Calypso on her island
               home of Ogygia. Odysseus's son Telemachus, a tod-
               dler when Odysseus left for war, but now a young
               man, initiates plans to search for his long-lost father.
Book II.   Telemachus chastizes the arrogant young men of Ithaca
               who have taken over the palace and who continue to
               court faithful Penelope, wife of Odysseus and mother
               of Telemachus. He then prepares to leave for Pylos,
               hoping to find information there about his father.
Book III.   Disappointment awaits Telemachus in Pylos, where the
               aged king Nestor cannot furnish information about
               the fate or whereabouts of Odysseus. Telemachus then
               travels to Sparta for an interview with the king,
               Menelaus.
Book IV.   Menelaus tells Telemachus that, according to the sea
               god Proteus, Odysseus was being detained by Calypso
               on Ogygia.
Book V.   Meanwhile, the goddess Athena (Odysseus's protector
               and benefactor) pleads with Zeus to help Odysseus.
               Zeus sends Hermes to Ogygia to command Calypso to
               release Odysseus. She obeys; and Odysseus builds a
               boat and sets sail, only to be shipwrecked on the
               island of Phaeacia.

Book VI.   Odysseus is awakened from a deep sleep by a group of young Phaeacian women who have come to the seashore to wash clothing. Odysseus enjoys a friendly conversation with one of these, Nausicaa, daughter of Alcinous, the Phaeacian king. She suggests that he ought to visit the palace.

Book VII.   Odysseus makes his way to the palace, where he is warmly received.

Book VIII.   Alcinous announces to his people that they must assist Odysseus in his efforts to reach his home. But first, Odysseus attends a banquet in his honor, where he agrees to tell the assembled Phaeacians about his wanderings.

Book IX.   Odysseus relates his story, including descriptions of his encounters with the Lotus-eaters and the Cyclopes.

Book X.   Odysseus's narrative continues, with accounts of his encounters with Aeolus (king of the winds), the man-eating Laestrygonians, and the goddess Circe.

Book XI.   Odysseus describes his descent into the Underworld, and the many souls he spoke to there, including Agamemnon, Achilles, and his own mother, Anticlea.

Book XII.   The narrative continues with descriptions of the Sirens and their seductive songs, the whirlpool Charybdis, the grotesque sea monster Scylla, and the eating of the sun god's cattle. Because of the latter offense, all of Odysseus's men are later drowned when washed overboard during a storm at sea.

Book XIII.   The Phaeacians transport Odysseus to Ithaca in one of their ships. When he disembarks, Athena meets him; together, they make plans for the destruction of Penelope's suitors. The goddess disguises Odysseus as a beggar, so that he may slip into the city to reconnoitre.

Book XIV.   The first man whom Odysseus encounters in Ithaca is the aged swineherd Eumaeus. Eumaeus does not recognize him, so Odysseus invents a story about his identity and background.

Book XV.   At the bidding of Athena, Telemachus returns (from Sparta) to Ithaca.

Book XVI.   Upon his arrival at Eumaeus's hut, Telemachus sees Odysseus, but does not recognize him. Athena advises Odysseus to reveal his true identity to his son, so that the two of them can plot the destruction of the suitors. Odysseus complies.

Book XVII.   Odysseus (resuming his disguise) and Eumaeus go to the palace, where Odysseus is insulted and mistreated by the ringleader of the suitors, Antinous.

Book XVIII.   Odysseus defeats the town tramp Irus in a boxing
               match, and then argues with Eurymachus, another of
               the suitors.
Book XIX.   After Odysseus and Telemachus stealthily transfer the
               suitors' weapons from the palace's hall to a storeroom,
               Odysseus visits his wife, Penelope, who does not
               recognize him. He fabricates a story about his identity
               and background, and tells Penelope that Odysseus
               will soon return to Ithaca. Penelope informs him that
               she plans to marry any man who can string Odysseus's
               famous bow and shoot an arrow through the hollows
               of 12 ax heads.
Book XX.   Odysseus and Telemachus are again taunted and in-
               sulted by the suitors, this time at a feast.
Book XXI.   Penelope announces to the suitors that she will marry
               the one who can string the bow and shoot an arrow
               through the ax heads. Odysseus alone succeeds.
Book XXII.   Odysseus, Telemachus, Eumaeus, and Philoetius
               (another of Odysseus's loyal servants) slaughter the
               suitors, who are unable to escape from the locked
               banquet hall.
Book XXIII.   Odysseus and Penelope are reunited; the following day,
               Odysseus visits his aged father, Laertes.
Book XXIV.   Odysseus meets resistance from the relatives of the dead
               suitors, and once more he must take up arms to
               reclaim his throne. The battle ends when Zeus sends a
               thunderbolt, and Athena brings peace.

The division of the two epics, the *Iliad* and the *Odyssey*, into 24 books each
did not occur until long after Homer's day. The Alexandrian scholar and editor
Zenodotus (the first head of Alexandria's great library, from about 284 to 260
B.C.) reportedly created the 24-book format for both poems.

The Twenty-Four Letters of the Greek Alphabet
The 24 letters of the Greek alphabet are as follows:

1. alpha(A, α)	13. nu (N, ν)
2. beta (B, β)	14. xi (Ξ, ξ)
3. gamma (Γ, γ)	15. omicron (O, o)
4. delta (Δ, δ)	16. pi (Π, π)
5. epsilon (E, ϵ)	17. rho (P, ϱ)
6. zeta (Z, ζ)	18. sigma (Σ, s)
7. eta (H, η)	19. tau (T, τ)
8. theta (Θ, θ)	20. upsilon (Υ, υ)
9. iota (I, ι)	21. phi (Φ, ϕ)
10. kappa (K, $\varkappa$)	22. chi (X, χ)
11. lambda (Λ, λ)	23. psi (Ψ, ψ)
12. mu (M, μ)	24. omega (Ω, ω)

Twenty-Four Prices for Goods and Services in Fifth-Century Athens

A variety of ancient sources, both literary and inscriptional, provides evidence about the cost of goods and services in the ancient world. The list below is an example.

The basic units of Athenian currency were the obol; drachma (worth six obols); and tetradrachma (four drachmas).

The price list that follows is adapted from Frank Frost's *Greek Society*.

Product or service	Athenian price
1. One quart of figs or olives	1/8 obol
2. Five pounds of wheat	2 obols
3. One gallon of domestic wine	3 obols
4. One gallon of olive oil	3 drachmas
5. One loaf of bread	1 obol
6. One salted fish	1 obol
7. One small pig	3 drachmas
8. One woollen cloak	5–20 drachmas
9. One pair of shoes	6–8 drachmas
10. A stool	1 drachma, 1 obol
11. A table	4–6 drachmas
12. An imported bed	8 drachmas
13. A cow or ox	About 50 drachmas
14. A sheep or goat	10–15 drachmas
15. A ring providing immunity against snakebite	1 drachma
16. A woman's cosmetic kit	2 obols
17. A small jug for oil	1 obol
18. Dream interpretation	2 obols per dream
19. The procurement of a prostitute (one night)	About 4 drachmas ·

(Numbers 20–24 indicate the prices for various kinds of slaves.)

20. A Carian goldsmith	360 drachmas
21. A Macedonian woman	310 drachmas
22. Syrians	240–300 drachmas
23. Thracians and Illyrians	About 150 drachmas
24. A donkey driver	140 drachmas

Twenty-Four Wage and Price Figures from Fourth-Century (A.D.) Rome

In an effort to control Rome's runaway inflation, the emperor Diocletian issued a decree that specified the maximum wages for various categories of workers, and the maximum prices for various commodities. This document, which appeared in A.D. 301 in the form of a lengthy inscription, is known as the Edict of Diocletian.

Wages and prices are expressed in denarii, one of the basic units of Roman currency. Units of measure and weight are expressed in the following terms:

sextarius (equivalent to about 1 pint); modius (equivalent to about ¼ bushel); Italian pound (equivalent to 12 ounces, or ¾ of a modern pound).

The 24 items that appear below have been adapted from Lewis and Reinhold's *Roman Civilization,* vol. II: *The Empire*

Product	Maximum price in denarii
1. One modius of wheat	100
2. One modius of barley	60
3. One modius of crushed beans	100
4. One modius of cleaned rice	200
5. One sextarius of Falernian wine	30
6. One sextarius of Egyptian beer	2
7. One sextarius of olive oil	40
8. One Italian pound of pork	12
9. One Italian pound of Tarentine wool	175
10. One pair of soldier's boots, without hobnails	100
11. One Italian pound of refined gold	50,000
12. One Italian pound of raw silk, dyed purple	150,000

Maximum wages for various occupations	In denarii
13. Farm laborer	25 per day
14. Carpenter	50 per day
15. Picture painter	150 per day
16. Baker	50 per day
17. Camel driver	25 per day
18. Shepherd	20 per day
19. Muleteer	25 per day
20. Barber	2 per man
21. Sewer cleaner	25 per day
22. Teacher of Greek or Latin language or literature	200 per student per month
23. Lawyer, for pleading a case	1,000 per case
24. Cloakroom attendant in a public bathing establishment	2 per bather

The Twenty-Five Dialogues of Plato

Over the course of some fifty years the philosopher Plato (427–347 B.C.) wrote 25 philosophical dialogues, all of which survive. Platonic scholars have divided the 25 dialogues into three classifications, based on style and content.

First classification (containing eight titles):

1. *Apology*
2. *Charmides*
3. *Crito*
4. *Euthyphro*

5. *Hippias Minor*	7. *Laches*
6. *Ion*	8. *Lysis*

Second classification (11 titles):

1. *Cratylus*	7. *Phaedrus*
2. *Euthydemus*	8. *Protagoras*
3. *Gorgias*	9. *Republic*
4. *Meno*	10. *Symposium*
5. *Parmenides*	11. *Theaetetus*
6. *Phaedo*	

Third classification (six titles):

1. *Critias*	4. *Politicus*
2. *Laws*	5. *Sophist*
3. *Philebus*	6. *Timaeus*

Other dialogues sometimes ascribed to Plato are *Alcibiades*; *Hippias Major*; and *Menexenus*.

Many of the dialogues, especially those in the first two classifications, feature Socrates in a leading role. Prominent topics in the dialogues include virtue; friendship; courage; justice; pleasure; wisdom; government; and the nature of good and evil. Two of the dialogues, *Apology* and *Crito*, deal with the trial and condemnation of Socrates; and the *Phaedo* relates his final hours and his execution. In some dialogues, notably *Euthydemus* and *Sophist*, Plato satirizes the sophists.

The *Republic*, undoubtedly Plato's most famous work, is divided into ten books. These are listed below, along with a summary of their contents.

Book I.	The participants meet at the house of Cephalus, near Athens, to consider the characteristics of justice.
Book II.	Socrates expounds upon his vision of justice within the state, including a detailed description of the requisite characteristics of the military class, the Guardians.
Book III.	A continuation of the discussion of the Guardians, with emphasis upon the kind of training that they should receive.
Book IV.	A return to the concept of justice, as it applies both to the state and to individual citizens.
Book V.	The roles of women and children within the Socratic state; and the difficulties inherent in attempting to create the ideal state.
Book VI.	A description of the philosopher-king, the ideal ruler of the state.
Book VII.	The celebrated allegory of the cave, in which hypothetical people, chained in a cave, observe only shadows on the cave walls. Just as a person who escapes this confinement would perceive reality rather

then merely shadows, so too can the unenlightened soul be set free from its ignorance through education.

Book VIII. A discussion of the five kinds of government, ordered by rank from best to worst:

1. Aristocracy
2. Timocracy
3. Oligarchy
4. Democracy
5. Tyranny

Book IX. An attack on tyranny, and praise for the just man, for whom happiness can be a reality.

Book X. A criticism of poetry; and the myth of the warrior Er, who returns to earth 12 days after being slain in battle, with his descriptions of the pleasures that await the just man in the afterlife.

In addition to the dialogues, 13 letters are sometimes credited to Plato; modern scholars, however, generally deem most of them, if not all, to be spurious.

Twenty-Five Scolia

In the fifteenth book of his *Deipnosophistae*, Athenaeus records the content of 25 *Scolia*, "drinking songs." The word *scolia* literally means "crooked," the supposed connection being that these short ditties were sung by guests "crookedly," that is, not in any set order.

The Twenty-Seven Kings, Lands, and Provinces Delivered, Protected, or Subdued by Pompey the Great

Most historians would agree that the crowning achievement of Pompey's military career was his subjugation of much of the eastern Mediterranean. To commemorate his deeds, a dedicatory plaque was set up in Rome, in 62 or 61 B.C. Among Pompey's accomplishments (according to Diodorus Siculus [40.4]) were the following:

Clearing the eastern seas of pirates;
Delivering from blockades

1. Asia
2. Cappadocia
3. Bithynia
4. Galatia

Offering protection to

5. Paphlagonia
6. Pontus
7. Armenia
8. (Scythian) Achaea
9. Iberia
10. Colchis
11. Mesopotamia
12. Sophene
13. Gordyene

Subduing

14. Darius, king of the Medes
15. Artoles, king of the Iberians
16. Aristobulus, king of the Jews
17. Aretas, king of the Nabataean Arabs
18. Syria   19. Judaea
20. Arabia   21. Cyrene
22. The Achaeans   23. The Iozygians
24. The Soanians   25. The Heniochians
26. Other tribes living along the north coast of the Black Sea
27. All other nations between the Black Sea and the Persian Gulf

Additionally, Pompey dedicated an offering to the goddess Minerva of 12,060 pieces of gold and 307 talents of silver.

Pliny the Elder adds that Pompey claimed to have put to flight, forced to surrender, or killed 12,183,000 people; sunk or captured 846 ships; and caused 1,538 towns and fortresses to surrender.

The Twenty-Seven Shrines of the Argei

Each May 14 the Romans celebrated a festival in which the Vestal Virgins carried bound bundles of bullrushes to the Pons Sublicius from the 27 shrines of the *argei* ("rush dummies," so called because the bundles were in the guise of humans). Upon reaching the bridge, they hurled these bundles into the river. The origin and purpose of this ritual are disputed, but it is generally believed that it may have some connection with a placation of the river god; and the flooding propensity of the Tiber is well documented.

The Twenty-Eight Augustan Legions

The number of legions in the Roman army varied from one era (or even generation) to the next, so it is difficult to discern the precise figure for any given year. The legion count under Augustus (reigned 27 B.C.–A.D. 14) has been variously put at 25, 27, or 28; the latter number is represented here. Legion names may derive from place names, for example, *Hispana* (Spain), or *Gallica* (Gaul); or names of gods, for example, *Apollinaris* (Apollonian, ultimately Apollo); or special characteristics of the legion, for example, *Ferrata* (iron), *Victrix* (victorious). Legions called *Gemina* (twin) are thought to have been formed from the consolidation of two or more preexisting legions. (Note: some legions have duplicate numbers because they formerly had been under the command of one of Augustus's rivals—Mark Antony, for example—but were later assimilated into Augustus's army. The legions on this list were founded in the mid to late first century B.C.) (Legions XVII–XIX were destroyed in a battle in Germany [A.D. 9] and never reconstituted. This so-called Varian disaster—named from the Roman commander Publius Quinctilius Varus—was one of Rome's most disastrous military setbacks.)

	Legion number	*Legion name*
1.	I	Unknown
2.	II	Augusta
3.	III	Augusta
4.	III	Cyrenaica
5.	III	Gallica
6.	IV	Macedonica
7.	IV	Scythica
8.	V	Alaudae
9.	V	Macedonica
10.	VI	Ferrata
11.	VI	Victrix
12.	VII	Macedonica(?)
13.	VIII	Augusta
14.	IX	Hispana
15.	X	Fretensis
16.	X	Gemina
17.	XI	Actiacus(?)
18.	XII	Fulminata
19.	XIII	Gemina
20.	XIV	Gemina
21.	XV	Apollinaris
22.	XVI	Gallica(?)
23–25.	XVII–XIX	Unknown
26.	XX	Valeria
27.	XXI	Rapax
28.	XXII	Deiotariana

The Twenty-Eight Kinds of Comic Masks

Julius Pollux, a second-century A.D. scholar, compiled a list of 28 different kinds of masks used by actors representing stock characters in Greek comic plays of the fourth and third centuries B.C. A comic mask was elaborate and distinctively crafted, and constructed in a manner so as to cover the entire face of the wearer. There were masks denoting old men, young men, slaves, and women, classified as follows:

Old Men (6)

	Character	*Mask description*
1.	Close-shaven old man	White hair; short beard
2.	Gray-haired old man	Gray, curly hair; prominent eyebrows
3.	Graying old man	Darkish hair; pallid complexion
4.	Dark-haired old man	Dark hair, beard and complexion
5.	Fair-haired old man	Blond, curly hair; healthful demeanor
6.	Fairer-haired old man	Similar to no. 5, but not as robust

Young Men (8)

7. Vigorous young man	Dark hair; robust complexion
8. Curly haired young man	Pale complexion; short, light-colored hair
9. Somewhat curly haired young man	Similar to no. 8, but more youthful
10. Delicate young man	Blond, curly hair; pallid complexion
11. Dirty young man	Dirty, mottled face; long hair
12. A second dirty young man	Similar to no. 11, but younger
13. Pale young man	Swollen, sickly facial appearance
14. Somewhat pale young man	Similar to No. 13, but more pallid

Slaves (3)

15. Leather-clad slave	White, straight hair; pallid complexion; protruding beard
16. Slave with wedge-shaped beard	Light hair; red face
17. Stiff-haired slave	Robust complexion; stiff hair; no beard

Women (11)

18. Gray, long-haired woman	Long, gray hair; pallid complexion
19. Free-born old hag	Fair complexion; long, unbound hair
20. Old servant woman	Wrinkled, aged face
21. Servant woman; hair parted in the middle	Fairly long, gray hair; pale complexion
22. Leather-clad woman	Similar to no. 21, but younger
23. Pale, long-haired woman	Pallid complexion; long, black hair
24. Pale woman, with hair parted in the middle	Similar to no. 23, but with shorter hair
25. Young woman, with hair parted in the middle	Similar to no. 23, but not as pale
26. Young woman, with hair cut close	Black, parted, combed-back hair; fairly pallid complexion
27. A second young woman, with hair cut close	Similar to no. 26, but without the part in the hair
28. Young girl	Youthful appearance

In addition to the stock comic masks, Greek artisans also fabricated masks for specific characters. Historical personages such as Socrates and Euripides—who appeared as characters in plays by Aristophanes—were portrayed by actors wearing masks that accurately caricatured them. The same held true for mythological figures such as Actaeon, Achilles, Priam, Phineus, the Muses, and others who might function as characters in tragic plays.

Twenty-Eight Roman Millionaires

During the imperial period, the 28 wealthiest Romans enjoyed fortunes ranging from 1.8 million to 400 million sesterces. The list that that appears below is adapted from Richard Duncan-Jones, *The Economy of the Roman Empire*, who in turn adapted his list from similar enumerations compiled by the historians Theodor Mommsen, Tenney Frank, and A. H. M. Jones. (All figures are expressed in sesterces.)

Name/approximate date of death	Size of fortune in millions	Occupation or status
1. Gn. Cornelius Lentulus/A.D. 25	400	Senator
2. Narcissus/A.D. 54	400	Freedman
3. L. Volusius Saturninus A.D. 56	300+	Senator
4. L. Annaeus Seneca/A.D. 65 (Seneca was also a well-known writer, and a counselor to the emperor Nero)	300	Senator
5. Q. Vibius Crispus/ca. A.D. 83/ 93	300	Senator
6. M. Antonius Pallas/A.D. 62	300	Freedman
7. G. Julius Licinus/after A.D. 14	200–300	Freedman
8. Tacitus/A.D. 275	280	Emperor
9. G. Julius Callistus/ca. A.D. 52	200+	Freedman
10. T. Clodius Eprius Marcellus/ca. A.D. 79	200	Senator
11. G. Sallustius Passienus Crispus/ ca. A.D. 46 or 47	200	Senator
12. M. Gavius Apicius/after A.D. 28	110	Senator
13. Ti. Claudius Hipparchus/after A.D. 81	100	Provincial entrepreneur
14. L. Tarius Rufus/A.D. 14	100	Senator
15. G. Caecilius Isidorus/8 B.C.	60	Freedman
16. M. Aquillius Regulus/ca. A.D. 105	60	Senator
17. Lollia Paulina/A.D. 49	40+	Senator
18. G. Stertinius Xenophon and 19. Q. Stertinius (joint estate)/ca. A.D. 41/54	30	Physicians
20. G. Plinius Caecilius Secundus/ A.D. 113 (Pliny the Younger, the well-known epistler	20	Senator
21. Crinias of Massilia/ca. A.D. 54/68	20	Physician

Name/approximate date of death	Size of fortune in millions	Occupation or status
22. P. Vergilius Maro/19 B.C. (Vergil, the celebrated author of the *Aeneid* and other poems)	10	Poet
23. M. Calpurnius Piso/uncertain	5 +	Senator
24. Aemilia Pudentilla/uncertain	4	Provincial entrepreneur
25. G. Licinius Marinus Voconius Romanus/A.D. 100	4	provincial entrepreneur
26. Herennius Rufinus/A.D. 158	3	Provincial entrepreneur
27. L. Apuleius/ca. A.D. 150	2	Provincial entrepreneur
28. M. Hortensius Hortalus/after A.D. 16	1.8 +	Senator

According to Pliny the Elder, Gaius Caecilius Isidorus (number 15, above) owned, in addition to the 60 million sesterces, 4,116 slaves, 3,600 pairs of oxen, and 257,000 heads of other varieties of cattle. In his will he allotted the sum of 1 million sesterces to cover his funeral expenses.

Twenty-Nine Epithets and Titles of Zeus

The prominent Greek gods and goddesses all required epithets or titles, usually descriptive of the particular deity's function or appearance. Zeus, as king of the gods, probably accumulated more of these nicknames than any other in the Greek pantheon. At various places in the Greek world, he was known as

1. Agoraios: guardian of assemblies
2. Alexikakos: defender against evil
3. Apobaterios: protector of persons landing
4. Apomuios: averter of flies
5. Astrapaios: lightning bringer
6. Bronton: thundering
7. Gamelios: presiding over marriage
8. Georgos: tiller of the ground
9. Eleutherios: the deliverer
10. Enalios: of the rivers
11. Erkeios: of the front court (that is, as a household god)
12. Ethrios: clear, bright (especially pertaining to weather)
13. Euanemos: bringer of good winds
14. Karpodotes: giver of (agricultural) produce
15. Kataibates: descending in thunder and lightning
16. Keraunios: thunder wielder

17. Keraunobolos: thunder hurler
18. Klarios: distributing by lot
19. Ktesios: protector of house and property
20. Leukaios: of the white poplar
21. Olbios: blessed
22. Olympios: Olympian; dweller on Mount Olympus
23. Ombrios: of rain
24. Ouranios: dweller in heaven
25. Ourios: of prosperous voyages
26. Plousios: wealthy
27. Polieus: guardian of the city
28. Soter: savior
29. Uetios: rain bringer

As the principal sky and weather god, it is not surprising that many of Zeus's epithets pertain to meteorological phenomena.

The Twenty-Nine Members of the Latin League

In about 500 B.C., 29 Latin cities decided to form an alliance to present a united front against the growing power of Rome. According to Dionysius of Halicarnassus (5.61), these 29 cities were as follows:

1. Ardea	16. Lavinium
2. Aricia	17. Nomentum
3. Bovillae	18. Norba
4. Bubentum	19. Pedum
5. Cabum	20. Praeneste
6. Carventum	21. Querquetula
7. Circeii	22. Satricum
8. Corq	23. Scaptia
9. Corbio	24. Setia
10. Corioli	25. Tibur
11. Fortinea	26. Tusculum
12. Gabii	27. Tolerium
13. Labici	28. Tellenae
14. Lanuvium	29. Velitrae
15. Laurentum	

Twenty-Nine Phantoms

In Book XI of the *Odyssey*, Homer describes Odysseus's descent into the Underworld, where he sees the ghosts of 29 specified individuals. These are listed in order as follows:

1. Elpenor	4. Tyro
2. Anticlea	5. Antiope
3. Tiresias	6. Alcmene

7. Megara	19. Achilles
8. Jocasta	20. Patroclus
9. Chloris	21. Antilochus
10. Leda	22. Ajax, son of Oileus
11. Iphimedia	23. Ajax, son of Telamon
12. Phaedra	24. Minos
13. Procris	25. Orion
14. Ariadne	26. Tityus
15. Maira	27. Tantalus
16. Clymene	28. Sisyphus
17. Eriphyle	29. Hercules
18. Agamemnon	

Anticlea was Odysseus's mother. Ajax, son of Telamon, refused to speak to Odysseus. Ajax was still sulking about the unfavorable result of the contest in which he and Odysseus had engaged over the armor of the dead Achilles.

The giant Tityus was said by Homer to have covered nine acres of ground.

Thirty Boys and Forty Girls and Other Trimalchionian Statistics

In Petronius's satirically ribald story about Trimalchio's dinner party, a slave appears who enumerates for his master the various events and transactions occurring on a single day (*Cena Trimalchionis* 53):

30 boys and 40 girls were born in Cumae, on one of Trimalchio's estates;
125,000 bushels of wheat were stored in barns belonging to Trimalchio;
500 oxen were broken to the plow; and
10 million sesterces were returned to Trimalchio's safe, after efforts to invest it were unsuccessful.

Additionally, the slave announced other information about public notices, wills, and prosecutions of Trimalchio's various servants and attendants.

The Thirty Characters of Theophrastus

The most well-known extant work of Theophrastus (370–287 B.C.), a writer of many interests, is a collection of 30 short essays entitled *Characters*. Each is on a certain human flaw or foible. The 30 character flaws, with examples from each essay are listed below:

1. Dissembling: a dissembler praises the same persons face to face whom she has criticized behind his back.
2. Flattery: a flatterer is the first to lavish praise on a host's wine, house, and furnishings.
3. Idle chatter: a chatterer habitually sits next to a stranger in a public place and proceeds to regale him endlessly with comments ranging from the weather, to the price of wheat, to the cost of living, to last night's dinner.

4. Crudity: a crude person is one who might remember in the middle of the night that he has lent a neighbor some farming tools, and immediately will pay a visit to his sleeping neighbor to demand their return.

5. Obsequiousness: an obsequious person tries to please all of the people all of the time.

6. Disreputableness: an intentionally disreputable person spends more time in jail than in his own house.

7. Talkativeness: if someone were to ask a talkative person about the day's political news, he will reply in such boring detail that the listener will have forgotten the question long before the answer is concluded.

8. Gossip mongering: a gossiper asks her listener not to repeat her information, even though the gossiper has been spreading the same information all over town.

9. Shamelessness: the shameless person tries to borrow more money from someone to whom he is already in debt.

10. Stinginess, I: the stingy person never makes a purchase on a shopping trip, and refuses to lend even the smallest item to a neighbor in need of it.

11. Grossness: the gross person might expose himself in public, or hiccup loudly during a play; and while idly conversing with an apple-seller, he might help himself to an apple—and not pay for it.

12. Tactlessness: a tactless person interrupts a friend at work with some trifling problem, or tells a story at a party where all the guests have heard it before.

13. Meddling: a meddler will try to break up a fight between two people she does not know, or, on a journey, will suggest an alternate route to her traveling companions, ultimately getting everyone lost.

14. Stupidity: a stupid man falls asleep in the theater, or returns to the wrong bedroom after relieving himself in the middle of the night, or ruins broth by salting it a second time.

15. Grouchiness: a grouch refuses to acknowledge a morning greeting from a friend, and replies brusquely to even the most innocuous question.

16. Superstitiousness: Theophrastus notes many superstitious behaviors, including avoidance of cats (of any color) in one's path; regular visits to dream interpreters; and fastidious observances of purification rituals.

17. Grumbling: a grumbler complains even when good fortune comes his way. Thus he frets over the cost of child-rearing when a healthy son is born to him; he laments that the money belt he finds in the street contains only a piddling amount; and he grumbles when he wins a court case because his lawyer neglected to put forth one or two additional arguments.

18. Suspiciousness: the suspicious person trusts no one. He sends two slaves to market (one to make the purchases, the other to verify the purchase prices) or, when in bed for the night, refuses to believe his wife when she tells him that she has locked the front door. Instead, he arises to check on it himself.

19. Disgusting offensiveness: the digusting man neglects personal health and cleanliness such as untreated cuts and sores; rotten, blackened

teeth; and has a habit of spitting when he talks, belching during social hours, and wearing unlaundered clothing.

20. Harmless mindlessness: this type of person will delay a friend with mindless conversation at the very moment when that friend is about to embark on a trip, or will discuss his bowel habits during meals.

21. Petty ambitiousness: this person habitually engages in ostentatious behavior—making a minor speech at a religious ceremony, for example, but afterward boasting about the power of his oratory.

22. Stinginess, II: at his daughter's wedding a tightwad sells the meat of a sacrificial animal (rather than allow the guests to consume it); he wears the same threadbare clothes; and he avoids anyone who might solicit a charitable contribution from him.

23. Braggadocio: a boastful man, like the pettily ambitious, has illusions of grandeur. He may claim to own his rented house, and that he plans to sell it because it is too small for the lavish parties he provides.

24. Snobbishness: a snobbish man has no time for public service. He never fails to remind people for whom he has done some favor of their indebtedness to him. He is imperious, never polite, in his dealings with others.

25. Cowardice: a coward fears the waves on a sea journey or, in battle, runs back to his tent to fetch a sword he has supposedly forgotten there.

26. Oligarchy: an oligarchical politician hates and distrusts the common person.

27. Learning too late: a late learner tries to memorize lines from plays that he should have learned as a child. Or he might compete in sports with men half his age.

28. Backbiting: a backbiter publicly discusses another's private affairs, eventually including friends, family, and even the dead in his litany of abuse.

29. Running with the crowd: this person associates with criminals and rogues to learn about the real world and, he would argue, there truly is honor among thieves.

30. Covetousness: the covetous person conveniently forgets his per diem allowance on a business trip, thereby necessitating his borrowing from his fellow travelers. He might leave town when a friend's daughter weds, so as to avoid the obligation of sending a wedding gift.

The Thirty Idylls of Theocritus

Some 30 poems are generally attributed to Theocritus (third century B.C.). Many of these are pastoral poems, but Theocritus also employed other settings for his poetry. His 30 idylls and a summary of their contents follow:

1. The shepherd Thyrsis requests of a goatherd a song about love and fidelity.

2. The young girl Simaetha prepares a love potion to regain the affections of her straying paramour.

3. The goatherd Tityrus serenades his mistress Amaryllis.

4. The goatherd Corydon receives an unexpected, albeit temporary, promotion.

5–9. Singing contests, usually between shepherds, goatherds, and other rustics.

10. Two reapers sing of love.

11. The Cyclops Polyphemus attempts to woo Galatea.

12. A poem on friendship.

13. The deification of Hylas.

14. A lovestruck man decides to join the army.

15. Two Alexandrian housewives attend the festival of Adonis.

16. A lament about contemporary materialism.

17. A panegyric in honor of Ptolemy II (reigned 285–246 B.C.).

18. A wedding song honoring Helen.

19. A bee stings Cupid.

20. A shepherd denounces a sophisticated city girl for spurning his attentions.

21. A fisherman's miraculous dream is interpreted.

22. The trials and tribulations of Castor and Pollux.

23. A neglected lover addresses his beloved.

24. Hercules' exploits as a toddler, and his education.

25. Hercules' slaying of the Nemean Lion.

26. The initiation of a young boy into the Dionysiac Mysteries.

27. A contest over a shepherd's pipe.

28. Theocritus bestows an ivory distaff upon a friend's wife.

29–30. Love poems.

Some scholars doubt the authenticity of poems 23, 25, and 27.

The Thirty Logistai

In ancient Athens 30 citizens were appointed each year to examine the accounts and records of any official who had responsibility for public monies; these *logistai*, or public auditors, were empowered to prosecute officeholders who had abused their fiscal responsibilities. Originally, there were 30 *logistai*, but by the fourth century B.C. their numbers had shrunk to ten.

The Thirty Members of the Spartan Gerousia

The Spartan *Gerousia* (council of elders) consisted of 30 members: the 2 kings, and 28 other men all over the age of 60. This council performed various deliberative and judicial functions.

The Thirty Trittyes

One of the democratic reforms of Cleisthenes (Athenian lawgiver, late sixth century B.C.) was the division of each of the ten tribes into *trittyes* ("thirds"). He based these divisions on geographical considerations; hence, each tribe encompassed a city, inland trittyes, and coastal trittyes.

The Thirty Tyrants

In the final days of the Peloponnesian War, with the Spartans at Athens's doorstep, the Athenian democracy was temporarily suspended and replaced with a ruling clique composed of 30 citizens (popularly called the Thirty Tyrants). It was their responsibility to devise a new constitution, but they quickly assumed autocratic roles, replete with the issuance and implementation of proscription lists. Their short-lived reign began in April 404 B.C. They were deposed early in the following year.

The THIRTY-ONES
through
the ONE HUNDREDS

The Thirty-One Crown Festival Victories of Milo of Croton

One of the more remarkable records in the history of athletic competition was set by the sixth-century B.C. wrestler Milo, who hailed from the southern Italian town of Croton. The four world-class athletic festivals in ancient Greece—the Olympic, Pythian, Nemean, and Isthmian games—attracted the best athletes in the Mediterranean basin, and to win a championship in any one of these festivals brought immediate fame and prestige to the victor. Milo claimed an incredible 31 such championships, all in wrestling: six each in the Olympic and Pythian games, ten in the Isthmian, and nine in the Nemean.

A Thirty-One–Letter Word

One of the endearing qualities of the comic playwright Aristophanes was his talent for creating neologisms. In his play *Lysistrata*, for example, he composed a 31-letter word: *spermagoraiolekitholachanopolides* (the "th" and "ch" combinations could be represented in Greek by one letter each). Roughly translated, the word means "lettuce-seed and pancake sellers of downtown [Athens]."

The Thirty-One Speeches Extant of Lysias

The orator Lysias (ca. 458–380 B.C.) reputedly composed some 425 speeches during his career, although subsequent ancient historians (for example, Dionysius of Halicarnassus) considered only a little over half to have been genuinely his work. Since Lysias was not an Athenian citizen, he was prohibited by law from addressing the courts or the assemblies; hence he had to content himself with his status as a logographer, or ghostwriter, for other pleaders and litigants. (There are two exceptions: he personally presented the *Olympiacus*, since the site of the speech was Olympia, not Athens; and he delivered the *Against Eratosthenes*, during a brief window of time in 403 when he had been granted Athenian citizenship, a decree that was nullified shortly after its enactment through some unknown technicality.)

At present, some 31 orations survive, as well as fragments of a few others. These 31 may be classified as epideictic (festival or funeral speeches) and forensic (courtroom speeches).

Epideictic (2)

> 1. *Olympiacus*, a plea for Panhellenism, dated 388 B.C.
> 2. *Epitaphios*, a funeral speech honoring soldiers who fell in the Corinthian War (395–386 B.C.).

Forensic (29 with title, followed by approximate date B.C.):

> 1. *Against Agoratus*; 398
> 2. *Against Alcibiades I (for desertion)*; 395
> 3. *Against Alcibiades II (for refusing to Serve in the Infantry)*; 395
> 4. *Against Andocides*; 399
> 5. *Against the Corndealers*; unknown
> 6. *Against Diogiton*; 400
> 7. *Against Epicrates*; 389
> 8. *Against Eratosthenes*; 403
> 9. *Against Ergocles*; 389
> 10. *Against Evander*; 382
> 11. *Against Nicomachus*; 399
> 12. *Against Pancleon*; unknown
> 13. *Against Philo*; between 404 and 395
> 14. *Against Philocrates*; 389
> 15. *Against Simon*; 394
> 16. *Against Theomnestus*; 384
> 17. *Defense on a Charge of Bribetaking*; 402
> 18. *Defense of a Charge of Seeking to Abolish Democracy*; 400
> 19. *For Callias*; unknown
> 20. *For the Disabled*; 403
> 21. *For Mantitheus*; 392
> 22. *For Polystratus*; between 411 and 405
> 23. *For the Soldier*; between 394 and 387
> 24. *On the Confiscation of Property of Nicias's Brother*; 395
> 25. *On the Murder of Eratosthenes*; unknown
> 26. *On the Property of Aristophanes*; 387
> 27. *On the Property of Erato*; 397
> 28. *On the Sacred Olives*; 395
> 29. *On Wounding with Intent*; unknown

Speeches of particular interest:

For the Disabled: there was a mechanism in place in Athens for providing financial support for poorer citizens whose physical handicaps prevented them from working. The lists of those eligible for this form of public assistance were revised and updated annually. This case involved an alleged instance of what in modern times might be termed welfare fraud: Lysias had to prove that the (unnamed) defendant, who was receiving one obol per day, should rightfully retain his eligibility for the subsidy.

The speeches against Alcibiades (the son of the flamboyant fifth-century politician and general) contain harsh words for the shortcomings of the father.

The speech on the Sacred Olive is interesting in that it highlights the Athenian veneration of certain olive trees and groves belonging to the state; these, in turn, were thought to provide a link to the original olive tree associated with Athena, the patron goddess of the city. To desecrate a so-called "sacred olive tree" was considered a serious violation of both civil and religious law, punishable by exile and loss of property.

The Thirty-Three Homeric Hymns

Thirty-three poems honoring the various deities of the Greek pantheon survive to the present day. They are grouped together under the title *Homeric Hymns*, given that Homer is thought to have been the author. They range in length from a mere three lines (the *Hymn to Demeter and Persephone* number 13) to 580 lines (the *Hymn to Hermes*, number 4). The 33 *Homeric Hymns* are as follows:

1. To Dionysus	18. To Hermes
2. To Demeter	19. To Pan
3. To Apollo	20. To Hephaestus
4. To Hermes	21. To Apollo
5. To Aphrodite	22. To Poseidon
6. To Aphrodite	23. To the Son of Cronus (Zeus)
7. To Dionysus	24. To Hestia
8. To Ares	25. To the Muses, Apollo and Zeus
9. To Artemis	26. To Dionysus
10. To Aphrodite	27. To Artemis
11. To Athena	28. To Athena
12. To Hera	29. To Hestia and Hermes
13. To Demeter and Persephone	30. To Earth
14. To the Mother of the Gods	31. To Helios
15. To Hercules	32. To Selene
16. To Asclepius	33. To Castor and Pollux
17. To Castor and Pollux	

Actaeon's Thirty-Three Hunting Dogs

A cruel fate befell Actaeon, the grandson of Cadmus, while he was journeying homeward through the forest with his 33 hounds after a successful day of hunting. He chanced to encounter the goddess Artemis unclothed, bathing. Artemis's six attendants were

1. Crocale	4. Phiale
2. Hyale	5. Psecas
3. Nephele	6. Rhanis

The six tried to shield their embarrassed mistress, but to no avail. The goddess in her shame and anger transformed Actaeon into a stag, whereupon he was beset by his own hunting dogs and devoured. According to Ovid's version of this myth (*Metamorphoses*, Book III), there were more than 33 dogs, but he provides these names:

1. Melampus, a Spartan dog, and the first to attack Actaeon
2. Ichnobates, from Crete, a "keen-nosed" dog
3. Pamphagus, an Arcadian dog
4. Dorceus, also from Arcadia
5. Oribasus, another Arcadian
6. Nebrophonus, a "strong" dog
7. Laelaps, described as "fierce"
8. Theron, another fierce dog
9. Pterelas
10. Agre (Ovid uses the adjective *utilis*, useful, serviceable, to apply to both Pterelas and Agre. Pterelas is *utilis* with respect to the feet [that is, a fast runner], while Agre is *utilis* with respect to the nose [that is, keen-nosed like Ichnobates])
11. Hylaeus, a fierce dog recently attacked by a wild boar
12. Nape, a dog "born from a wolf"
13. Poemenis, a dog that follows the flocks—a sheepdog
14. Harpyia, a female dog who had recently given birth; she was accompanied by two of her puppies
15. Ladon, from Sicyon, its flanks bound (possibly by a leash or a harness)
16. Dromas
17. Canace
18. Sticte
19. Tigris
20. Alce
21. Leucon, "Whitey," a dog with snow-white hair
22. Asbolus, a dog with dark hair
23. Lacon, a very strong dog
24. Aëllo, a stout-hearted hunting dog
25. Thoos
26. Cyprio, a fast dog, as was its brother,
27. Lycisce
28. Harpalus, a black dog distinguished by white marking on its forehead
29. Melaneus
30. Lachne, a shaggy dog
31. Labros, a dog whose father was Cretan and whose mother was Spartan
32. Argiodus, a dog with parentage similar to that of Labros;
33. Hylactor, a dog with an ear-piercing bark

Ovid concludes the list by noting that there were other dogs in the pack, but to mention them all would take too much time. The attack on Actaeon was commenced by three dogs not named in the original Ovidian list: Melanchaetes, Therodamas, and Oresitrophus.

The Thirty-Four Participants in the Calydonian Boar Hunt

Because Oeneus, king of Calydon, failed to offer proper sacrifices to the goddess Artemis, she sent a vicious boar to ravage the Calydonian countryside. It was a fearsome creature, with glowing eyes, a hide with bristles like spear shafts, tusks as long as an elephant's, and exhaling lightning bolts. Oeneus's son, Meleager, organized a cadre of famous mythological figures to hunt down the beast. Ovid (*Metamorphoses*, Book VIII) lists the participants as follows:

Name	Ovid's comment (if any); brackets indicate additional information, not in the Ovidian text
1. Acastus	Noted for his skill with the javelin
2. Admetus	Son of Pheres
3. Amphiaraus	Still safe from his wife [his wife, Eriphyle, persuaded him to accompany the Seven against Thebes, none of whom was destined to return home alive]
4. Ancaeus	From Arcadia
5. Atalanta	From Tegea [see additional comments below]
6. Caeneus	No longer a woman [Caeneus had been born a woman, but was granted by her father Poseidon the power to change her sex]
7–8. Castor and Pollux	Twin sons of Leda, the former noted for his boxing skills, the latter for horsemanship
9.–10. Cleatus and Eurytus	Sons of Actor
11. Dryas	—
12. Echion	Unbeatable in running
13. Eurytion	Energetic
14. Hippasus	Fierce
15. Hippothous	—
16. Hyleus	—
17. Idas	Swift [brother of Lynceus, below]
18. Iolaus	From Boeotia
19. Jason	Builder of the first ship [*Argo*]
20. Laertes	Father-in-law of Penelope [and father of Odysseus]
21. Lelex	From Locri

Name	Ovid's comment (if any); brackets indicate additional information, not in the Ovidian text
22. Leucippas	Fierce
23. Lynceus	Son of Aphareus
24. Mopsus	Shrewd [a noted prophet]
25. Nestor	Then in his prime
26. Panopeus	—
27. Peleus	Achilles' father
28. Phoenix	Son of Amyntor
29. Phyleus	From Elis
30–31. Plexippus and Toxeus	Sons of Thestius [and Meleager's uncles]
32. Telamon	—
33–34. Theseus and Pirithous	Well-matched friends

Also included in Ovid's list is an unnumbered contingent of warriors from Amyclae, sent by Hippocoon.

Ovid's most detailed portrayal is reserved for the last participant he mentions, Atalanta. He describes her clothing, her hair, her weaponry, and her face, the last with a nicely turned phrase: *virgineam in puero, puerilem in virgine*, a face that one could say was "girlish in a boy, boyish in a girl."

When the boar was finally dispatched, Meleager awarded its hide to Atalanta, since she was the first to wound it (with one of her arrows).

Thirty-Four Roman Provinces

Rome annexed its first province, Sicily, in 241 B.C. The growth of Roman power in subsequent centuries resulted in the acquisition of additional provinces. Thirty-four of these are listed below, together with the approximate date of their annexation.

1. Achaea; 146 B.C.
2. Africa; 146 B.C.
3. Alpes Maritimae; 14 B.C.
4. Arabia; A.D. 105
5. Armenia maior; A.D. 114
6. Asia; 133 B.C.
7. Assyria; A.D. 114
8. Bithynia-Pontus; 74 B.C.
9. Britain; A.D. 43
10. Cappadocia; A.D. 17
11. Cilicia; 102 B.C.
12. Crete-Cyrene; 74/67 B.C.
13. Cyprus; 58 B.C.
14. Dacia; A.D. 106
15. Egypt; 30 B.C.
16. Epirus; 146 B.C.
17. Galatia; 25 B.C.
18. Germany (upper and lower); A.D. 90
19. Illyricum; 167 B.C.
20. Judaea; 63 B.C.
21. Lycia-Pamphylia; A.D. 43
22. Macedonia; 146 B.C.
23. Mauretania; A.D. 40
24. Mesopotamia; A.D. 114
25. Moesia; date uncertain
26. Noricum; 15 B.C.
27. Pannonia; A.D. 10
28. Raetia; 15 B.C.
29. Sardinia-Corsica; 227 B.C.
30. Sicily; 241 B.C.
31. Spain (nearer and farther); 197 B.
32. Syria; 64 B.C.
33. Thrace; 168/129 B.C.
34. Transalpine Gaul; 58–51 B.C.

Thirty-Six Ingredients in a Preparation to Prevent Poisoning

In the fifth book of Celsus's *De Medicina*, a prescription appears that, if consumed, will immunize a person against poisoning; this prescription was said to have been a favorite of King Mithridates VI of Pontus (d. 63 B.C.). It must have been effective, since, in the final desperate hours of the king's life, he ordered a guard to kill him, for he knew that suicide by poison was impossible.

Ingredient	Amount (in grams)	Ingredient	Amount (in grams)
1. Costmary	1.66	19. Storax	21
2. Sweet flag	20	20. Castoreum	24
3. Hypericum	8	21. Frankincense	24
4. Gum	8	22. Hypocistis juice	24
5. Sagapenum	8	23. Myrrh	24
6. Acacia juice	8	24. Opopanax	24
7. Illyrian iris	8	25. Malabathrum leaves	24
8. Cardamon	8	26. Flower of round rush	24.66
9. Anise	12	27. Turpentine resin	24.66
10. Gallic nard	16	28. Galbanum	24.66
11. Gentian root	16	29. Cretan carrot seeds	24.66
12. Dried rose leaves	16	30. Nard	25
13. Poppy tears	17	31. Opobalsam	25
14. Parsley	17	32. Shepherd's purse	25
15. Casia	20.66	33. Rhubarb root	28
16. Saxifrage	20.66	34. Saffron	29
17. Darnel	20.66	35. Ginger	29
18. Long pepper	20.66	36. Cinnamon	29

To make this melange palatable, Celsus suggests pounding it together and consuming it with honey.

The Thirty-Seven Books of Pliny's Natural History

Pliny the Elder, ancient Rome's preeminent natural historian, wrote a massive treatise on the subject. Pliny prefaces the work by listing the names of 473 authors from those writings, 2000 in all, he gleaned information. Additionally, he notes that his *Natural History* contains some 20,000 facts. It was divided into 37 books:

Book I.	Table of contents; bibliographies.
Book II.	Astronomical phenomena.
Book III.	Rivers, mountains, islands, harbors and towns of Spain, France, Italy.
Book IV.	Rivers, mountains, islands, harbors and towns of Greece, the Black Sea area, northern Europe.
Book V.	Rivers, mountains, islands, harbors and towns of Africa and the eastern Mediterranean area.
Book VI.	Rivers, mountains, islands, harbors and towns of miscellaneous places from India to the Black Sea.

Book VII.   Human physiology and psychology.
Book VIII.   Land animals: elephants, snakes, lions, tigers, camels,
                 lizards, dogs, horses, apes, etc.
Book IX.   Sea animals: whales, lobsters, tortoises, dolphins, seals,
                 various species of fish, etc.
Book X.   Birds: eagles, hawks, vultures, owls, peacocks, cranes,
                 storks, swallows, thrushes, etc.; reproduction, senses,
                 food of land animals.
Book XI.   Insects — bees, spiders, grasshoppers, moths, and beetles;
                 and classification of animals.
Book XII.   Native shrubs and trees — apple, thorn, pepper, balsam,
                 cyprus, and cotton.
Book XIII.   Foreign trees — palm, fig, citrus, and pomegranate; per-
                 fumes; and papyrus.
Book XIV.   Fruit trees; and wines.
Book XV.   More on fruit trees — olive, pear, peach, plum, and cherry.
Book XVI.   Forest trees — oak, pine, maple, ash, and poplar; and
                 water plants.
Book XVII.   Cultivated trees; and vineyards.
Book XVIII.   Crops — corn, barley, wheat, beans, and oats.
Book XIX.   Flax; gardens; and garden plants.
Book XX.   Drugs and medicines from garden plants.
Book XXI.   Flowers — uses, cultivation, and diseases; and classifica-
                 tions of various kinds of plants.
Book XXII.   Drugs and medicines from various kinds of herbs.
Book XXIII.   Drugs and medicines from cultivated trees.
Book XXIV.   Drugs and medicines from forest trees.
Book XXV.   Noncultivated plants — nature and uses.
Book XXVI.   Other kinds of drugs and medicines.
Book XXVII.   Other kinds of plants.
Book XXVIII.   Drugs and medicines from animals (both wild and
                 domestic).
Book XXIX.   A brief historical survey of the medical profession; and
                 more information on drugs and medicines.
Book XXX.   More information on drugs and medicines from animals.
Book XXXI.   Different kinds of water.
Book XXXII.   Drugs and medicines from sea animals.
Book XXXIII.   Metals — gold and silver.
Book XXXIV.   Metals — copper, bronze, iron, and lead.
Book XXXV.   Painting, sculpture, and pottery production.
Book XXXVI.   Stone — marble, tufa, flint, lime, pumice, and pyrite;
                 and uses in construction.
Book XXXVII.   Gems — diamonds, amber, opals, onyx, sapphires,
                 agates, and turquoise.

When the violent and catastrophic volcanic eruption of Mount Vesuvius occurred in A.D. 79, Pliny hurried to the scene; as a scientist, he was eager to
gather data on the phenomenon. It was here that he met his death.

The Thirty-Nine Victims of Hercules

The redoubtable hero Hercules subdued many men and beasts — not to mention his own children, killed in a fit of madness — over the course of his storied career. The following list of his human victims is based upon the account found in the second book of Apollodorus' *Library*:

1. Linus, his music teacher: Hercules was provoked to slay Linus when Linus used corporal punishment to discipline his famous student.

2. Erginus, king of the Minyans: Hercules killed him in battle, near Thebes.

3. Diomedes: he was the owner of the man-eating mares. Hercules' Eighth Labor was to herd them to Mycenae, where King Eurystheus awaited them.

4. Chryses: son of King Minos.

5. Eurymedon: son of King Minos.

6. Nephalion: son of King Minos.

7. Philolaus: son of King Minos.

8. Mygdon: he was the king of the Bebryces.

9. Hippolyta: she was an Amazon queen, the procuring of whose girdle was Hercules' Ninth Labor.

10. Sarpedon: the excessively arrogant son of Poseidon.

11. Polygonus: Hercules killed him in a wrestling match.

12. Telegonus: he was another of Hercules' wrestling victims.

13. Eurytion: he was a shepherd whom Hercules killed while attempting to corral the cattle of Geryon, his Tenth Labor.

14. Geryon: the owner of the cattle (see above).

15. Ialebion: he attempted to take Geryon's cattle from Hercules, and paid with his life.

16. Dercynus: he died under the same circumstances as did Ialebion, above.

17. Eryx: Eryx was a Sicilian king whom Hercules killed in a wrestling match.

18. Antaeus: Antaeus drew his considerable strength from physical contact with the earth; Hercules subdued him in a wrestling match by lifting him off the ground.

19. Busiris: he was a king of Egypt who sacrificed strangers, one per year, allegedly in response to an oracular command to do so. When he attempted to honor Hercules in this dubious fashion, Hercules slew him before the sacrifice could be carried out.

20. Amphidamas: son of Busiris.

21. Emathion: a resident of Arabia.

22. Iphitus: Hercules hurled him from the walls of Tiryns in a fit of madness.

23. Syleus: Syleus customarily forced strangers to help him dig furrows for his vines. He lost his life when he tried to compel Hercules to assist in this endeavor.

24. Xenodoce: a daughter of Syleus.

25. Laomedon and his sons: Hercules killed them at Troy.

26. Eurypylus: Hercules killed this king of Cos in battle.

27. Eurytus: Hercules ambushed this Elean general.

28. Cteatus: another Elean general, whose fate was similar to that of Eurytus.

29. Periclymenus: Poseidon granted to the Pylian Periclymenus the power to transform himself in battle into various creatures: an eagle, an ant, a bee, a fly or a snake. He had apparently assumed the form of a fly or a bee when Hercules killed him.

30. Neleus and his sons: These men Hercules slew in battle at Pylos.

31. Hippocoön and his sons: These Hercules killed in battle at Sparta.

32. Eunomus: Hercules accidentally hit this young man while Eunomus was pouring water for him. The blow was apparently of sufficient force to kill the unfortunate youth.

33. Nessus: He attempted to rape Hercules' wife Deianira; Hercules shot him in the heart with an arrow. As he expired, he gave Deianira a concoction which he claimed was a love potion. (Although Nessus was a centaur, not a man, he is included in the list because of the consequence of his "gift.")

34. Laogoras: An arrogant king of the Dryopes; Hercules killed him during a banquet.

35. Cycnus: Cycnus challenged Hercules to fight; in the ensuing contest, Hercules killed him.

36. Amyntor: Hercules killed King Amyntor when the king refused to grant him passage through Ormenium.

37. Eurytus and his sons: Eurytus was the king of Oechalia.

38. Lichas: Lichas was a herald, and a servant to Hercules. It was he who delivered to Hercules a tunic that Deianira had smeared with Nessus's love potion. No one knew that the potion was in reality a poisonous substance that caused the garment to cling to Hercules' skin and burn his flesh. In his agony he threw Lichas over a cliff.

The Forty

Forty judges in ancient Athens — four from each of the ten tribes — presided over petty lawsuits, where the sum in question was less than ten drachmas.

The Forty Books of Diodorus's History

The historian Diodorus Siculus, "the Sicilian" (ca.80–20 B.C.), wrote a history of Rome in 40 books, as follows (the fragmentary books are designated with an asterisk):

Book I.	Military, political, and religious history of Egypt.
Book II.	Descriptions and history of Asia, Assyria, India, and Arabia.
Book III.	Descriptions and history of Ethiopia, Libya, and a place called Atlantia, described as being "on the edge of the ocean."

Book IV.	Greek myths, including those pertaining to Hercules, Theseus, Pelops, Tantalus, and Jason and the Argonauts.
Book V.	Sicilian myths; and descriptions of Britain, Gaul, and various islands, including Naxos, Rhodes, Crete, and Lesbos.
Book VI.	Pre–Trojan War legends.
Book VII.	Events from the time of the Trojan War to the death of Alexander the Great.
Book VIII.*	Various events from Athenian history; and the founding of Rome by Romulus.
Book IX.*	More events from Athenian history, including a number of stories about, and maxims of, Solon.
Book X.*	Roman legends and Greek philosophy, especially Pythagoreanism.
Book XI.	Events from Athenian and Sicilian history (480–451 B.C.).
Book XII.	Athenian and Sicilian history (450–416 B.C.).
Book XIII.	Athenian and Sicilian history (415–405 B.C.).
Book XIV.	Athenian and Sicilian history (404–387 B.C.); and the Gallic invasion of Italy (387 B.C.).
Book XV.	Greek, Sicilian, and Carthaginian history (386–360 B.C.).
Book XVI.	Greek history (360–345 B.C.), including the rise to power of Philip of Macedonia.
Book XVII.	The conquests of Alexander the Great.
Book XVIII.	Military history of Greece in the years following Alexander's death.
Book XIX.	A continuation of the contents of Book XVIII.
Book XX.	A continuation of the contents of Book XVIII.
Book XXI.*	Greek military history (301–285 B.C.).
Book XXII.*	Military activities in Italy and Sicily of Pyrrhus, the Epirote mercenary (280–269 B.C.).
Book XXIII.*	Initial stages (264–255 B.C.) of the First Punic War.
Book XXIV.*	Latter stages of the First Punic War (to 241).
Book XXV.*	Carthaginian history in the years following the end of the First Punic War.
Book XXVI.*	Hannibal's military activities in Italy (218–205 B.C.).
Book XXVII.*	The latter stages of the Second Punic War.
Book XXVIII.*	Roman, Greek, and Carthaginian history (204–193 B.C.).
Book XXIX.*	Roman affairs (192–172 B.C.); and evaluations of Philopoemen, Hannibal, and Scipio Africanus.
Book XXX.*	Roman affairs (171–169 B.C.); and the conflicts with Perseus (Third Macedonian War).
Book XXXI.*	Roman affairs (169–153 B.C.).
Book XXXII.*	Roman affairs (150–146 B.C.), including the destruction of Carthage. The book concludes with a bizarre description of hermaphroditism.

Book XXXIII.*   Various events in Egypt, Greece, and Asia Minor (145–138 B.C.).

Books XXXIV–   Sicilian, African, and Roman affairs (135–105 B.C.),
XXXV.*   including a discussion of the slave rebellion in Sicily in 135, and brief accounts of the Gracchan brothers.

Book XXXVI.*   Unrest in Sicily and southern Italy (104–98 B.C.); and an account of the career of Gaius Marius.

Book XXXVII.*   Roman affairs (91–86 B.C.), including a description of the Social War and a survey of virtuous Roman statesmen such as Quintus Mucius Scaevola, Lucius Asyllius, and Marcus Livius Drusus.

Books XXXVIII–   Roman affairs (88–72 B.C.)—Sulla's dictatorship; and
XXXIX.*   conflicts between Marius and Sulla.

Book XL.*   Roman, Syrian, and Judaean affairs (71–61 B.C.); and the Catilinarian conspiracy.

The Forty-Plus Rooms of Pliny's Laurentine Villa

Pliny the Younger wrote a letter (2.17) to his friend Gallus in which he described the rooms and other amenities of his villa in Laurentum, 17 miles from Rome. These include:

1. Apotheca: storeroom
2. Area: courtyard
3. Atrium: entrance hall
4. Cavaedium: inner courtyard
5. Cella frigidaria: cooling room (for the bath)
6. Cenatio: small dining room

7–18. Cubicula: bedrooms. The home contained at least 12 bedrooms, including one described as *amplum* (large, perhaps the master bedroom); another termed *politissimum* (very exquisite); and another called *munimentis hibernum* (insulated for winter).

19–24. Diaetae: six sitting rooms
25. Heliocaminus: sun room
26. Hibernaculum: winter apartment
27. Horreum: storeroom for grain
28. Hortus: garden
29–30. Hypocausta: two saunas
31. Piscina: fish pond
32–33. Procoeta: two anterooms
34. Propnigeon: room with hot bath
35. Sphaeristerium: handball court
36–37. Triclinia: two formal dining rooms
38. Unctorium: anointing, or massage, room
39. Vestibulum: entrance court
40. Zotheca: day room

Pliny also mentions several other features of the house, including other storerooms of various kinds, passageways, porticos, and servants' quarters.

A Forty-Year Military Career

Dionysius of Halicarnassus (10.37) records the extraordinary statement of a 58-year-old Roman soldier named Lucius Siccius Dentatus. Dentatus claims the following, in a speech before an assembly of the people, about 453 B.C.:

1. He served in the army for 40 years, including 30 years in various command positions.

2. He fought in 120 battles, sustaining 45 wounds; and he was careful to note that he took all 45 wounds on the front, not back, part of his body. He received 12 of these wounds in a single day.

3. He earned 14 civic crowns (for saving the life of a fellow soldier in battle); three mural crowns (for being the first to breach an enemy's wall); and eight others for various acts of bravery. He was also awarded 83 gold collars, 160 gold bracelets, 18 spears, and 25 other decorations.

Dentatus reviewed his military career as a prologue to his lament that, despite his sacrifices, he did not have even the smallest portion of land on which to farm or live.

Forty-One Greek Colonies

In the eighth century B.C. the ancient Greeks embarked upon a massive colonization movement, extending westward to France, Sicily, and southern Italy, south to Africa, and east to Turkey and the Black Sea area. (A detailed account of colonization in Sicily may be found at the beginning of Book VI of Thucydides' treatise on the Peloponnesian War.) Hundreds of colonies were founded in this period; gaps in the evidence would make it impossible to list them all, but many of the prominent ones appear below.

A Greek colony, once founded, became an independent city-state. The modern concept of colonization, which implies subservience on the part of the colony toward the colonizer, does not apply to the ancient Greeks.

Colony	Colonizer(s)	Approximate date
Colonies in Italy		
1. Pithecusae	Chalcis, Eretria	8th century B.C.
2. Cumae	Chalcis	8th century B.C.
3. Rhegium	Chalcis	8th century B.C.
4. Sybaris	Achaeans	720 B.C.
5. Paestum	Sybaris	600 B.C.
6. Croton	Achaeans	708 B.C.
7. Metapontum	Achaeans	650 B.C.
8. Tarentum	Sparta	706 B.C.
9. Locri Epizephyrii	Locrians	673 B.C.
10. Elea	Phocaeans	6th century B.C.

Colonies in Sicily

11. Naxos	Chalcis	734 B.C.
12. Leontini	Naxos	728 B.C.
13. Catana	Naxos	728 B.C.
14. Zancle	Chalcis	8th century B.C.
15. Megara, Hyblaea	Megara	8th century B.C.
16. Selinus	Megara, Hyblaea	7th century B.C.
17. Gela	Rhodes, Crete	7th century B.C.
18. Syracuse	Corinth	733 B.C.
19. Acragas	Gela	6th century B.C.
20. Himera	Zancle	648 B.C.

Colony in France

21. Massilia	Phocaeans	600 B.C.

Colonies in Thrace

22. Maronea	Chios	7th century B.C.
23. Thasos	Paros	700 B.C.
24. Abdera	Clazomenae	7th century B.C.
25. Aenos	Aeolians	7th century B.C.

Colonies in Turkey and the Black Sea area

26. Chalcedon	Megara	7th century B.C.
27. Byzantium	Megara	7th century B.C.
28. Perinthus	Samos	600 B.C.
29. Sestos	Aeoians	7th century B.C.
30. Elaious	Athens	600 B.C.
31. Apollonia	Miletus	Unknown
32. Tomis	Miletus	Unknown
33. Istrus	Miletus	Unknown
34. Olbia	Miletus	7th–6th century B.C.
35. Tanais	Miletus	Unknown
36. Cyzicus	Miletus	756 B.C.
37. Trapezus	Miletus or Sinope	756 B.C.
38. Amisus	Miletus or Phocaeans	6th century B.C.
39. Heraclea	Megara, Boeotians	6th century B.C.

Colonies in Africa

40. Cyrene	Thera	631 B.C.
41. Naucratis	Merchants	Unknown

The Forty-Two Orations of Demosthenes

The public career of Demosthenes (384–322 B.C.), the orator nonpareil of the ancient world, spanned over 40 years. Some 58 extant orations are credited to his name, although modern critics consider several of these to have been produced by other writers of the time. (The list of 42, which follows, is based upon the scholarly consensus, as nearly as it can be determined, of the authentically

Demosthenic works. The same holds true for the dates given, which are problematic for several of the orations.)

The surviving speeches can be conveniently divided into three categories:

1. Private speeches, argued on behalf of citizens with various legal grievances. The private speeches are concerned with such matters as inheritances; wills; breaches of contract; debt payments; assault; and perjury.

2. Semi-public speeches, argued on behalf of citizens directly involved in public affairs or public policy issues. Within the realm of semi-public speeches are such items as: taxation; constitutionality of laws; and rights and privileges of public officials.

3. Public speeches, orations presented to assemblages of the people, on issues such as national security; military preparedness and other military matters; international leagues and treaties; and rights of independent states.

The 42 orations are as follows:

Title/approximate date B.C.	Private, semi-public, or public
1. *First Oration Against Aphobus*/363	Private
2. *Second Oration Against Aphobus*/363	Private
3. *Third Oration Against Aphobus*/363	Private
4. *First Oration Against Onetor*/362	Private
5. *Second Oration Against Onetor*/362	Private
6. *Against Callicles*/361	Private
7. *Against Spudias*/361	Private
8. *On the Trierarchic Crown*/361	Public
9. *Against Polycles*/359	Semi-public
10. *Against Conon*/356	Private
11. *Against Androtion*/355	Semi-public
12. *Against Leptines*/354	Semi-public
13. *On the Navy Boards*/354	Public
14. *For the People of Megalopolis*/354	Public
15. *Against Timocrates*/353	Semi-public
16. *Against Aristocrates*/352	Semi-public
17. *On the Liberty of the Rhodians*/351	Public
18. *First Oration Against King Philip*/351	Public
19. *For Phormio*/350	Private
20. *First Oration Against Boeotus*/350	Private
21. *First Oration Against Stephanus*/349	Private
22. *First Olynthiac Oration*/349	Public
23. *Second Olynthiac Oration*/349	Public
24. *Third Olynthiac Oration*/348	Public
25. *Against Midias*/347	Semi-public
26. *On Peace*/346	Public

Title / approximate date B.C.	Private, semi-public, or public
27. *Against Pantaenetus* / 345	Private
28. *Against Nausimachus* / 345	Private
29. *Against Eubulides* / 345	Private
30. *Second Oration Against King Philip* / 344	Public
31. *On the Embassy* / 343	Semi-public
32. *On the Halonnese* / 342	Public
33. *On the Chersonese* / 341	Public
34. *Against Apaturius* / 341	Private
35. *Third Oration Against King Philip* / 341	Public
36. *Fourth Oration Against King Philip* / 341	Public
37. *Against Lacritus* / 340	Private
38. *On the Crown* / 330	Semi-public
39. *Against Phormio* / 326	Private
40. *Against Dionysodorus* / 322	Private
41. *Against Leochares* / date uncertain	Private
42. *Against Zenothemis* / date uncertain	Private

In addition, the following 16 speeches, occasionally thought to have been written by Demosthenes, are now generally considered to be the work of others: *First and Second Orations Against Aristogiton*; *Second Oration Against Boeotus*; *Against Callippus*; *Against Euergus*; *Against Macartatus*; *Against Neaera*; *Against Nicostratus*; *Against Olympiodorus*; *Against Phaenippus*; *Second Oration Against Stephanus*; *Against Theocrines*; *Against Timotheus*; *The Funeral Speech*; *On Organization*; and *On the Treaty with Alexander*.

Demosthenes' father died when Demosthenes was seven years of age. He left the management of his estate to two brothers (some sources say nephews), Aphobus and Demophon, and a family friend, Therippides. When Demosthenes turned 18 and attempted to claim his inheritance, he discovered to his dismay that the three guardians has mismanaged and plundered it to the point of bankruptcy. Demosthenes took them to court over this issue (and eventually won, although the amount he actually collected was a mere fraction of the value of the estate). The orator described in detail the estate's worth (as follows) in the *First Oration Against Aphobus*:

Item	Net value
A sword manufacturing company, employing 32 or 33 slaves (each worth from 3 to 6 minas), and turning a profit of 30 minas per year.	195 minas
A sofa manufacturing company, employing 20 slaves, and turning a profit of 12 minas per year, given to Demosthenes' father as collateral for a 40-mina loan.	52 minas
Money loaned at 12 percent interest.	1 talent
Ivory, iron, and wood used in the factories.	80 minas

Item	Net value
Wood stains and copper.	70 minas
A house.	3,000 drachmas
Furnishings and clothing from the house.	10,000 drachmas
Silver from the house.	80 minas
Loan to a certain Xuthus.	70 minas
In the *trapeza* (bank) of Pasion.	2,400 drachmas
In the *trapeza* of Pylades.	600 drachmas
In the *trapeza* of Demomeles.	1,600 drachmas
No-interest loans.	1 talent

Total: 10 talents, 233 minas, or (considering 233 minas equal to 3 talents, 53 minas) 13 talents, 53 minas.

The Last Forty-Three Consuls Before the Crossing of the Rubicon

When Tarquinius Superbus, the seventh and final king of Rome was expelled in 510 B.C., the monarchy was replaced by a republican form of government headed by two executive officials called consuls. The consulship was an annual magistracy, and for centuries two new consuls assumed power each January 1. (A complete list of all Roman consuls may be found in T. R. S. Broughton's *The Magistrates of the Roman Republic*.)

However, the 60s and 50s B.C. form one of the most turbulent—and best documented—time periods in Roman history. In 49 B.C. Julius Caesar crossed the Rubicon River with his army, thereby touching off a civil war that ultimately doomed the Roman Republic. The last consuls of those final years were as follows, together with the date B.C. of their consulship:

1-2. Marcus Licinius Crassus and Gnaeus Pompeius Magnus, 70
3-4. Quintus Hortensius Hortalus and Quintus Caecilius Metellus, 69
5-6. Lucius Caecilius Metellus and Quintus Marcius Rex, 68
7-8. Gaius Calpurnius Piso and Manlius Acilius Glabrio, 67
9-10. Manlius Aemilius Lepidus and Lucius Volcatius Tullus, 66
11-12. Lucius Aurelius Cotta and Lucius Manlius Torquatus, 65
13-14. Lucius Julius Caesar and Gaius Marcius Figulus, 64
15-16. Marcus Tullius Cicero and Gaius Antonius, 63
17-18. Decimus Junius Silanus and Lucius Licinius Murena, 62
19-20. Marcus Pupius Piso and Marcus Valerius Messalla, 61
21-22. Quintus Caecilius Metellus Celer and Lucius Afranius, 60
23-24. Gaius Julius Caesar and Marcus Calpurnius Bibulus, 59
25-26. Lucius Calpurnius Piso and Aulus Gabinius, 58
27-28. Publius Cornelius Lentulus Spinther and Quintus Caecilius Metellus Nepos, 57
29-30. Gnaeus Cornelius Lentulus Marcellinus and Lucius Marcius Philippus, 56
31-32. Gnaeus Pompeius Magnus and Marcus Licinius Crassus, 55
33-34. Lucius Domitius Ahenobarbus and Appius Claudius Pulcher, 54
35-36. Gnaeus Domitius Calvinus and Marcus Valerius Messalla Rufus, 53

37. Gnaeus Pompeius Magnus, 52

38–39. Servius Sulpicius Rufus and Marcus Claudius Marcellus, 51

40–41. Lucius Aemilius Lepidus Paullus and Gaius Claudius Marcellus (cousin of the Marcellus who was consul in 51), 50

42–43. Lucius Cornelius Lentulus Crus and Gaius Claudius Marcellus (brother of the Marcellus who was consul in 51), 49

Cotta and Torquatus (numbers 11 and 12) assumed their consulships after the duly elected consuls for the year (Publius Cornelius Sulla and Publius Autronius Paetus) had both been removed after being convicted of bribery. Due to the civil violence that was erupting in Rome with increasing frequency in the late 50s, it was decided that a single consul might be able to deal with it more effectively. Hence, Gnaeus Pompeius Magnus (Pompey the Great) (number 37) was chosen *consul solus* for the year 52 B.C., although his father-in-law, Quintus Caecilius Metellus Nepos, was his nominal colleague for the last several months of 52.

The Forty-Five Epinician Odes of Pindar

The Greek epinician poet Pindar (ca.518–438 B.C.) wrote numerous odes in honor of athletes who had won championships at the four major athletic festivals in ancient Greece: the Olympian, Pythian, Nemean, and Isthmian games. Of these, 45 are still extant: 14 in honor of Olympian victors, 12 for Pythian, 11 for Nemean, and 8 for Isthmian winners (although the tenth Pythian ode celebrates a champion flute player, while the eleventh Nemean ode honors a man who had been elected as a member of the town board where he lived).

Pindar's 45 extant odes are as follows:

Ode		*Event*	*Winner/hometown*
Olympian	*1*	Horse race	Hieron of Syracuse
Olympian	*2*	Chariot race	Theron of Acragas
Olympian	*3*	Chariot race	Theron of Acragas
Olympian	*4*	Chariot race	Psaumis of Camarina
Olympian	*5*	Chariot race	Psaumis of Camarina
Olympian	*6*	Chariot race	Hagesias of Syracuse
Olympian	*7*	Boxing	Diagoras of Rhodes
Olympian	*8*	Boys' wrestling	Alcimedon of Aegina
Olympian	*9*	Wrestling	Epharmostus of Opus
Olympian	*10*	Boys' boxing	Hagesidamus of western Locri
Olympian	*11*	Boys' boxing	Hagesidamus of western Locri
Olympian	*12*	Dolichos race	Ergoteles of Himera
Olympian	*13*	Stade race/pentathlon	Xenophon of Corinth
Olympian	*14*	Boys' stade race	Asopichus of Orchomenus
Pythian	*1*	Chariot race	Hieron of Aetna
Pythian	*2*	Chariot race	Hieron of Syracuse
Pythian	*3*	Horse race	Hieron of Syracuse
Pythian	*4*	Chariot race	Arcesilas of Cyrene
Pythian	*5*	Chariot race	Arcesilas of Cyrene

Ode	Event	Winner/hometown
Pythian 6	Chariot race	Xenocrates of Acragas
Pythian 7	Chariot race	Megacles of Athens
Pythian 8	Boys' wrestling	Aristomenes of Aegina
Pythian 9	Race in armor	Telesicrates of Cyrene
Pythian 10	Boys' double stade	Hippocleas of Thessaly
Pythian 11	Boys' stade race	Thrasydaeus of Thebes
Pythian 12	Flute playing	Midas of Acragas
Nemean 1	Chariot race	Chromius of Aetna
Nemean 2	Pankration	Timodemus of Acharnae
Nemean 3	Pankration	Aristoclides of Aegina
Nemean 4	Boys' wrestling	Timasarchus of Aegina
Nemean 5	Boys' pankration	Pytheas of Aegina
Nemean 6	Boys' wrestling	Alcimidas of Aegina
Nemean 7	Boys' pentathlon	Sogenes of Aegina
Nemean 8	Double stade race	Dinias of Aegina
Nemean 9	Chariot race	Chromius of Aetna
Nemean 10	Wrestling	Theaeus of Argos
Nemean 11	Installation into office	Aristagoras of Tenedos
Isthmian 1	Chariot race	Herodotus of Thebes
Isthmian 2	Chariot race	Xenocrates of Acragas
Isthmian 3	Chariot race	Melissus of Thebes
Isthmian 4	Pankration	Melissus of Thebes
Isthmian 5	Pankration	Phylacidas of Aegina
Isthmian 6	Boys' pankration	Phylacidas of Aegina
Isthmian 7	Pankration	Strepsiades of Thebes
Isthmian 8	Boys' pankration	Cleander of Aegina

Forty-Eight of the Largest Amphitheaters in the Roman World

Although the Coliseum in Rome is undoubtedly the most famous ancient amphitheater, the Romans built hundreds of such structures throughout their empire. A list of the 48 largest amphitheaters follows. (Amphitheaters were usually oval-shaped; hence, two figures are provided for the dimensions.)

Location (city followed by country or region)	Dimensions (in meters)
1. Rome, Italy	188 × 156
2. Faleria, Italy	178.8 × 106.2
3. Capua, Italy	169.9 × 139.6
4. Julia Caesarea, North Africa	168 × 88
5. Italica, Spain	156.5 × 134
6. Augustodunum, France	154 × 130
7. Verona, Italy	152 × 123
8. Cyzicus, Asia	150*
9. Divodurum Mediomatricorum, France	150 × 124
10. Puteoli (Amphitheatrum Flavium), Italy	149 × 116

Location (city followed by country or region	Dimensions (in meters)
11. Tarraco, Spain	148.1 × 118.9
12. Thysdrus, North Africa	148 × 122
13. Augusta Treverorum, Germany	ca. 145 × ca. 102
14. Caesarodunum Turonum, France	143 × 124
15. Syracuse, Sicily	140 × 119
16. Augustoritum Limovicum, France	138 × 116
17. Pictavis, France	138 × 115
18. Leuci, France	137.6 × 61
19. Pergamum, western Turkey	136.2 × 128.1
20. Arelate, France	136.2 × 106.8
21. Parma, Italy	136 × 106
22. Lugdunum, France	135 × 115.5
23. Pompeii, Italy	135 × 104
24. Nemausus, France	133.4 × 101.4
25. Pola, Italy	132.5 × 105.1
26. Burdigala, France	132.3 × 110.6
27. Luceria, Italy	131.4 × 99.2
28. Carnuntum, the former Yugoslavia	ca. 130 × 110
29. Puteoli (Amphitheatrum Augustum), Italy	130 × 95
30. Mediolanum, Italy	ca. 129.5 × 105.3
31. Cumae, Italy	ca. 129 × 104
32. Lutetia Parisiorum, France	128*
33. Augusta Emerita, Spain	126.3 × 102.7
34. Catana, Sicily	125 × 105
35. Luca, Italy	123.9 × 96.4
36. Arretium, Italy	121 × 68
37. Ariminum, Italy	120 × 91
38. Aventicum, Germany	115 × 87
39. Spoletium, Italy	115 × 85
40. Forum Julii, France	113.9 × 82.6
41. Vindonissa, Germany	112 × 98
42. Aquae Segetae, France	108 × 90
43. Lambaesis, North Africa	104*
44. Baeterrae, France	103 × 74
45. Lupiae, Italy	102 × 83
46. Florentia, Italy	101*
47. Colonia Agrippinensis, Germany	100 × 60
48. Vetera, Germany	99 × 87.5

This list has been adopted from Herbert Benario's article "Amphitheaters of the Roman World," who notes that many of the dimensions may vary from one source to the next, depending on the time that the measurements were taken (*noted at numbers 8, 32, 43 and 46 are instances in which Benario does not provide a second figure; it could be these are circular). J.-C. Golvin's *L'Amphithéâtre Romain* enumerates 186 known amphitheaters in the Roman world, and another 86 structures that likely were used as amphitheaters.

The Fifty Plutarchian Biographies

Plutarch (ca. A.D. 45–120) who, along with his Roman counterpart Suetonius, was the preeminent biographer of the ancient world, wrote 50 biographies
of famous Greeks and Romans. Forty-six of these he composed in pairs—hence
the title *Parallel Lives* is sometimes applied to his work—matching a Greek with
a comparable Roman. Four biographies are independent of pairing. The 22
pairs—one of the pairs (see number 19) consists of four, rather than two
entries—in their traditional order are as follows:

Greek subject	Roman subject
1. Theseus	Romulus
2. Lycurgus	Numa
3. Solon	Publicola
4. Themistocles	Camillus
5. Pericles	Fabius Maximus
6. Alcibiades	Coriolanus
7. Timoleon	Aemilius Paulus
8. Pelopidas	Marcellus
9. Aristides	Cato the Elder
10. Philopoemen	Flamininus
11. Pyrrhus	Gaius Marius
12. Lysander	Sulla
13. Cimon	Lucullus
14. Nicias	Crassus
15. Eumenes	Sertorius
16. Agesilaus	Pompey
17. Alexander the Great	Julius Caesar
18. Phocion	Cato the Younger
19. Agis and Cleomenes	Tiberius and Gaius Gracchus
20. Demosthenes	Cicero
21. Demetrius	Mark Antony
22. Dion	Brutus

The unpaired biographies are

1. Aratus	3. Galba
2. Artaxerxes	4. Otho

In grouping number 19 the two Spartan kings are compared to the second
century B.C. Roman reformer brothers.

The Fifty-Year Period Between Wars

The period of time between the end of the Persian Wars (479 B.C.) to the
beginning of the Peloponnesian War (431 B.C.) is sometimes referred to as the
Pentecontaetia, or "50-Year Period" (so-called, despite the fact that it covers
somewhat fewer than 50 years). The title Pentecontaetia is applied to chapters
89–118 of the first book of Thucydides' treatise on the Peloponnesian War,

wherein the author described some of the major events that took place during that period.

The Fifty-Talent Ransom

When Julius Caesar was a young man, he was taken captive by pirates while en route to the island of Rhodes. After a 40-day detainment, the ransom — 50 talents, according to Suetonius (*Julius Caesar* 4) — arrived, and Caesar was permitted to continue on his way. Soon thereafter, however, he gained revenge by organizing a fleet, hunting down the pirates, and crucifying them all.

A Voice as Loud as Fifty Warriors

In Book V of the *Iliad*, Homer states that the herald of the Greek army, Stentor, had a voice like bronze, with volume equal to that of 50 other men (compare the modern word "stentorian"). In the same book Homer describes a fight between Ares and Diomedes; when Diomedes (with Athena's assistance) struck the god in the midsection with a spear, his scream of pain was as piercing as that made by 9,000 or 10,000 men.

The Fifty-Six Argonauts

The quest of Jason for the Golden Fleece is one of the most famous stories in Greek mythology. In a book (*Argonautica*) on the subject by Apollonius of Rhodes (third century B.C.), brief biographies of all 56 Argonauts appear. Apollonius's enumeration, in Book I, lines 23–227, of the 56 Argonauts includes the following:

1. Acastus		21. Erginus	
2. Admetus		22. Eribotes	
3. Aethalides		23. Erytus	
4. Amphidamas		24. Euphemus	
5. Amphion		25. Eurydamas	
6. Ancaeus (of Arcadia)		26. Eurytion	
7. Ancaeus (of Parthenia)		27. Hercules	
8. Areius		28. Hylas	
9. Argus		29. Idas	
10. Asterion		30. Idmon	
11. Asterius		31. Iphiclus (of Aetolia)	
12. Augeias		32. Iphiclus (of Phylace)	
13. Butes		33. Iphitus (of Phocia)	
14. Calais		34. Iphitus (origin unstated)	
15. Canthus		35. Jason	
16. Castor		36. Laocoon	
17. Cepheus		37. Leodocus	
18. Clytius		38. Lynceus	
19. Coronus		39. Meleager	
20. Echion		40. Menoetius	

41. Mopsus
42. Nauplius
43. Oileus
44. Orpheus
45. Palaemonius
46. Peleus
47. Periclymenus
48. Phalerus
49. Phlias
50. Polydeuces
51. Polyphemus
52. Talaus
53. Telamon
54. Theseus
55. Tiphys
56. Zetes

Apart from *Jason* himself, the two most famous Argonauts were undoubtedly Theseus, the legendary founder and king of Athens, and Hercules, perhaps the most widely documented of all the myriad of characters in the panoply of Greek mythology. But several other Argonauts enjoyed their own small claims to fame.

Admetus was the husband of Alcestis, who volunteered to die in his stead; their story is portrayed in Euripides' play *Alcestis*. Argus was the builder of the *Argo*, the ship that carried Jason and his men on their quest. Calais and Zetes, twin brothers, freed the aged Phineus from the scourge of the Harpies. Castor and Polydeuces, another set of twins, were conveyed to the heavens and transformed into a constellation (Gemini, "twins") when they died. Laocoon, a priest who advised the Trojans not to drag the Wooden Horse into the city, was strangled (along with his two sons) by a serpent sent from Athena. Meleager was the leader of the Calydonian Boar Hunt, an effort to rid Calydonia of a wild boar terrorizing the region; many famous mythological characters took part in this adventure, including Meleager's fellow Argonauts Admetus, Castor and Polydeuces, Theseus and Peleus.

Famous fathers on the expedition included Oileus, father of the Lesser Ajax; Peleus, father of Achilles; and Telamon, father of the Greater Ajax.

A Fifty-Seven–Year Sleep

In his biography of the sixth century B.C. Cretan philosopher Epimenides, Diogenes Laertius relates that one day his father sent him out to the hills to look for a lost sheep. Epimenides (rightly noted as the Rip Van Winkle of antiquity) wandered into a cave, where he reputedly slept for 57 years.

Diogenes also states that Epimenides lived an exceedingly long life—although perhaps not surprising in light of the fact that he did not grow older while slumbering for those five-plus decades. Various sources placed his age at death at 154, 157, or 299 years.

The Fifty-Eight Orations of Marcus Tullius Cicero

Marcus Tullius Cicero (106–43 B.C.), perhaps the ancient world's finest orator, has 58 extant speeches to his credit. Most of these are revised transcripts of speeches he delivered in court; a few deal with other topics, such as proposed laws. The 58 are as follows:

Speeches on miscellaneous topics

Latin title of the oration	English title	Date B.C.
1. Pro Lege Manilia	On Behalf of the Law of Manilius	66
2–4. De Lege Agraria I–III*	Concerning the Agrarian Law	63
5. Post Reditum ad Quirites	After Returning [from exile], to his fellow citizens	57
6. Post Reditum in Senatu	After returning, in the Senate	57
7. De Domo Sua	Concerning His Own House	57
8. De Haruspicum Responso	Concerning the Response of the Soothsayers	56
9. De Provinciis Con- sularibus	Concerning the Consular Provinces	56

Court cases in which Cicero served as a defense attorney

Title of the oration	Cicero's client	Date B.C.
10. Pro Quinctio	Publius Quinctius	81
11. Pro Sexto Roscio Amerino	Sextus Roscius of Ameria	80
12. Pro Q. Roscio Comoedo	Quintus Roscius the comedian	77(?)
13. Pro Tullio	Marcus Tullius	69
14. Pro Fonteio	Marcus Fonteius	69
15. Pro Caecina	Aulus Caecina	69
16. Pro Cluentio	Aulus Cluentius Habitus	66
17. Pro Rabirio	Gaius Rabirius	63
18. Pro Murena	Lucius Licinius Murena	63
19. Pro Sulla	Publius Cornelius Sulla	62
20. Pro Archaia Poeta	Aulus Licinius Archias the poet	62
21. Pro Flacco	Lucius Valerius Flaccus	59
22. Pro Sestio	Publius Sestius	56
23. Pro Caelio	Marcus Caelius Rufus	56
24. Pro Balbo	Lucius Cornelius Balbus	56
25. Pro Scauro	Aemilius Scaurus	54
26. Pro Plancio	Gnaeus Plancius	54
27. Pro Rabirio Postumo	Gaius Rabirius Postumus	54
28. Pro Milone	Titus Annius Milo	52
29. Pro Marcello	Marcus Marcellus	46
30. Pro Ligario	Quintus Ligarius	46
31. Pro Rege Deiotaro	King Deiotarus	45

*Cicero delivered three speeches in opposition to a land reform bill proposed by a tribune named Publius Servilius Rullus; these speeches are sometimes alternatively entitled Contra Rullum, Against Rullus.

Court cases in which Cicero served as a prosecutor; public speeches in which he attacked or criticized a rival ("defendant" applies in both situations):

Title of the oration	Defendant(s)	Date B.C.
32. *In Caecilium*	Quintus Caecilius Niger	Summer 70
33. *In Verrem I*	Gaius Verres	Summer 70
34–38. *In Verrem II**	Gaius Verres	Summer 70
39. *In Catilinam I*	Lucius Sergius Catilina	November 63
40. *In Catilinam II*	Lucius Sergius Catilina	November 63
41. *In Catilinam III*	Lucius Sergius Catilina	December 63
42. *In Catilinam IV*	Lucius Sergius Catilina	December 63
43. *In Vatinium*	Publius Vatinius	56
44. *In Pisonem*	Lucius Calpurnius Piso	55
45. *Philippic I*	Mark Antony	September 44
46. *Philippic II*	Mark Antony	October 44
47. *Philippic III*	Mark Antony	December 44
48. *Philippic IV*	Mark Antony	December 44
49. *Philippic V*	Mark Antony	January 43
50. *Philippic VI*	Mark Antony	January 43
51. *Philippic VII*	Mark Antony	January 43
52. *Philippic VIII*	Mark Antony	January 43
53. *Philippic IX*	Mark Antony**	January 43
54. *Philippic X*	Mark Antony; his brother Gaius	March 43
55. *Philippic XI*	Mark Antony; Publius Cornelius Dolabella	March 43
56. *Philippic XII*	Mark Antony	March 43
57. *Philippic XIII*	Mark Antony	April 43
58. *Philippic XIV*	Mark Antony	April 43

The *Pro Quinctio* (of 81 B.C.) is the earliest of Cicero's surviving orations. The fourteenth *Philippic*, delivered on April 21, 43 B.C., is the last of the surviving speeches. The famous orator was murdered at the behest of Mark Antony during the proscriptions of December 43 B.C.

The Fifty-Nine Wives and Mistresses of Hercules

In Book II of *Library*, by the second-century B.C. grammarian Apollodorus, the following list of 59 names of wives and (mostly) mistresses of Hercules appears:

1. Aeschreis	3. Anthea	5. Antiope
2. Aglaia	4. Anthippe	6. Argele

*Cicero's second oration against Verres, in actuality a series of five short speeches, was never delivered; Verres fled from Rome after Cicero's first speech.
**The ninth Philippic is more a eulogy of Cicero's recently deceased friend Servius Sulpicius Rufus than it is an attack on Antony.

7. Asopis	25. Eubote	43. Nice
8. Astydamia	26. Eurypyle	44. Nicippe
9. Astyoche	27. Eurytele	45. Olympusa
10. Auge	28. Exole	46. Omphale
11. Autonoe	29. Hebe	47. Oria
12. Calametis	30. Heliconis	48. Panope
13. Certhe	31. Hesychia	49. Parthenope
14. Chalciope	32. Hippo	50. Patro
15. Chryseis	33. Hippocrate	51. Phyleis
16. Clytippe	34. Iphis	52. Praxithea
17. Deianira	35. Laothoe	53. Procris
18. Elachia	36. Lyse	54. Pyrippe
19. Eone	37. Lysidice	55. Stratonice
20. Epicaste	38. Lysippe	56. Terpsicrate
21. Eurybia	39. Marse	57. Tiphyse
22. Epilais	40. Megara	58. Toxicrate
23. Erato	41. Meline	59. Xanthis
24. Euboea	42. Menippis	

Most of these 59 are near-anonymities; a few are subjects of mythological stories. King Creon of Thebes gave his daughter Megara in marriage to Hercules, for services that Hercules had rendered to Thebes. Later, during a bout of insanity induced by Hera, Hercules killed his wife and their three children. To gain Deianira's hand in marriage, Hercules had to defeat the river god Achelous in a wrestling contest. Deianira unknowingly caused Hercules' death by sending him a robe imbued with the lethal blood of the centaur Nessus. After his death and deification, he married Hebe, daughter of Hera, thus effecting a reconciliation with the goddess who had long been his tormentor.

The Sixty Hippocratic Treatises

Antiquity's most famous physician, Hippocrates (ca.460–370 B.C.) is generally associated with a voluminous output of medical treatises, perhaps 60. However, modern scholars doubt that Hippocrates himself wrote all, or even any, of these; it is thought instead that the works attributed to him were probably authored by a consortium of fourth-century physicians. Even the celebrated Hippocratic oath seems likely to have been composed by some unknown medical practitioner.

Some of the major topics in what might be termed the "Hippocratic Collection" are

1. Air; wind; water, and their effects on health
2. Epidemics
3. Nutriments
4. The art of prognosis
5. Epilepsy (sometimes called the "Sacred Disease" due to its supposed divine origin)

6. Fractures and dislocations
7. Medical aphorisms
8. Treatments for various diseases and disorders

The Sixty-Plus Who Conspired Against Caesar

According to the biographer Suetonius (*Julius Caesar* 80), more than sixty Romans, many of them senators, conspired to assassinate Julius Caesar. The plot unfolded successfully on March 15 (the "Ides of March"), 44 B.C. Suetonius notes that Caesar absorbed 23 stab wounds at the hands of the conspirators.

A Sixty-Year Kingship

Masinissa (ca.240–150 B.C.), king of Libya, lived to the age of 90, having ruled for some 60 years. He had ten sons—one of whom he fathered at the age of 86!—and at his death he left each of them farms of 10,000 plethra (or about 7,000 acres).

The Sixty-Five Sketches and Essays of Lucian

The Greek satirist and essayist Lucian (second century A.D.) authored works on rhetoric, literature, and philosophy, as well as numerous satirical dialogues, for which he is best known. Much of his satirical writing mocks philosophy, oratory, and religious customs and beliefs.

Controversy swirls around the authenticity of several sketches often ascribed to Lucian. The list that appears below contains the titles of those writings generally considered to be Lucian's work. Some of the entries have variant titles, depending upon which edition of Lucian or which reference book one consults. An effort has been made to offer the most common or descriptive title, along with the genre or topic for each.

1. *Alexander the False Prophet*: satirical biography
2. *Amber, or The Swans*: rhetoric
3. *Anacharsis*: satirical dialogue
4. *Assembly of the Gods*: satirical dialogue
5. *Charon, or The Inspectors*: satirical dialogue
6. *The Dance*: satirical dialogue
7. *On the Death of Peregrinus*: satirical essay
8. *Defense of the Essay on Dependent Scholars* [see note at the end of list]
9. *Demonax*: philosophy
10. *Dependent Scholars*: satirical essay
11. *Dialogues of the Dead*: satirical dialogues
12. *Dialogues of the Gods*: satirical dialogues
13. *Dialogues of the Prostitutes*: satirical dialogues
14. *Dialogues of the Sea Gods*: satirical dialogues
15. *Dionysus*: rhetoric

16. *Dipsads*, or *Vipers*: essay on Libyan wildlife
17. *Discussion with Hesiod*: essay on poetry writing
18. *Disowned*: satirical essay
19. *Double Indictment*: satirical dialogue
20. *The Dream*: satirical dialogue
21. *Drinking Party*, or *The Lapiths*: satirical dialogue
22. *The Eunuch*: satirical dialogue
23. *On Funerals*: satirical essay
24. *The Goddess of Syria*: satirical essay
25. *The Hall*: rhetoric
26. *Harmonides*: essay directed to a patron
27. *Hercules*: rhetoric
28. *Hermotimus*: satirical dialogue
29. *Herodotus*: literary essay
30. *How to Write History*: historiographical essay
31. *Icaromenippus*, or *Above the Clouds*: satirical dialogue
32. *Images*: satirical dialogue
33. *On the Images*: satirical dialogue
34. *Judgment of the Goddesses*: satirical dialogue
35. *Lexiphanes*: satirical dialogue
36. *Life of Lucian*: autobiographical essay
37. *Lover of Lies*: satirical dialogue
38. *Menippus*: satirical dialogue
39. *The Mistaken Critic*: satirical essay
40. *The Parasite*: satirical dialogue
41. *Phalaris I*: rhetoric
42. *Phalaris II*: rhetoric
43. *In Praise of a Fly*: rhetoric
44. *Prometheus*: satirical dialogue
45. *A Prometheus in Words*: essay on dialogues and comedy
46. *Return to Life*, or *The Fishermen*: satirical dialogue
47. *The Runaways*: satirical dialogue
48. *On Sacrifices*: satirical essay
49. *Sailing Down to Hades*: satirical dialogue
50. *Sale of Lives*: satirical dialogue
51. *Saturnalia*: satirical dialogue
52. *The Scythian*: essay directed to a patron
53. *The Ship*: satirical dialogue
54. *Slander*: rhetoric
55. *A Slip of the Tongue in Greeting*: essay on the forms of salutation
56. *Teacher of Rhetoric*: satirical essay
57. *Timon*, or *The Grouch*: satirical dialogue
58. *Toxaris*, or *Friendship*: ten stories on the theme of friendship
59. *The Tragic Zeus*: satirical dialogue
60. *True Story*: short satirical novel
61. *Tyrannicide*: satirical essay
62. *The Uneducated Book Collector*: satirical essay
63. *Wisdom of Nigrinus*: satirical dialogue

64. *Zeus Cross-examined*: satirical dialogue
65. *Zeuxis the Artist*: essay on Zeuxis's work of art

Lucian's sketch entitled *Dependent Scholars* was a satire on educated Greeks who accepted employment in the households of wealthy Romans, a line of work that Lucian apparently considered demeaning. But later he had to eat his own words when he himself took up such a post; hence, the *Defense*.

Several other essays, satires, and stories are sometimes attributed to Lucian, most notably, perhaps, the short novel entitled *Lucian or the Ass*.

The Sixty-Seven Sons of Hercules

The names and number of children ("Heraclids") ascribed to the prolific Hercules vary from one author to the next. A list of 67 Herculean sons appears in Apollodorus's *Library* (Book II).

1. Agelaus	24. Deicoön	46. Lycurgus
2. Alexiares	25. Dynastes	47. Lyncaeus
3. Alopius	26. Entelides	48. Mentor
4. Amestrius	27. Erasippus	49. Nephus
5. Anicetus	28. Erythras	50. Nicodromus
6. Antiades	29. Eumedes	51. Oestrobles
7. Antileon	30. Eurycapys	52. Olympus
8. Antimachus	31. Euryopes	53. Onesippus
9. Antiphus	32. Eurypylus	54. Onites
10. Archedicus	33. Everes	55. Palaemon
11. Archemachus	34. Glenus	56. Patroclus
12. Astyanax	35. Halocrates	57. Phalias
13. Astybies	36. Hippeus	58. Polylaus
14. Atromus	37. Hippodromus	59. Telephus
15. Bucolus	38. Hippozygus	60. Teles
16. Buleus	39. Homolippus	61. Teleutagoras
17. Capylus	40. Hyllus	62. Therimachus
18. Celeustanor	41. Iobes	63. Thestalus
19. Cleolaus	42. Laomedon	64. Thettalus
20. Creon	43. Laomenes	65. Threpsippas
21. Creontiades	44. Leucippus	66. Tigasis
22. Ctesippus I	45. Leucones	67. Tlepolemus
23. Ctesippus II		

Ironically, only a few of these sons enjoyed any prominence apart from their birthrights. Tlepolemus commanded a squadron of nine Rhodian ships during the Trojan War. Telephus also fought on the Greek side during the Trojan War, even though he was the son-in-law of the aged Trojan king, Priam. According to some stories, Agelaus was an ancestor of the sixth-century B.C. King Croesus of Lydia, reputedly one of the ancient world's richest men. Hyllus killed King Eurystheus, the one who assigned Hercules the Twelve Labors, although some versions of the story state that Hercules' nephew, Iolaus, dispatched Eurystheus.

The assorted wives, mistresses, and lovers who produced these 67 children are listed under number 59.

Seventy-Five Roman Wars

The study of Roman history inevitably involves a heavy concentration on military matters, given that the Romans were seemingly engaged in almost constant warfare. A historian by the name of Lucius Annaeus Florus (second century A.D.) compiled a summary of all known Roman wars from the period of the kings down to the time of Augustus, an epitome *bellorum omnium annorum DCC*, "of all the wars of 700 years" of Roman history.

The 75 wars described by Florus (some of the wars this historian catalogued were actually multiple conflicts, for example, entries number 3, 5, and 9 — and thus accounted for a list total of 69 instead of 75) were as follows:

War/chief Roman commander (according to Florus)	Approximate date
1. The Etruscan War with Lars Porsenna/Junius Brutus	509 B.C.
2. The Latin War/L. Quinctius Cincinnatus	mid–fifth century B.C.
3. The War with the Etruscans, Faliscians, Veientines, Fidenates/various leaders	mid–fifth century B.C.
4. The Gallic War/Marcus Manlius and Camillus	390 B.C.
5. More Wars with the Gauls/Manlius Torquatus	mid–fourth century B.C.
6. The [Second] Latin War/Manlius Torquatus and Decius Mus	340 B.C.
7. The Sabine War/Curius Dentatus	290 B.C.
8. The [Second] Samnite War/the consuls Veturius and Postumius were the vanquished generals in the Battle of Caudine Forks (321), one of Rome's most devastating defeats	328–304 B.C.
9. The Etruscan and [Third] Samnite Wars; more wars with the Gauls/Fabius Maximus	300–290 B.C.
10. The Tarentine War/Curius and Fabricius	first battle: 280 B.C.
11. The Picenian War/Sempronius	280 B.C.
12. The Sallentine War/Marcus Atilius	280 B.C.
13. The Volsinian War/Fabius Gurges	280 B.C.
14. The First Four Plebeian Secessions	494, 450, 445, 367 B.C.

15. The First Punic War/Lutatius   264–241 B.C.
Catulus
16. The Ligurian War/Fulvius, Baebius,   235 B.C.
Postumius
17. [Another] Gallic War/Aemilius,   222 B.C.
Flaminius, Marcellus
18. The [First] Illyrian War/Gnaeus
Fulvius Centimalus   220 B.C.
19. The Second Punic War/Scipio   218–202 B.C.
Africanus
20. The First Macedonian War/Valerius   216–205 B.C.
Laevinus
21. The Syrian War with King An-   192–188 B.C.
tiochus/Lucius Cornelius Scipio
22. The Aetolian War/Fulvius Nobilior   189 B.C.
23. The Istrian War/Appius Pulcher   178 B.C.
24. The Gallo-Greek War/Manlius Vulso   178 B.C.
25. The Second Macedonian War/Paulus   200–197 B.C.
26. The Second Illyrian War/L. Aemilius   219 B.C.
Paulus
27. The Third Macedonian War/Lucius   171–168 B.C.
Aemilius Paulus Macedonicus
28. The Third Punic War/Scipio   149–146 B.C.
Aemilianus
29. The Achaean War/Q. Caecilius   148 B.C.
Metellus
30. The Numantine War/Scipio   143–133 B.C.
Aemilianus
31. The Asiatic War/Aquilius, Marcus   130–129 B.C.
Perperna
32. The Jugurthine War/Gaius Marius   111–105 B.C.
33. The Allobrogian War/Gnaeus Domi-   121 B.C.
tius Ahenobarbus, Fabius Maximus
34. The War against the Cimbrians,   102–101 B.C.
Teutones, and Tigurinians/Gaius
Marius
35. The Thracian War/Marcus Livius   112–100 B.C.
Drusus, Titus Didius
36. The Mithridatic War/Sulla, Pompey,   88–67 B.C.
Lucullus
37. The War against the Pirates/Pompey   67 B.C.
38. The Cretan War/Marcus Antonius,   72–66 B.C.
Quintus Caecilius Metellus Creticus
39. The Balearic War/Q. Caecilius   121–120 B.C.
Metellus Balearicus
40. The Expedition to Cyprus/Marcus   58 B.C.
Porcius Cato
41. The Gallic War/Gaius Julius Caesar   58–50 B.C.

42. The Parthian War/Marcus Licinius   54–53 B.C.
    Crassus
43. The Social Wars/Cato, Carbo, Sulla,   91–88 B.C.
    Pompeius Strabo
44. The [Sicilian] Slave War/Marcus   135–132 B.C.
    Perperna
45. The War against Spartacus/M.   72–70 B.C.
    Licinius Crassus
46. The Civil War between Marius and   87–86 B.C.
    Sulla
47. The War against Sertorius/Metellus   80–72 B.C.
    Pius
48. The Civil War under Lepidus   78 B.C.
49. The War against Catiline/Gaius An-   63–62 B.C.
    tonius
50. The Civil War between Caesar and   49–48 B.C.
    Pompey
51. The [Civil] War near Mutina/Octa-   43 B.C.
    vianus, Marcus Antonius
52. The [Civil] War near Perusia/Octa-   41 B.C.
    vianus, Lucius Antonius
53. The [Civil] War against Cassius and   42 B.C.
    Brutus/Octavianus
54. The [Civil] War against Sextus   38–36 B.C.
    Pompeius
55. The Parthian War under Ventidius   39–38 B.C.
56. The Parthian War under Marcus An-   36 B.C.
    tonius
57. The [Civil] War against Antonius   31 B.C.
    and Cleopatra/Octavianus
58. The Norican War/Nero Claudius   15–9 B.C.
    Drusus
59. [Another] Illyrian War/Augustus   13–9 B.C.
60. The Pannonian War/Vinnius   13 B.C.
61. The Dalmatian War/Vibius   A.D. 7
62. The Moesian War/Marcus Crassus   29 B.C.
63. [Another] Thracian War/Piso   12–9 B.C.
64. The Dacian War/Gnaeus Cornelius   Uncertain
    Lentulus
65. The Sarmatian War/Lentulus   Uncertain
66. The German War/Publius Quinc-   A.D. 9
    tilius Varus
67. The Gaetulian War/Cossus   Uncertain
68. The Armenian War/Gaius Caesar   A.D. 4
    (Augustus's adopted son)
69. The War against the Cantabrians
    and Asturians/Augustus, Marcus   26–19 B.C.
    Agrippa

The First Samnite War (343–341), considered fictitious by some historians, is not mentioned by Florus.

Modern historians divide the Mithridatic War into three separate conflicts: the First, Second, and Third Mithridatic Wars.

Octavianus, the future emperor, was not granted the title Augustus until 27 B.C.

Florus also includes several other disturbances on his list, including the uprisings resulting from the reform movements of the Gracchan brothers and Apuleius Saturninus.

Plutarch's Seventy-Eight Moral Essays

Although Plutarch (ca. A.D. 46–120) is best remembered as a biographer, he also wrote a collection of short essays usually entitled *Moralia*, or *Moral Essays*. The individual essays have variant English titles, depending on the whims or preferences of editors and translators; the most commonly used titles appear in the list. The variety of topics (as illustrated by the titles) indicate the breadth of the erudite Plutarch's learning and interests.

1. *On the Education of Children*
2. *How a Young Person Ought to Study Poetry*
3. *On Listening to Lectures*
4. *How to Distinguish a Flatterer from a Friend*
5. *On Progress in Virtue*
6. *How to Profit from Your Enemies*
7. *On Having Many Friends*
8. *On Fortune*
9. *On Virtue and Vice*
10. *Consolation to Apollonius*
11. *Instructions for Maintaining Health*
12. *Advice on Marriage*
13. *The Banquet of the Seven Sages*
14. *On Superstition*
15. *Sayings of Kings and Commanders*
16. *Spartan Sayings*
17. *The Bravery of Women*
18. *Roman Questions, Greek Questions*
19. *Greek and Roman Parallels*
20. *On the Fortune of the Romans*
21. *On the Fortune and Courage of Alexander the Great*
22. *Were the Athenians More Famous in War or Peace?*
23. *Isis and Osiris*
24. *The Delphic* E
25. *On the Pythian Prophecies*
26. *On the Decline of Oracles*
27. *Can Virtue Be Taught?*
28. *On Moral Virtue*

29. *On Controlling Anger*
30. *On the Tranquillity of the Mind*
31. *On Brotherly Love*
32. *On the Love of Offspring*
33. *Does Vice Alone Cause Unhappiness?*
34. *Which Is Worse: the Ills of the Mind or the Ills of the Body?*
35. *On Talkativeness*
36. *On Curiosity*
37. *On the Love of Riches*
38. *On Harmful Scrupulousness*
39. *On Envy and Hatred*
40. *On Praising Oneself*
41. *On the Gods' Slowness to Punish*
42. *On Fate*
43. *On Socrates' Sign*
44. *On Exile*
45. *Consolation to My Wife*
46. *Nine Dinner Conversations*
47. *Love Book*
48. *Love Stories*
49. *Philosophers and Rulers*
50. *To the Uneducated Ruler*
51. *Should Old Men Take Part in Politics?*
52. *Advice on Public Life*
53. *On Monarchy, Democracy, and Oligarchy*
54. *On Borrowing*
55. *Lives of the Ten Orators*
56. *Comparison of Aristophanes and Menander*
57. *On Herodotus's Malice*
58. *On the Doctrines of the Philosophers*
59. *Natural Questions*
60. *On the Face in the Moon*
61. *On the Primary Cold*
62. *Is Fire or Water More Useful?*
63. *Are Land or Sea Animals More Clever?*
64. *Animals Are Rational*
65–66. *On Eating Flesh* (two essays)
67. *Platonic Questions*
68. *On the Creation of the Soul in Plato's* Timaeus
69. Epitome of number 68
70. *On Stoic Contradictions*
71. *Stoic Paradoxes Are More Absurd Than Poets'*
72. *On the Common Notions Against the Stoic View*
73. *Not Even a Pleasant Life Is Possible on Epicurean Principles*
74. *Against Colotes*
75. *On the Unnoticed Life*
76. *On Music*
77–78. Two fragmentary essays on aspects of the soul

Seventy-Nine Roman Emperors

The transition from one Roman emperor to the next was relatively orderly in the first and second centuries A.D. Such was not the case in the third, fourth, and fifth centuries, when emperors frequently had short reigns, when often two or more emperors ruled concurrently, or when volatile political and military conditions bred rapid imperial turnover. This instability causes a certain degree of difficulty in composing an accurate list of emperors for the latter three centuries. The following list provides the names of 81 Roman emperors, along with the years of their reigns. It has been drawn primarily from the lists in D. M. Low's abridgement of Gibbon's *Decline and Fall of the Roman Empire*, and the list appearing in M. Cary's *A History of Rome*:

1. Augustus 27 B.C.–A.D. 14
2. Tiberius 14–37
3. Caligula 37–41
4. Claudius 41–54
5. Nero 54–68
6. Galba 68–69
7. Otho 69
8. Vitellius 69
9. Vespasian 69–79
10. Titus 79–81
11. Domitian 81–96
12. Nerva 96–98
13. Trajan 98–117
14. Hadrian 117–138
15. Antoninus Pius 138–161
16. Marcus Aurelius 161–180
17. Lucius Verus 161–169
18. Commodus 180–192
19. Pertinax 193
20. Didius Julianus 193
21. Septimius Severus 193–211
22. Caracalla 211–217
23. Geta 211–212
24. Macrinus 217–218
25. Diadumenianus 218
26. Elagabalus 218–222
27. Severus Alexander 222–235
28. Maximinus Thrax 235–238
29. Gordian I 238
30. Gordian II 238
31. Balbinus 238
32. Pupienus Maximus 238
33. Gordian III 238–244
34. Philip the Arab 244–249
35. Philip, son of Philip the Arab 247–249
36. Decius 249–251
37. Trebonianus Gallus 251–253
38. Aemilianus 253
39. Valerianus 253–260
40. Gallienus 253–268
41. Claudius Gothicus 268–270
42. Aurelianus 270–275
43. Tacitus 275–276
44. Florianus 276
45. Probus 276–282
46. Carus 282–283
47. Carinus 283–284
48. Numerianus 283–284
49. Diocletian 284–305
50. Maximian 284–305
51. Galerius 293–311
52. Constantius I 292–306
53. Valerius Severus 305–307
54. Licinius 308–324
55. Constantine (the Great) 306–337
56. Maximinus Daza, or Daia 305–313
57. Constantine II 317–340
58. Constantius II 337–361
59. Constans 337–350
60. Julian 361–363
61. Jovian 363–364
62. Valentinian I 364–375
63. Valens 364–378
64. Gratian 367–383
65. Valentinian II 375–392
66. Theodosius I 378–395

67. Arcadius 383–408
68. Honorius 392–423
69. Theodosius II 408–450
70. Valentinian III 425–455
71. Petronius Maximus 455
72. Avitus 455–456
73. Majorian 457–461

74. Libius Severus 461–465
75. Anthemius 467–472
76. Olybrius 472
77. Glycerius 473–474
78. Julius Nepos 474–475
79. Romulus Augustulus 475–476

It is one of the ironies of Roman history that the first king (in 753 B.C.) and the last emperor shared the name Romulus, and also ironic that the first and last emperors both claimed the title Augustus, with a fittingly pejorative diminutive suffix for fifth-century emperor.

The Eighty Extant Speeches of Dio Chrysostom

A native of Bithynia, Dio Chrysostom ("Golden-mouthed"; ca. A.D. 40–after 112) eventually took up residence in Rome, where he became an orator and philosopher. About 80 of his speeches still survive; some deal with actual cases, but the majority involve hypothetical situations, devised for the enlightenment and entertainment of the listeners. A representative sampling of the topics follows, with the speech number given for each.

IX: Dio offers an account of the manner in which Diogenes the Cynic belittled the champion sprint racer at the Isthmian games.

XI: Dio questions Homer's credibility, and argues that the Greeks did not capture Troy.

XIII: He discusses his banishment from Rome (in A.D. 82), brought on by his alleged participation in a plot against the emperor Domitian.

XX: The attitudes and activities appropriate for retirement form the basis of this speech.

XLVI: A rise in the price of grain in Bithynia sparked a riot; the rioters believed that the wealthy Dio should have done something to alleviate the situation. He rises to speak in his own defense.

LIV: Dio presents a panegyric on Socrates.

LXI: This speech is interesting primarily because it focuses on one of the minor characters of the *Iliad*, Chryseis, whose kidnapping by Agamemnon fueled his violent argument with Achilles in the opening scene of the epic.

Many of Dio's other speeches deal with abstract concepts, such as virtue, reputation, trust, envy, and freedom.

The One Hundred–Eyed Watchdog

In Greek mythology Io was one of the many objects of Zeus's affection. Therefore, his jealous wife Hera assigned the giant Argus the task of guarding Io.

Argus had many eyes — the number varies from author to author — but 100 seems to be the commonly accepted figure. He was the ideal watchman because some of his 100 eyes stayed open while others slept.

The One Hundred-Foot Column of Trajan

In A.D. 113 the Roman emperor Trajan (reigned A.D. 98–117) dedicated a 100-foot-tall marble column commemorating his victory over the Dacians in 106. The column was decorated throughout its length with sculpted scenes from the Dacian Wars and Roman military life in general. Some additional statistics about Trajan's Column include the following:

Number of column drums: 17
Number of contiguous, sculpted spirals: 23
Number of windows in the shaft: 43
Total length of the 23 spirals: 670 feet
Number of figures depicted: over 2,500

The One Hundred-Handed Giants, or Hecatonchires

Three of the offspring of Uranus and Ge, oldest of the gods, were terrible giants with 100 arms and 50 heads. Their names were Briareus, Cottus, and Gyges.

A One Hundred-Headed Dragon

The Apples of the Hesperides (whose retrieval was Hercules' Eleventh Labor) were guarded by a multilingual dragon with 100 heads.

One Hundred Talents for a Painting

The emperor Augustus is said to have paid 100 talents for a painting (of Aphrodite rising from the sea), the work of one of the ancient world's greatest painters, Apelles of Colophon (fourth century B.C.).

One Hundred Talents for Earthquake Relief

About 227 B.C. an earthquake shook the island of Rhodes; this disaster destroyed, among other things, the colossal statue of Apollo, one of the ancient world's seven wonders. The Sicilian tyrants Hieron and Gelon sent 100 talents to the citizens of Rhodes to aid in the reconstruction of the city.

One Hundred Voices, One Hundred Mouths, and One Hundred Tongues

Persius begins his fifth *Satire* by noting that epic poets sometimes use the imagery of tens or hundreds of voices, mouths, and tongues required to call attention to a particular fact or circumstance. For example, in Book II of the *Iliad*,

Homer states that he could not provide a complete tally of the Greek soldiers and commanders who sailed to Troy, not even if he had ten tongues, ten mouths, a tireless voice, and a heart of bronze. And in Book VI of the *Aeneid*, Vergil suggests that to describe the terrors of the Underworld even 100 tongues, 100 mouths, and a voice of iron would not suffice.

ONE HUNDRED EIGHT
through
the FIVE HUNDREDS

Penelope's One Hundred Eight Suitors

Penelope, the faithful wife of Odysseus, was beset by a horde of aggressive and arrogant suitors. Although her husband had been away for 20 years, she clung to the hope that he might one day return to her, and so she refused the advances of the suitors. In the *Odyssey* (Book XVI), Homer says that there were 108 suitors: 52 from Doulichion, 24 from Same, 20 from Zakynthos, and 12 from Ithaca.

The One Hundred Thirteen Poems of Catullus

One of Rome's greatest lyric poets, Catullus (84–54 B.C.) wrote 113 poems. Several of these are a mere two lines in length; the longest contains over 400 lines. The following is a sampling of the topics:

Poem number	Length (in lines)	Content summary
III	18	The death of the pet sparrow of Lesbia, Catullus's enamorata.
VIII	19	The end of Catullus's romance with Lesbia.
XII	17	The "art" of the napkin thief, Asinius Marrucinus.
XVII	26	The bridge at Colonia—and an elderly townsman incapable of satisfying his young bride; for such a lapse, the old man ought to be tossed from the bridge.
XXII	21	The inferior poet Suffenus, who has written 10,000 lines of literary garbage (10,000 lines being the approximate length of an epic poem).

199

Poem number	Length (in lines)	Content summary
XXIII	27	Furius, a man so poor that he need not fear a house fire since he has no house.
XXXI	14	Sirmio, a peninsula on Lake Benacus (in northern Italy), and a favorite retreat of Catullus.
XXXIX	21	Egnatius and his annoyingly ever present toothy grin.
XLIX	7	The oratorical skill of Marcus Tullius Cicero.
LXI	228	A hymn in honor of a marriage, thought to be that of Manlius Torquatus and Junia.
LXIV	408	The Argonauts; marriage of Peleus and Thetis; and the story of Theseus and Ariadne. (This is Catullus's longest extant poem.)
LXX	4	The fickleness of a woman.
XCIII	2	Catullus's antipathy toward Julius Caesar.

One Hundred Twenty Asses per Day, and Other Legal Limits on Dinner Expenditures

Roman politicians (especially of the third, second, and first centuries B.C.), were fond of enacting sumptuary laws to limit the amount of money that could be spent on formal dinners. Aulus Gellius (2.24) provides the following examples (*as* [*asses*, plural] being a bronze coin of the Roman Republic):

120 asses. In 161 B.C. a senatorial decree placed a limit of 120 asses on daily dinner expenses; it also specified that no more than 100 pounds of silverware could be used. This decree was subsequently modified by the consul Gaius Fannius to permit only ten asses per day, except for ten days of any given month, on which 30 could be spent, and certain holidays, when 100 was the limit. Not surprisingly, some Romans chafed under these restrictions. The satirist Lucilius, for example, railed at the *Fanni centussis misellus*, "Fannius's cheapskate 100-as [law]."

200 asses. A law passed around 103 B.C., while observing the provisions of Fannius's law, permitted 200 asses to be spent on wedding dinners.

300 sesterces. In about 80 B.C. the dictator Lucius Cornelius Sulla proposed that 300 sesterces could be spent for dinners on certain designated days (holidays, for example), but that on all other days, 30 sesterces should be the limit.

1,000 sesterces. At some point in Augustus's reign—the exact date is unknown—the emperor proposed that on business days no more than 200 sesterces ought to be spent on dinners, but that the limit should be raised to 300 on certain holidays, and 1,000 for wedding banquets. (The final provision was no doubt inserted as an incentive to marry, the encouragment

of which was one of the primary components of Augustus's social legislation.) Augustus's law was later amended to allow the expenditure of 2,000
sesterces on holidays.

The One Hundred Twenty-Foot-Tall Statue

The vestibule of Nero's *Domus Aurea* (Golden House) was sufficiently
capacious to accommodate a 120-foot-tall statue of the emperor. The mansion
also boasted a one-mile-long covered colonnade with a triple row of columns.

The One Hundred Twenty-Three–Day Spectacle

When the emperor Trajan returned from Rome to Dacia (A.D. 107), his arrival was commemorated with a 123-day celebration, which included the killing
of 11,000 animals in mock beast hunts and gladiatorial bouts in which 10,000
men fought.

The One Hundred Thirty-Nine Demes of Attica

Ancient Athens and its environs—collectively referred to as Attica—were
divided into ten administrative units called tribes. The tribes were subdivided
into demes (from the Greek word *demos*, "people"). This organizational structure resulted from the reforms of the lawgiver Clisthenes (ca. 510 B.C.).

The exact number of demes has been disputed, due to inconsistencies in
the ancient evidence. The figure has been placed between 120 and 170; the most
recent research indicates that 139 may be correct. The list of the 139 deme names
presented below has been adapted from David Whitehead's *The Demes of
Attica*.

1. Acharnai	22. Bate
2. Acherdous	23. Besa
3. Agryle, Lower	24. Boutadai
4. Agryle, Upper	25. Cholargos
5. Aigilia	26. Cholleidai
6. Aithalidai	27. Daidalidai
7. Aixone	28. Deiradiotai
8. Alopeke	29. Dekeleia
9. Amphitrope	30. Diomeia
10. Anagyrous	31. Eiresidai
11. Anakaia	32. Eitea (Tribe V: Akamantis)
12. Anaphlystos	33. Eitea (Tribe X: Antiochis)
13. Angele	34. Elaious
14. Ankyle, Lower	35. Eleusis
15. Ankyle, Upper	36. Epiekidai
16. Aphidna	37. Epikephisia
17. Araphen	38. Erchia
18. Atene	39. Erikeia
19. Athmonon	40. Eroiadai (Tribe VIII: Hippothontis)
20. Auridai	41. Eroiadai (Tribe X: Antiochis)
21. Azenia	42. Euonymon

43. Eupyridai
44. Gargettos
45. Hagnous
46. Halai Aixonides
47. Halai Araphenides
48. Halimous
49. Hamaxanteia
50. Hecale
51. Hermos
52. Hestiaia
53. Hippotomadai
54. Hybadai
55. Ikarion
56. Ionidai
57. Iphistiadai
58. Kedoi
59. Keiriadai
60. Kephale
61. Kephisia
62. Kerameis
63. Kettos
64. Kikynna
65. Koile
66. Kollytos
67. Kolonai (Tribe IV: Leontis)
68. Kolonai (Tribe X: Antiochis)
69. Kolonos
70. Konthyle
71. Kopros
72. Korydallos
73. Kothokidai
74. Krioa
75. Kropidai
76. Kydantidai
77. Kydathenaion
78. Kytheros
79. Lakiadai
80. Lamptrai, Lower
81. Lamptrai, Upper
82. Leukonoion
83. Lousia
84. Marathon
85. Melite
86. Myrrhinous
87. Myrrhinoutta
88. Oa
89. Oe
90. Oinoe (Tribe VIII: Hippothontis)
91. Oinoe (Tribe IX: Aiantis)
92. Oion Dekeleikon
93. Oion Kerameikon
94. Otryne
95. Paiania, Lower
96. Paiania, Upper
97. Paionidai
98. Pallene
99. Pambotadai
100. Peiraieus
101. Pelekes
102. Pergase, Lower
103. Pergase, Upper
104. Perithoidai
105. Phaleron
106. Phegaia
107. Phegous
108. Philaidai
109. Phlya
110. Phrearrhioi
111. Phyle
112. Pithos
113. Plotheia
114. Poros
115. Potamos Deiradiotes
116. Potamos, Lower
117. Potamos, Upper
118. Prasiai
119. Probalinthos
120. Prospalta
121. Ptelea
122. Rhamnous
123. Semachidai
124. Skambonidai
125. Sounion
126. Sphettos
127. Steiria
128. Sybridai
129. Sypalettos
130. Teithras
131. Themakos
132. Thorai
133. Thorikos
134. Thria
135. Thymaitadai
136. Trikorynthos
137. Trinemeia
138. Tyrmeidai
139. Xypete

One's demotic affiliation became, in effect, a last name. Hence (for example) the fifth-century statesman Pericles was called "Pericles, of the deme Cholargos," while the admiral Themistocles, whose successful strategies were implemented at the Battle of Salamis (480 B.C.), was known as "Themistocles, of the deme Phrearrhioi."

The One Hundred Forty-Two Books of Livy's History of Rome

The Roman historian Titus Livius (Livy, 59 B.C.–A.D. 17) spent 40 years of his life composing his massive work on the history of Rome from its earliest beginnings down to his own time (Latin title, *Ab Urbe Condita*, *From the City's Founding*). Livy's history was divided into 142 books; of these, Books I–X, XXI–XL, and XLII–XLV are intact, although abridgements of most of the others also survive. The following are synopses of the extant books:

Book I.	Aeneas's actions in Italy; the founding of Rome by Romulus; the deeds of the kings; expulsion of the last king; and the founding of the Roman Republic.
Book II.	Many tales of the early noble Romans, including Horatius Cocles, Mucius Scaevola, Menenius Agrippa, and Coriolanus.
Book III.	Fifth-century B.C. land laws; two censuses taken, the second of which indicated a citizen population of 117, 219; and Cincinnatus's actions as dictator.
Book IV.	Conflicts between patricians and plebeians; creation of the office of censor; and a military campaign against Fidenae.
Book V.	Siege of Veii; the Gauls attacked Rome and were repulsed, thanks in part to the heroics of the dictator Camillus.
Book VI.	Military campaigns against the Volscians, the Aequians, and the Praenestinians; and plebeians gained the right to hold the consulship (367 B.C.?).
Book VII.	A melange of information about laws, trials, creation of new tribes, and magistracies; and the First Samnite War.
Book VIII.	Quarrels with the Latins and battles with the Samnites.
Book IX.	The (disastrous) Battle of the Caudine Forks (321 B.C.); the creation of new tribes and colonies; the construction of the first aqueduct (Aqua Appia) and the first paved road (Via Appia) under the leadership of the censor Appius Claudius Caecus; and battles with various neighboring peoples.
Book X.	Additional tribes and colonies; continuing conflicts with the Samnites; and a census taken in 292 B.C. indicated a citizen population of 262,321.

Book XXI.	The Second Punic War began (219 B.C.); Hannibal's miraculous crossing of the Alps is described; and the Roman defeat at the Trebia River (217).
Book XXII.	Fabius Maximus was appointed dictator; his tactics are described and the Battle of Cannae is related (216 B.C.) and its impact.
Book XXIII.	Hannibal's successes in gaining Campanian allies; and Roman successes in Spain against the Carthaginians stationed there.
Book XXIV.	Syracuse aligned with Carthage; the siege of Syracuse (herein included is a description of Archimedes ingenious devices used in the city's defense); and more Roman successes in Spain.
Book XXV.	Hannibal captured Tarentum; Syracuse fell to the Romans after a two-year siege.
Book XXVI.	Hannibal camped within three miles of Rome, but did not attempt to capture the city; the Roman siege and retaking of Capua; and military events in Spain.
Book XXVII.	Retaking of Tarentum; and Roman successes in Spain continued.
Book XXVIII.	Successful conclusion of Roman operations in Spain.
Book XXIX.	Publius Cornelius Scipio arrived in Africa with the army; a census taken in 204 B.C. indicated a citizen population of 214,000.
Book XXX.	The decisive Battle of Zama (202 B.C.), which brought despair to Carthage and glory to Rome, and especially to Scipio, hereafter styled Africanus.
Book XXXI.	Problems with King Philip of Macedonia are described.
Book XXXII.	The successes of Titus Quinctius Flamininus against King Philip; and the number of annually elected praetors raised to six.
Book XXXIII.	Flamininus defeated Philip at the Battle of Cynoscephalae (197 B.C.); and Hannibal fled from Africa to Syria.
Book XXXIV.	The repealing of the Oppian Law, which regulated expenditures by women on luxurious clothing and jewelry; Flamininus's continuing military campaigns in Greece are described.
Book XXXV.	A conversation between Scipio and Hannibal in Ephesus: Scipio asked him to rank in order the three generals whom he considered the greatest in history. Hannibal's response was one, Alexander the Great; two, Pyrrhus; and three, Hannibal. (By not naming Scipio, Hannibal supposedly paid him the greatest compliment, as a general with skills far beyond those named in the list, and hence not comparable to them.)

Book XXXVI.   Roman military victories against the Seleucid King
                   Antiochus III (reigned 223–187 B.C.).
Book XXXVII.   Successful conclusion of the war against Antiochus.
Book XXXVIII.   Battles in Greece and Asia are described; and the
                   prosecution of Africanus on a charge of embezzle-
                   ment.
Book XXXIX.   Asiatic influences on Roman society; the censorship
                   (184 B.C.) of Cato the Elder.
Book XL.   Macedonian politics; an extraordinary story about a
                   chance discovery of some books written by Numa
                   Pompilius (Rome's second king). Since the books
                   contained antireligious sentiments, they were
                   ordered to be burned.
Book XLII.   War was declared against Perseus of Macedonia; and
                   battles with Perseus are described.
Book XLIII.   Prosecutions of corrupt Roman governors are related;
                   and military activities of Perseus.
Book XLIV.   The consul Lucius Aemilius Paulus moved against
                   Perseus.
Book XLV.   Paulus captured Perseus and returned to Rome in
                   triumph.

The One Hundred Forty-Seven Temples of Rome

Hundreds of temples graced the ancient Roman landscape. The major
ones, as noted by Platner (*Topography and Monuments of Ancient Rome*) include the following 148, with name and date:

1. Aesculapius: 292 B.C.
2. Deified Antoninus: ca. A.D. 193
3. Antoninus and Faustina: A.D. 141
4. Apollo (on the Palatine Hill): 28 B.C.
5. Apollo (near the Porta Carmentalis): 431 B.C.
6. Deified Augustus: ca. A.D. 40
7. Bacchus: uncertain
8. Bellona: 3rd century B.C.
9. Bona Dea Subsaxana: uncertain
10. Camenae: seventh century B.C.
11. Castor (near the Circus of Flaminius: uncertain)
12. Castor (in the forum): 484 B.C.
13. Ceres Liber and Libera: 494 B.C.
14. Deified Claudius: ca. A.D. 75
15. In the Colonna gardens; uncertain
16. Concordia (on the citadel): 217 B.C.
17. Concordia (in the forum): 367 B.C.
18. Concordia (in the portico of Livia): ca.7 B.C.
19. Diana (on the Aventine Hill): sixth century B.C.
20. Diana (near the Circus Flaminius): 179 B.C.

21. Diana (on the Esquiline Hill): uncertain
22. Deus Fidius (on the Quirinal Hill): fifth century B.C.
23. Dis Pater: uncertain
24. Divi (on the Palatine Hill): ca. A.D. 40
25. Elagabalus: ca. A.D. 220
26. Eventus Bonus: late first century B.C.
27. Faunus: 194 B.C.
28. Felicitas (in the forum): late first century B.C.
29. Felicitas (in the theater of Pompey): 55 B.C.
30. Felicitas (in the forum boarium): ca.150 B.C.
31. Fides (on the Capitoline Hill): seventh century B.C.
32. Fides (on the Palatine Hill): uncertain
33. Flora (near the Circus Maximus): ca.240 B.C.
34. Flora (on the Quirinal Hill): uncertain
35. Fors Fortuna: sixth century B.C.
36. Fortuna: sixth century B.C.
37. Fortuna Equestris: 173 B.C.
38. Fortuna Huiusce Diei: 101 B.C.
39. Fortuna Primigenia: 194 B.C.
40. Fortuna Publica: uncertain
41. Fortuna Publica populi Romani: uncertain
42. Fortuna Redux: A.D. 93
43. Fortuna Respiciens: uncertain
44. Fortuna novum: uncertain
45. Gens Flavia: late first century A.D.
46. Hadrian: mid–second century A.D.
47. Hercules: uncertain
48. Hercules Custos: between 221 and 189 B.C.
49. Hercules Fundanus: uncertain
50. Hercules Invictus: uncertain
51. Hercules Musarum: ca.187 B.C.
52. Hercules Pompeianus: uncertain
53. Hercules Sullanus: first century B.C.
54. Honor (near the Porta Collina): uncertain
55. Honor (in the Theater of Pompey): 55 B.C.
56. Honor et Virtus: 234 B.C.
57. Honor et Virtus (built by Marius): second century B.C.
58. Janus (in the forum): seventh century B.C.
59. Janus (in the forum of Nerva): late first century A.D.
60. Janus (near the Theater of Marcellus): restored A.D. 17
61. Isis: uncertain
62. Isis and Serapis: late first century B.C.
63. Isis Patricia: uncertain
64. Deified Julius: ca.30 B.C.
65. Juno: ca.147 B.C.
66. Juno Lucina: 375 B.C.
67. Juno Moneta: 344 B.C.
68. Juno Regina (on the Aventine Hill): 392 B.C.

69. Juno Regina (near the Circus Flaminius): 179 B.C.
70. .Juno Sospita (in the Forum Holitorium): 194 B.C.
71. Juno Sospita (on the Palatine Hill): second century B.C.
72. Jupiter Custos: late first century A.D.
73. Jupiter Dolichenus: uncertain
74. Jupiter Dolichenus (on the Aventine Hill): uncertain
75. Jupiter Dolichenus (on the Esquiline Hill): uncertain
76. Jupiter Feretrius: ca. eighth century B.C.
77. Jupiter Optimus Maximus: sixth century B.C.
78. Jupiter Propugnator: uncertain
79. Jupiter Redux: third century A.D.
80. Jupiter Stator: eighth century B.C.
81. Jupiter Stator (in the Porticus Octavia): 147 B.C.
82. Jupiter Tonans: A.D. 29
83. Jupiter Victor: 293 B.C.
84. Juturna (in the Campus Martius): 78 B.C.
85. Juventas: 193 B.C.
86. Lares: uncertain
87. Lares Permarini: 179 B.C.
88. Libertas: 238 B.C.
89. Luna: sixth century B.C.
90. Luna Noctiluca: second century B.C.
91. Magna Mater: uncertain
92. Magna Mater (on the Palatine Hill): 191 B.C.
93. Marius: third century A.D.
94. Mars (near the Circus Flaminius): 138 B.C.
95. Mars (outside the Porta Capena): ca.388 B.C.
96. Mars Ultor (in the forum of Augustus): 2 B.C.
97. Mars Ultor (on the Capitoline Hill): A.D. 20
98. Mater Matuta: sixth century B.C.
99. Mens: ca.217 B.C.
100. Mercury: 495 B.C.
101. Minerva: uncertain
102. Minerva (on the Aventine Hill): uncertain
103. Minerva (in the forum of Nerva): first century A.D.
104. Minerva Chalcidica: ca.62 B.C.
105. Minerva Medica: uncertain
106. Neptune: uncertain
107. Nymphae: uncertain
108. Ops (on the Capitoline Hill): uncertain
109. Pax: first century A.D.
110. Penates: seventh century B.C.
111. Pietas (near the Circus Flaminius): uncertain
112. Pietas (in the Forum Holitorium): 181 B.C.
113. Portunus: uncertain
114. Quirinus: uncertain; possibly 453 B.C.
115. Romulus: uncertain
116. Deified Romulus: fourth century A.D.

117. Sacra Urbs: first century A.D.
118. Salus: 303 B.C.
119. Salus (near the Circus Maximus): A.D. 65
120. Saturn: 497 B.C.
121. Semo Sancus: fifth century B.C.
122. Serapis: third century A.D.
123. Sol Aurelianus: A.D. 273
124. Sol et Luna: uncertain
125. Sol Elagabali: third century A.D.
126. Spes: third century B.C.
127. Spes (new): uncertain
128. Spes (old): uncertain
129. Summanus: uncertain
130. Tellus: uncertain
131. Tempestas: 259 B.C.
132. Trajan and Plotina: second century A.D.
133. Veiovis (on the Tiber island): uncertain
134. Veiovis (between the two summits of the Capitoline Hill): uncertain
135. Venus (near the Circus Maximus): 295 B.C.
136. Venus Erycina: 181 B.C.
137. Venus Erycina (on the Capitoline Hill): second century B.C.
138. Venus Genetrix: 46 B.C.
139. Venus (in the Gardens of Sallust): first century B.C.
140. Venus and Rome: second century A.D.
141. Venus Victrix: ca.217 B.C.
142. Deified Vespasian: A.D. 80
143. Vesta: seventh century B.C.
144. Victoria (on the Palatine Hill): 294 B.C.
145. Virtus (in the Theater of Pompey): 55 B.C.
146. Volcan: uncertain
147. Vortumnus: ca.264 B.C.

One Hundred Fifty Dogs

Strabo (15.1) recounts a story that a part of India ruled by a provincial chief named Sopithes was noted for the excellence of its dogs, and that Sopithes gave Alexander the Great a gift of 150 of these famous dogs as Alexander was journeying through the area.

The One Hundred Fifty-Mile Run

Prior to the Battle of Marathon (490 B.C.), with the Persians almost literally on their doorsteps, the Athenians appealed to Sparta for help. The appeal was carried to Sparta by a long-distance runner named Phidippides. According to the historian Herodotus (6.106), Phidippides arrived in Sparta the day after he left Athens, hence running the 150 miles in two days. (The Spartans, by the way, refused to send assistance.)

The One Hundred Sixty-Two Books of Cato's De Agricultura

Cato the Elder, although perhaps better known as one of ancient Rome's outstanding statesmen-politicians, never lost touch with his rural roots. His treatise on agriculture (*De Agricultura*) is the earliest extant work in prose Latin, and it is divided into 162 books. Some of the topics that Cato discussed (followed by the book number[s] in parentheses) are listed below:

1. How to buy a farm (I).
2. Building animal pens and farm houses (IV).
3. Hired hands and equipment necessary for cultivating olives (X), vineyards (XI), and wine-pressing rooms (XII, XIII).
4. Fodder for cattle and sheep (XXX, LIV).
5. Methods of planting beans, wheat, and barley (XXXV).
6. Fertilizers (XXXVI) and composting (XXXVII).
7. Olive harvesting (LXIV).
8. Treatments for sick oxen (LXX, LXXI), and for an ox bitten by a snake (CII).
9. A method of controlling caterpillars (XCV).
10. A recipe for wine-making (CXII).
11. A method of preserving grape juice (CXX).
12. Methods of grafting fruit trees (CXXXIII).
13. A harvest sacrifice (CXXXIV).
14. Good places to buy farm clothes, scythes, axes, shovels, carts, jars, water pitchers, plows, yokes, nails, pails, baskets, and rope (CXXXV).
15. Suggested terms and prices for olives on the tree (CXLVI), grapes on the vine (CXLVII), wine in jars (CXLVIII), and leasing of pastureland (CXLIX).
16. Constructing drainage ditches (CLV).
17. The curative powers of cabbage (CLVII).
18. Remedies for constipation (CLVIII).
19. A method for preserving ham (CLXII).

One Hundred Seventy Bathing Establishments

According to Pliny the Elder, early first-century A.D. Rome was graced by some 170 public bathing establishments (although his figure has been called into question).

The One Hundred Ninety-Three Centuries

The citizens of the Roman Republic were divided into 193 voting blocks called centuries; assignment to a particular century was based primarily on the degree of wealth, and also upon military status. The so-called Centuriate Assembly elected many of the important government officials, and also passed laws. The system was not entirely democratic, however; the wealthiest classes, though smaller numerically than the lower-income groups, controlled 98 of the 193 centuries, and thus enjoyed a clear voting majority whenever the Centuriate Assembly convened for elective or legislative purposes.

According to the historian Dionysius of Halicarnassus (4.18), the sixth Roman king, Servius Tullius, ordained the following six divisions for the Centuriate Assembly:

Division number	Number of centuries	Comments
1	98	Infantry, cavalry; the wealthiest and most eminent citizens
2	22	Soldiers of the second rank (in terms of wealth); artisan and craftsmen
3	20	Soldiers of lesser means
4	22	Low income soldiers; trumpeters
5	30	The least wealthy soldiers
6	1	All the poorest citizens, who did not possess the financial means to purchase weapons or armor, and hence did not serve in the army

Two Hundred Lines of Poetry

According to Horace (*Satires* 1.4), the poet Lucilius could churn out 200 lines of poetry in an hour *stans pede in uno*, "standing on one foot," that is, without taking a break or changing positions. Horace (*Satires* 1.10) also refers to a certain poet named Cassius who could write 200 lines before dinner, and another 200 afterward. (A popular story making the rounds at the time had it that Cassius's poetry was so bad that his manuscript pages were used for fuel for his funeral pyre.)

The Two Hundred–Plus Athenian Jurors

Modern juries usually consist of "twelve good men (or women) and true," but ancient Athenian juries were much larger, consisting of 200 or more citizens; the most common number was 501. Jurors were chosen by lot.

Sometimes juries numbered in the thousands. According to Plutarch (*Pericles* 32), 1,500 jurors were called to sit in judgment at the fifth-century (B.C.) trial of Pericles' courtesan, Aspasia. There was a pool of 6,000 potential jurymen (600 from each of the ten tribes); they were paid two (later three) obols per day for their services, a small sum, but one that elderly jurors in particular depended upon to supplement their savings.

Two Hundred Seven Fables Attributed to Aesop

The most famous fabulist of the ancient world, Aesop, may not have been a real person, although he is mentioned by a number of credible ancient writers, including Aristophanes, Herodotus, Plato, and Aristotle. He might have been a sixth-century B.C. slave, but, in any event, his tales were not committed to paper until much later—in the second century A.D. by the Roman poet Valerius Babrius.

Another noted fabulist was Gaius Julius Phaedrus (ca.15 B.C.–A.D. 50), to whom 126 fables are credited.

The Two Hundred Eight Letters of Fronto

Marcus Cornelius Fronto (ca. A.D. 100–166), regarded in antiquity as one of the preeminent orators in Roman history, is known today primarily through his correspondence. Many of his extant letters are to or from Marcus Aurelius, both prior to and during the latter's reign as emperor. His 208 letters may be itemized as follows:

To Marcus Aurelius:	65
From Marcus Aurelius:	78
To Lucius Verus:	8
From Lucius Verus:	6
To Antoninus Pius:	6
From Antoninus Pius:	2
To various friends:	40
From friends:	1
To the mother of Marcus Aurelius:	2
Total:	208

The Three Hundred Achaeans and Polybius

After the battle of Pydna (167 B.C., in the Third Macedonian War), 1,000 influential Achaeans were deported from Greece to Rome and detained there for the next 17 years. At the end of the 17 years the 300 who were still alive were permitted to return home, by a special decree of the Roman Senate. Among the 300 survivors was the noted historian Polybius, at whose urging the decree was passed.

The Three Hundred–Member Roman Senate

The Roman Senate was traditionally composed of 300 members, although that number fluctuated from time to time. The dictator Sulla raised the number to 600, and Julius Caesar to 900. Later, Augustus reduced it once more to 600.

Three Hundred Roman Deaths in Civil Violence

The rioting between the supporters and opponents of Tiberius Sempronius Gracchus (in 133 B.C.) resulted in 300 deaths, including Gracchus himself. It was, says Plutarch, the first time in the history of the Roman Republic that a civil dispute had led to bloodshed and death.

The Three Hundred Romans and Gaius Mucius

In 508 B.C., when Rome was suffering from the effects of an Etruscan blockade, a young nobleman by the name of Gaius Mucius volunteered to try to penetrate the Etruscan defenses and kill the king. He succeeded in slipping behind the enemy's line, but the assassination attempt failed. The guards seized Mucius and brought him before the king, who asked of him some pointed questions about the daring attack. Mucius defiantly replied that there were 300 young men in Rome, who would singly, as he had, embark upon a similar mission, and that sooner or later one of them would inevitably succeed. As a further sign of his bravery, he thrust his right hand into a sacrificial fire that was burning nearby.

The astonished king released Mucius, who was thereafter known as *Scaevola*, the "left handed man."

The Three Hundred Spartans and Leonidas

In 480 B.C. the Persian king Xerxes embarked upon his fabled march from Asia to Greece, with the intention of crushing the Greeks, and in particular Athens. His route took him through a narrow mountain pass called Thermopylae, about 100 miles northwest of Athens. Although the Persian army was massive (over one million men, according to some accounts), the Greeks sent only a small force, under the command of the Spartan king Leonidas, to guard the pass; their nationalities and numbers were as follows (according to Herodotus [7.202-203]):

Number of soldiers	From
300	Sparta
500	Tegea
500	Mantinea
120	Orchomenus, in Arcadia
1,000	The rest of Arcadia
400	Corinth
200	Phlius
80	Mycenae
700	Thespiae
400	Thebes
Exact number not stated	Opus
1,000	Phocis

Total: 5,200

When Xerxes' scouts informed him of the small size of the Greek force defending Thermopylae, he was incredulous; for four days he delayed, expecting the Greeks to retreat. Finally, on the fifth day he attacked, but without success. Once more, on the following day Xerxes' army advanced, but with similarly disappointing results. At that point, however, a local man approached the increasingly frustrated Xerxes with information about a narrow path around the pass that, if taken, would enable the Persians to surround and obliterate the Greeks. Xerxes was overjoyed; and he gave the marching orders immediately.

Meanwhile, Leonidas and the Greeks knew that indefinite resistance was impossible, and when their lookouts observed the flanking movement of the Persian army, their worst fears were confirmed. Many of the Greek contingents now deserted; Leonidas dismissed the rest, leaving only the 300 Spartans to face the advancing Persians. All 300 fell in the battle that ensued. Herodotus claims to have memorized the 300 names, although he does not list them in his account of this battle. Only two Spartans survived; one was a man named Pantites, who was carrying a message to Thessaly when the fighting took place. He subsequently committed suicide.

The stand made by Leonidas and the 300 Spartans at Thermopylae was long noted and remembered in the annals of Greek literature. A famous epitaph was placed at the site:

> Go tell the Spartans, you who read,
> We obeyed the orders, and now are dead.

The other Spartan survivor was a certain Aristodemus. Leonidas had dismissed him from the camp prior to the battle, due to illness (ophthalmia, according to Herodotus [7.229]). Because of these circumstances, his countrymen branded him a coward. He incurred their wrath, not for missing the battle but rather because his traveling companion and fellow Spartan soldier Eurytus (who was suffering from the same ailment) returned immediately to Thermopylae when he learned that the Persians were about to attack. Aristodemus could have done likewise, but his courage failed him.

Three Hundred Sixty Bronze Statues for Demetrius

For ten years (318–308 B.C.) Demetrius of Phalerum ruled Athens as a sort of military governor. A capable administrator and a skilled orator, he enjoyed such repute in Athens that some 360 bronze statues were fashioned of him, most of them depicting him riding a horse or driving a chariot. Diogenes Laertius (5.75) states that these 360 statues were fabricated in less than 300 days.

The Three Hundred Sixty Votes Against Socrates

In 399 B.C. one of the most famous trials in history took place when the philosopher Socrates was prosecuted for impiety and for corrupting the youth of Athens. (Socrates' stirring defense is recorded and preserved in Plato's *Apology*.) In the end, however, his arguments were not sufficiently persuasive; 360 jurors voted to condemn him to death, with only 141 dissenting. He committed suicide by drinking hemlock. (On the size of the Athenian juries, see The Two Hundred–Plus Athenian Jurors.)

Socrates constantly maintained that he had done nothing deserving of punishment; however, he did offer to pay a fine of 100 drachmas, a sum estimated to have been about one-fifth of his net worth. Several of his friends—

Plato, Crito, Critobulus, and Apollodorus—offered to provide 3,000 drachmas for him from their own resources, but the jury did not consent to these arrangements, instead insisting upon the death penalty.

The Three Hundred Sixty-Eight Letters in Pliny's Correspondence

Gaius Plinius Caecilius Secundus (Pliny the Younger, ca. A.D. 62–114) enjoyed a distinguished career as an orator, statesman, diplomat, and litterateur. Still extant are 247 letters, divided into nine books, that he wrote to friends. An additional 121 letters also remain, written to and received from the emperor Trajan while Pliny was serving as his representative in the province of Pontus-Bithynia. One speech also survives, the *Panegyricus* in honor of Trajan.

Each of the nine books contains between 20 and 40 letters, as follows:

Book I:	24 letters	Book VI:	34 letters
Book II:	20 letters	Book VII:	33 letters
Book III:	21 letters	Book VIII:	24 letters
Book IV:	30 letters	Book IX:	40 letters
Book V:	21 letters	Total:	247 letters

The following is a list of summaries of the content of one letter from each of the nine books:

Book I, number 6. To the historian Cornelius Tacitus, in which Pliny explains why he took writing materials with him on a hunting trip.

Book II, number 18. To Junius Mauricus, in which Pliny promises to seek a tutor for Junius's nephews.

Book III, number 5. To Baebius Macer, in which Pliny describes his uncle's writings and mode of working.

Book IV, number 8. To Maturus Arrianus, on Pliny's appointment as an augur.

Book V, number 3. To Titius Aristo, in which Pliny explains why he dabbles in writing poetry, and why public readings (of one's literary works) can be useful.

Book VI, number 20. To Cornelius Tacitus, on the eruption of Mount Vesuvius.

Book VII, number 9. Advice to Fuscus Salinator on ways to improve his writing ability.

Book VIII, number 17. To Caecilius Macrinus on the damage done by floods of the Tiber and Anio rivers.

Book IX, number 26. To Lupercus, on the art and practice of oratory.

The correspondence with Trajan often involves a request of some sort made by Pliny on behalf of the provincials, usually for money to initiate or continue some public works project. In many cases he requests that Trajan send engineers, architects, or surveyors from Rome to assist in these endeavors. In some letters he asks for official (if after-the-fact) approval for some course of action that he had taken. The following are some examples:

Letter number/Pliny's request	Trajan's response or action
5. A request for Roman citizenship for his therapist Arpocras, and also for two freedwomen, Hedia and Antonia Maximilla.	Granted.
19. A request that soldiers be employed as prison guards.	Rejected; soldiers should not be called away from their official duties
23. A request that the public bath at the town of Prusa be renovated.	Granted, as long as this could be done without levying additional taxes.
33. A request to form a fire brigade from among the provincials in Nicomedia.	Rejected; such an association could rapidly evolve into a political or conspiratorial faction.
37. The citizens of Nicomedia had wasted over 3.5 million sesterces on two unfinished aqueducts; Pliny requested the services of an engineer from Rome to do a feasibility study on completing an aqueduct.	The request for an engineer was ignored; a stern injunction was directed at Pliny to discover why so much money had been squandered on the first two aqueducts.
75. A bequest that authorized Pliny either to construct public buildings in Trajan's name, or establish quinquennial games in Trajan's honor; Pliny wrote to learn of the emperor's wishes.	Trajan directed Pliny to use his own judgment in this matter.
90. A request that a survey be done for the town of Sinope to determine the feasibility of constructing an aqueduct.	Granted, as long as the town bore all expenses.

Three Hundred Seventy Votes for Peace

The year 50 B.C. was a tumultuous one in ancient Rome. Julius Caesar was bearing down on the city with his legions; and it looked as if civil war were imminent. At the behest of a tribune named Gaius Scribonius Curio the Roman Senate voted on a compromise proposal aimed at averting war: if Caesar would disarm, then his primary foe — Pompey the Great — would likewise. The measure passed by the overwhelming count of 370 to 22. However, the vote was disregarded, Caesar crossed the Rubicon River with his army intact, and war broke out soon thereafter.

The Four Hundred

The Four Hundred was a special council organized in Athens in spring 411 B.C. Several years earlier the Athenians had suffered a disastrous and unexpected defeat in Sicily, and the prime objectives of the Four Hundred were to revive morale after the calamity and to ameliorate a deteriorating military situation. The Four Hundred's short-lived reign ended with its overthrow in September 411.

Four Hundred Captured Cities

Cato the Elder served as the governor of farther Spain in the year 195 B.C. His military conquests proved so overwhelming that he later boasted that he captured more cities (400) than the number of days he remained in Spain.

Four Hundred Ships

According to Strabo (9.1), Athens's harbor at Piraeus could accommodate 400 ships, the minimum number required for Athenian expeditions and military forays.

Four Hundred Slaves, and Other Statistics About the Rebellion of 135 B.C.

A slave named Eunus led a major servile uprising in Sicily in 135 B.C. Eunus (whose name means "well-minded") was something of a mystical figure: magician, fortune-teller, and soothsayer. When the oppressed slaves began to organize their rebellion, they consulted Eunus about the question of divine approbation; when he informed them of the gods' support, they made him their leader. Some statistics pertaining to this revolt, from Diodorus of Sicily (34.10ff.) are as follows:

400. The number of slaves involved at the outset.

6,000. The number of slaves involved after three days.

10,000. The number of slaves involved after 30 days.

5,000. The number of slaves serving under Cleon, who had organized a revolt in another part of Sicily.

8,000. The number of soldiers under the command of Lucius Plautius Hypsaeus, the Roman general who was sent to Sicily to deal with the situation.

20,000. The number of slaves involved after the merger with Cleon's contingent, plus additional recruits.

200,000. Eunus's ultimate slave/troop strength.

Eunus's rebellion produced a ripple effect in other parts of the Mediterranean world, as slaves in the following locales also revolted:

Number of slaves	Location
150	Rome
1,000 +	Attica
Unstated	Delos
Unstated	"Many other places"

1,000. The size of Eunus's personal bodyguard.

4. The number of attendants with Eunus when he was captured (in 132 B.C.) by the Romans. The 4 attendants were a cook, a baker, a masseuse, and a jester.

The rebellion died out soon after Eunus's demise in 132.

Four Hundred Slaves Executed

In A.D. 61 the City Prefect, Pedanius Secundus, was murdered by one of his slaves, either because (as Tacitus [*Annals* 14.42] relates) Secundus had reneged on a promise of freedom for the slave, or because he and the slave were two of the principals in a love triangle. In any event, tradition demanded that all 400 of Secundus's slaves be executed. After some debate in the Roman Senate about the propriety of killing so many innocent people, the order was given and carried out.

The Four Hundred Forty-Five–Day Year

Prior to Julius Caesar's reform of the Roman calendar, the year consisted of only 355 days; the missing 11 days were accounted for by the insertion of an intercalary "month" between February 23 and February 24.

However, those responsible for the intercalating often did their jobs so ineptly that by Caesar's time the solar year was hopelessly out of synchronization with the civic year. So Caesar's first move was to add three months to the year 46 B.C. (two new months, plus the intercalary month), thus resulting in a 445-day year—the *ultimus annus confusionis* ("last year of confusion," as Macrobius [1.14] put it). He then reformed the calendar by basing it on the solar (not lunar) year, with 365 days and a quadrennial leap year.

The Council of Five Hundred

The Council of 500, sometimes called the *Boule*, was a governmental body in ancient Athens. Its chief functions were the supervision of state finances; the care of public buildings and archives; and the preparation of the agenda for the Athenian assembly. It was formed by selecting (by lot) 50 representatives from each of the ten tribes.

A Five Hundred–Drachma Sophist's Fee

Greek philosophers and other itinerant teachers—called sophists—often found themselves embroiled in controversy over the fees that they charged for their services. (It was just such a controversy that spelled trouble for Socrates, although he claimed never to have accepted any payments.) Socrates' contemporary, the sophist Evenus of Paros, was said to have demanded 500 drachmas for his pedagogical activities, whereas another sophist, Protagoras (born ca.485 B.C.) commanded the astronomical fee of 10,000 drachmas.

Five Hundred Jugera

The second century B.C. was fraught with social and economic problems for the ancient Romans. Among other things, the agricultural lands were increasingly falling under the ownership and dominance of wealthy absentee landlords, thus forcing many small farmers out of business. In 133 B.C. the reformer-tribune Tiberius Sempronius Gracchus attempted to remedy the situation by proposing that a 144-year-old law limiting land ownership to 500 jugera (about 310 acres) be enforced. Although his proposal was eventually implemented, Gracchus was slain in a riot before he could see the fruit of his labors.

Manius Curius Dentatus, a third-century B.C. Roman general, noted especially for his victory over King Pyrrhus in 275, gained additional fame for his statement that seven acres of land should be sufficient for a virtuous citizen.

Rebirth in the Five Hundredth Year

According to Herodotus and Tacitus, the mythological phoenix, a crimson, eagle-like bird, was said to nest and die every 500 years; from the next a new phoenix appeared, to regenerate the species.

The OVER
FIVE HUNDREDS

The Eight Hundred Sixty-Four Letters
to and from Cicero

Marcus Tullius Cicero was a prolific epistler; over 850 of the letters that he wrote — or which were written to him — have survived to the present time. They may be categorized thus: letters to and from various friends and family members (*Ad Familiares*); letters to his brother Quintus (*Ad Quintum Fratrem*); letters to Marcus Brutus (*Ad Marcum Brutum*); and letters to his close friend Atticus (*Ad Atticum*).

It is probable that Cicero had no intention of publishing his correspondence. However, his secretary, Tiro, preserved and organized his letters, and it is primarily due to him that Cicero's letters — many quite personal in content — are extant. In the aggregate they provide a unique glimpse into the private thoughts of a very public man in Rome's chaotic first century B.C. (Included in the letters to friends and family members are letters to a great many people, including his wife, Terentia, his daughter Tullia, and some of the notable political figures of the day, such as Gnaeus Pompeius [Pompey], Julius Caesar, Marcus Caelius Rufus, Marcus Porcius Cato [Cato the Younger], and Servius Sulpicius Rufus.) Cicero's letters:

To friends (particularly Atticus) and family members:	774
From friends:	90
Total	864

One Thousand and Thirty Thousand as Arbitrary Figures

Occasionally, and for reasons that are unknown, the ancient Greek and Romans chose the figures 1,000 and 30,000 as estimates, to represent large numbers in cases and situations where more numerical specificity was inappropriate or impossible. These figures are used frequently when reporting sums of money or numbers of soldiers. The following are some examples:

1,000

1. The learned Roman Marcus Terentius Varro (116–27 B.C.) noted that the Greeks sent 1,000 ships to Troy for the Trojan War.

2. In one of his poems addressed to his girlfriend Lesbia, the poet Catullus asked for 1,000 kisses, and then 100 more.

3. One of the characters in Petronius's novel *Satyricon* complained about a government official (an aedile) who raked in 1,000 gold coins for doing little or no work.

4. The poet Horace advised his friend Numicius to revel in the fact that 1,000 eyes were upon him when he gave a speech.

5. Strabo noted that some historians credited Iberia (in Spain) with 1,000 cities, but he was skeptical of that estimate, stating that the region was not large enough to accommodate that many cities.

6. Horace claimed that a second-rate poet could churn out 1,000 lines of poetry per day. He also satirized the parsimonious person who would drink vinegar even though he owned 1,000 bottles of fine wine.

7. Ovid recounted the story of 306 members of the Fabian family who defended a fort against thousands of attackers from the city of Veii (ca.477 B.C.). He also tells a story about the woodland god Silenus, who attempted to extract honey from a beehive and received 1,000 stings on his bald head.

8. The biographer Suetonius reported that the emperor Nero never set out on a journey with fewer than 1,000 carriages in his entourage.

9. Juvenal complained in his sixteenth *Satire* that 1,000 delays face a plaintiff seeking to prosecute thieves or deadbeats.

10. In his fifth *Satire* Persius referred to the diversity of the human race: *mille hominum species*, 1,000 kinds of people.

11. According to Diodorus Siculus, the Romans won the decisive battle of the First Punic War (the Battle of the Aegates Islands, 241 B.C.) in part thanks to the 1,000 ships that they brought to bear.

12. Gaius Acilius, a Roman historian (of the second century B.C.) quoted by Dionysius of Halicarnassus, wrote that it once cost 1,000 talents to clean the sewers of Rome, when regular maintenance had been neglected for a period of time.

13. After the fall of Troy, Ajax (son of Oileus) of Locri raped Cassandra, after dragging her from the temple of Athena, where she had sought refuge. For the next 1,000 years the Locrians were required to send two young women annually to Troy, to serve as slaves in the temple, as an atonement for this crime.

14. Columella stated that oxen could be trained to walk 1,000 paces in a calm and orderly fashion.

15. According to Varro, the price for a pair of breeding pigeons was 1,000 sesterces.

16. One of Aulus Gellius's essays was concerned with the proper use

of the Latin word for 1,000, *mille*, with examples drawn from the works of
Cicero, Lucilius, Varro, Cato the Elder, and Quintus Claudius Quadrigarius.

30,000

1. In the opening speech of Aristophanes' play *Acharnians*, the protagonist, Dicaeopolis, refers to 30,000 drachmas that the demagogue Cleon was compelled to surrender to the Athenian treasury. Although the circumstances surrounding this incident are unclear, it appears that Cleon had accepted a bribe in that amount, which the authorities discovered and required him to forfeit.

2. When Alexander the Great sacked Thebes in 336 B.C., he sold 30,000 citizens into slavery. Some sources suggest that Alexander's troop strength in 334 B.C., when he crossed the Hellespont to fight the Persians, was 30,000.

3. In 330 B.C. Alexander stopped at the Asian city of Hyrcania, where he arranged for 30,000 Hyrcanian youth to be taught Greek and to be schooled in Macedonian military strategy.

4. The number of men who worked on the project to drain Lake Fucinus in Italy (A.D. 41–54) was said to have been 30,000.

5. The emperor Augustus stated in his autobiography that he returned 30,000 runaway slaves to their masters during the civil war of 44–31 B.C.

6. The number of Roman soldiers killed at the Battle of the Trebia River (217 B.C.), and the number of Roman soldiers who fought in the Second Macedonian War (200–197 B.C.), was reportedly 30,000.

7. Julius Caesar habitually exaggerated the number of enemy soldiers his men could expect to face in battle. On one such occasion, prior to a battle with King Juba of Numidia, he told his troops that the king had at his disposal 30,000 cavalrymen.

8. According to Strabo, the people of Tarentum (in southern Italy) were at one time so powerful that they could field an army of 30,000 soldiers.

9. Strabo was also the source for a report that the Roman general Quintus Fabius Maximus Aemilianus (second century B.C.) defeated 200,000 Celts with a force of Romans numbering less than 30,000.

10. In 87 B.C. the Roman general Lucius Cornelius Sulla landed in Greece with an army numbering 30,000 men.

11. Plutarch related that the troop strength of Mithridates VI, king of Pontus, was 30,000 in 63 B.C. when Pompey moved against him.

12. Diodorus Siculus stated that the Amazons, under the leadership of a certain Myrina, assembled a force of 30,000 infantry in preparation for a war against the Atlantians.

13. Diodorus also noted that King Eumenes of Pergamum (second century B.C.) once promised the people of Rhodes a gift of 30,000 measures of wheat.

The Face That Launched 1,186 Ships

When Helen, Queen of Sparta, was kidnapped by the Trojan prince Paris and taken to Troy, the Greeks amassed a huge fleet to sail to Troy to retrieve her. Helen's beauty gave rise to the popular phrase "the face that launched a thousand ships," the rounded-off number of vessels that set out for Troy.

In Book II of the *Iliad*, Homer provides a lengthy enumeration of the fleet; this section of Book II is generally known as the "Catalogue of Ships." Although there has been (and continues to be) a good deal of scholarly debate about the authenticity of this portion of Book II, it does provide many details about the nature, composition, and size of the fleet. The following is a list of the points of origin of the ships, the leaders, and the number of ships contributed:

Point of origin	Leader(s)	Number of ships
Boeotia	Leitus, Penelaus et al.	50
Orchomenus	Ascalaphus, Ialmenus	30
Phocis	Schedius, Epistrophus	40
Locris	Ajax (son of Oileus)	40
Euboea	Elephenor	40
Athens	Menestheus	50
Salamis	Ajax (son of Telamon)	12
Argos and neighboring towns	Diomedes, Sthenelus, Euryalus	80
Mycenae and neighboring towns	Agamemnon	100
Sparta and neighboring towns	Menelaus	60
Pylos and neighboring towns	Nestor	90
Arcadia	Agapenor	60
Western Peloponnesus	Thalpius, Amphimachus, Diores, Polyxinus	40
Western islands	Meges	40
Ithaca and other islands	Odysseus	12
Aetolia	Thoas	40
Crete	Idomeneus	80
Rhodes	Tlepolemus	9
Syme	Nireus	3
Cos and neighboring islands	Phidippus, Antiphus	30
Phthia and northern Greece	Achilles	50
Phylace and neighboring towns	Podarces	40
Pherae and neighboring towns	Eumelus	11
Methone and neighboring towns	Medon (substituting for Philoctetes	7
Tricce and neighboring towns	Podalirius, Machaon	30

Point of origin	Leader(s)	Number of ships
Ormenion and neighboring towns	Eurypylus	40
Argissa and neighboring towns	Polypoetes, Leonteus	40
Cyphus and neighboring towns	Gouneus	22
Magnesia	Prothous	40
Total		1,186

One Thousand Two Hundred Wagons and Other Statistics from Aemilius's Triumphal Procession

When Lucius Aemilius Paulus Macedonicus defeated the Macedonian commander Perseus in 168 B.C., he commemorated the victory with a magnificent three-day celebration in Rome, featuring the triumphal processions on each day. Diodorus Siculus (31. 10–12) provides the particulars.

First day:

> 1,200 wagons filled with animal-hide shields
> 1,200 wagons filled with bronze shields
> 300 wagons filled with lances, spears, and bows
> "Many other wagons," also filled with weapons
> 800 suits of armor displayed on poles.

Second day:

> Coins whose total value was set at 1,000 talents
> 2,200 talents' worth of silver
> "Many drinking cups"
> 500 wagons filled with various statues (both of gods and mortals)
> "Very many" gold shields and inscriptions.

Third day:

> 120 white oxen
> 220 conveyances filled with (an unspecified number of) talents of gold
> A bowl worth 10 talents, and adorned with jewels
> Various other items made of gold, with a total value of ten talents
> 2,000 elephants' tusks, each five feet long
> An ivory chariot, decorated with gold and jewels
> A horse in golden battle garb, with bejeweled cheek pieces
> A golden couch covered with floral tapestries
> A golden litter with red curtains
> The defeated Perseus, with his three children and 250 of his officers
> 400 wreaths, the gifts of various cities and rulers
> The triumphant Aemilius, riding in an ivory chariot.

A little over 100 years later (in 62 B.C.), Pompey the Great celebrated a triumph upon his return to Rome from the east; according to the historian Appian (*Mithridatic Wars* 116, 117), this celebration was unprecedented in its magnificence. The festivities were spread over two days; the representatives of many nations participated, including those from Armenia, Cappadocia, Cilicia, Pontus, and Syria. A display (in the harbor at Ostia) of 700 undamaged ships was also featured.

In the triumphal procession were the following:

> Carriages bearing golden ornaments and household furnishings belonging to the defeated Mithridates, as well as a 12-feet-tall, solid gold statue of Mithridates
> 75.1 million drachmas' worth of silver coins
> Wagons carrying innumerable weapons and prows of ships, as well as a multitude of prisoners
> 324 captured generals and family members of the various rulers whose armies Pompey defeated, including five of Mithridates' sons
> A plaque with the following statistics: 800 ships captured, 29 cities founded, including 8 in Cappadocia, 20 in Cilicia and Syria, and 1 in Palestine
> 6 kings defeated:

1. Tigranes of Armenia	4. Darius of Persia
2. Artoces of Iberia	5. Aretas of Nabataea
3. Oroezes of Albania	6. Antiochus of Commagene

Riding in a bejeweled chariot came Pompey himself, wearing what was purported to be a cloak that once belonged to Alexander the Great.

Xerxes' One Thousand Two Hundred Seven Triremes

Herodotus (7.89–95) reports that when the Persian king Xerxes invaded Greece in 481 B.C., he brought with him a fleet of 1,207 warships, composed of the following contingents:

Contingent	Number of ships contributed
1. Phoenicians, Syrians of Palestine	300
2. Egyptians	200
3. Cyprians	150
4. Cilicians	100
5. Pamphylians	30
6. Lycians	50
7. Asiatic Dorians	30
8. Carians	70
9. Ionians	100
10. Aegean islanders	17
11. Aeolians	60
12. Pontus	100
Total	1,207

When transport ships and other, smaller craft are considered, the overall armada totaled 3,000.

The One Thousand Four Hundred Sixty-Two Chariot Racing Wins of Appuleius Diocles

The career of the second-century A.D. Roman charioteer Appuleius Diocles is chronicled in the form of a lengthy inscription that provides the details of his 24 years of competition on the track. Among the statistics are the following: 4,257 races; 1,462 victories; and a staggering prize money total of over 35 million sesterces—a sizable fortune.

Four Thousand One Hundred Sixteen Slaves

The will (dated 8 B.C.) of a certain Gaius Caecilius Isidorus stated the following information about his net worth:

Number of pairs of oxen: 3,600
Number of slaves: 4,116
Number of others kinds of stockyard animals: 257,000
Cash: 60 million sesterces

Additionally, the will specified that 1 million sesterces be spent on Caecilius's funeral.

Five Thousand Deaths for a Triumph

Victorious Roman generals could be granted the honor of a triumphal procession in Rome to celebrate their military success, but only if at least 5,000 enemy soldiers had been killed, according to the provisions of a law reputedly passed in 143 B.C.

The Five Thousand–Man Legion

The basic organizational unit of the Roman army was the legion. While its numbers naturally fluctuated, the preferred troop strength for a legion was 5,000.

The Five Thousand–Sesterce Fish

A four and one-half pound mullet once came into the possession of the emperor Tiberius. He quietly ordered it to be sold at auction, with a wry prediction that one of the two leading gastronomists of the time, Publius Octavius or Marcus Gavius Apicius, would buy it. His prophecy was fulfilled, when the two of them bid for it. Octavius offered the higher sum, an astronomical 5,000 sesterces, and, ironically, presented the 5,000-sesterce fish to Tiberius as a gift.

Six Thousand Ostracism Votes

For a time in fifth century Athens any politician thought to be too ambitious or a potential threat to the state could be exiled for ten years by a vote of the Athenian Assembly, as long as his name was entered at least 6,000 times. (If fewer than 6,000 votes were cast, the entire proceeding was declared invalid.)

The voters scratched the name of the person whom they wished exiled on broken pieces of pottery (*ostraca*); hence, the term "ostracism."

Seven Thousand One Hundred Talents

Ancient Rome's wealthiest individual was probably Marcus Licinius Crassus (112–53 B.C.). He amassed much of his wealth through his machinations as a sort of slum landlord. His net worth at the beginning of his public career amounted to 300 talents; at the end he had increased that to 7,100 talents, a huge sum, making him easily the equivalent of a billionaire by modern standards.

The Ten Thousand

In 401 B.C. the Persian king Cyrus recruited an army of 10,000 mercenary Greeks to do battle with the forces of his estranged brother, Artaxerxes. Their arduous march from Sardis to Babylonia (site of the Battle of Cunaxa, where Cyrus died) and the equally arduous retreat of the Ten Thousand, is recounted in Xenophon's *Anabasis*.

Sixty-eight years later Alexander the Great regaled his troops with the tale of the Ten Thousand in order to embolden them for their upcoming battle with the Persians at Issus.

Ten Thousand Picked Men

In response to an impassioned plea by Vercingetorix, the various Gallic tribes offered 10,000 picked men to assist in the defense of Avaricum against Caesar's onslaught in 52 B.C.

Ten Thousand versus One Hundred Thirty Thousand

Strabo (6.1) recounts a story about a 10,000-man army from the Italian town of Rhegium defeating a force of 130,000 from its near neighbor, Croton (Battle of Sagra, fifth century B.C.). This disaster reputedly hastened the downfall of Croton.

There is also a tradition — mentioned by Cicero (*De Natura Deorum* 2.2) — that the news of this battle reached Olympia (where the quadrennial games were under way) on the very day that it happened.

Eleven Thousand Dangerous Beasts, and Other Enumerations of Animals

The ancient Romans had a love of the exotic, including an interest in viewing wild animals, both on display and (more grimly) as victims in mock beast hunts in the amphitheaters. Many ancient authors provide statistics on the kinds and numbers of animals displayed or hunted at various times in the showplaces of Italy. Some of these statistics are as follows:

11,000. The emperor Trajan (reigned A.D. 98–117) celebrated his victory over the Dacians with the killing of 11,000 wild beasts.

5,000. According to the biographer Suetonius, 5,000 wild beasts were displayed by the emperor Titus as part of the celebration to commemorate the opening of the Coliseum in A.D. 80. The historian Dio Cassius puts the number at 9,000.

600. In his dedication of the Theater of Marcellus in 13 B.C. the emperor Augustus caused 600 wild animals from Africa to be killed as part of the dedication ceremony.

500. In 55 B.C. the consul Pompey sponsored games, including mock beast hunts, in which 500 lions and 18 elephants were killed.

400. In A.D. 37 the emperor Caligula sponsored games that resulted in the deaths of 400 bears and 400 various other wild beasts.

300 (etc.). In the third century A.D. the future emperor Gordian exhibited in Rome 300 ostriches, 200 ibexes, 200 gazelles, 200 stags, 150 boars, 100 bulls, 100 bears, 100 wild sheep, 30 wild horses, 30 wild donkeys, and 10 elk.

260. The dedication of the Temple of Mars by Augustus in 2 B.C. was celebrated in part with the slaying of 260 lions and 36 crocodiles.

Fifteen Thousand (Twice) Stolen Talents

In a temple in the Gallic town of Tolosa there was said to be stored 15,000 ill-gotten talents—plunder from Apollo's temple at Delphi. The Roman general Quintus Servilius Caepio sacked Tolosa in 106 B.C. and removed the 15,000 talents. The treasure mysteriously disappeared en route to Rome, and although Caepio was widely suspected of having stolen it, no proof of his guilt or innocence could be uncovered.

The geographer Strabo (4.1) states that some Tolosans, and others living in the area, threw their gold and silver into nearby lakes, to prevent the advancing Romans from coming into possession of these valuables.

Fifteen Thousand-Plus Seating Capacities

Estimated seating capacities for four of the ancient world's most famous entertainment centers were as follows:

The Theater of Dionysus in Athens: 15,000
The Theater at Ephesus: 25,000

The Coliseum in Rome: 45,000
The Circus Maximus in Rome: 250,000

Fifteen Thousand Six Hundred Ninety-Three Lines: The Lengths (in Lines) of Some Notable Greek and Roman Plays and Poems

Author	Title	Length
Homer	*Iliad*	15,693
Silius Italicus	*Punica*	12,202
Homer	*Odyssey*	12,110
Ovid	*Metamorphoses*	11,986
Vergil	*Aeneid*	9,896
Lucretius	*On the Nature of Things*	7,415
Aristophanes	*Birds*	1,765
Sophocles	*Oedipus Rex*	1,530
Euripides	*Medea*	1,419
Aeschylus	*Persians*	1,076
Pindar	*Olympian XIII*	115
Horace	*Carmen Saeculare*	76

Twenty Thousand Gladiators

According to Pliny the Elder, the emperor Caligula owned a training school with a complement of 20,000 gladiators. Only two of these 20,000 did not blink when suddenly confronted by some danger, a sign that these two would be unconquerable.

Twenty Thousand Residents, and Other Statistics on Pompeii

In the summer of A.D. 79 one of history's most famous volcanic eruptions occurred, when Mount Vesuvius exploded, burying the city of Pompeii (and nearby Herculaneum) under tons of ash, stone, and lava. Not rediscovered until the eighteenth century, Pompeii has proven to be an archaeologist's dream, yielding a plethora of artifacts and inscriptions. Some statistics on Pompeii are as follows:

1. 20,000 residents, 2,000 casualties. The extent of the city—some 160 acres—and its general plan suggest that there may have been between 15,000 and 20,000 residents there in the year 79. Archaeologists speculate that perhaps 2,000 were killed by the volcano; but most fatalities probably resulted from a refusal to leave town, although there was adequate warning and ample time to do so. Those who remained apparently believed either that the prospects for survival were better at home than in flight, or that they had to defend their property against looting. In a building that served as a laundry, archaeologists found a skeleton and with it a cache of 107 gold and silver coins. And in a villa just outside Pompeii they discovered a silver cup decorated with four embossed skeletons and an

inscription with the (ironic, as it turned out) advice to "live for today, for one does not know what the future might bring."

Among Vesuvius's victims was the noted natural scientist Pliny the Elder, who had come to Pompeii to observe and study the volcano.

2. Seating capacities of 12,000, 5,000, and 800. Pompeii possessed an amphitheater with an estimated seating capacity of 12,000. There were also two theaters in the city, a large one that could accommodate about 5,000 spectators, and a smaller one with space for 800 theatergoers.

3. 9,184 inscriptions. Not surprisingly, thousands of inscriptions turned up in Pompeii, including election notices, tradesmen's advertisements, lost and found notices, information about upcoming gladiatorial shows, and, of course, numerous examples of graffiti, some quite obscene. The authoritative collection of Latin inscriptions, the massive *Corpus Inscriptionum Latinarum*, contains transcripts of 9,184 Pompeian inscriptions; this number will certainly increase annually as more inscriptions are discovered.

4. Four styles of wall painting. Archaeologists and art historians have classified the wall paintings found in Pompeian homes into four distinct groupings, based on chronological and stylistic considerations:

Name	Approximate dates	Characterized by
1. Incrustation style	150–80 B.C.	Representations of marble blocks, colums, and retaining walls
2. Architectural style	80 B.C.–A.D. 14	Representations of architectural patterns
3. Egyptianizing style	A.D. 14–62	Representations of architectural motifs, with designs from tapestries
4. Ornamental style	A.D. 62–79	Representations of scenes from nature, mythology, and architecture

Twenty Thousand Sesterces for a Talking Raven

Macrobius (2.4) recounts an amusing story about Augustus's triumphant return to Rome after his victory at Actium (31 B.C.) over Mark Antony and Cleopatra. A man approached him with a talking raven, which he had taught to say: "Hail, Caesar, general and conqueror." The amazed Augustus forthwith bought the bird for 20,000 sesterces.

But the trainer had a partner with whom he refused to share the money;

the partner, therefore, approached Augustus and told him that his colleague owned another talking raven, and that he ought to show off the second one, too.

Augustus so ordered. It turned out that the second raven had been trained to say: "Hail, Antony, general and conqueror." Augustus was not roused to anger by this disloyal statement; he merely directed the trainer to divide the 20,000 sesterces equally with his partner.

Twenty-Two Thousand Tables

Upon Caesar's triumphant return to Rome in 46 B.C., he provided a feast for the people on such a magnificent scale that 22,000 tables were required to accommodate the diners.

Twenty-Five Thousand: Standing Room Only

The Pnyx, a Greek word roughly meaning "people closely packed," was a rocky Athenian hillside, west of the Acropolis; this hill served as the meeting place for the Athenian Assembly, whose meetings any citizen was eligible to attend. There was room for an estimated 25,000 standees, possibly 18,000 if the assemblage sat on the ground.

Forty Thousand Workers

According to Polybius, as quoted by Strabo, 40,000 miners worked the silver veins near New Carthage in Spain; they extracted 25,000 drachmas' worth of silver per day.

Fifty Thousand Casualties, I

The Athenians lost some 50,000 men, and nearly all of their 134 triremes, during their ill-fated invasion of Sicily (415–413 B.C.), while the Romans lost a like number in a single day at the Battle of Cannae (216 B.C.), during the Second Punic War.

Fifty Thousand Casualties, II

In A.D. 27 a certain Atilius initiated the construction of an amphitheater in Fidena, a small town near Rome. This amphitheater was poorly designed and located; and, in particular, its foundations were not properly reinforced. Not surprisingly, the entire edifice collapsed under the weight of the spectators who flocked there to view a gladiatorial show sponsored by Atilius. Tacitus states that 50,000 people were injured or killed in the catastrophe; while Suetonius reports that more than 20,000 lost their lives.

Atilius, as the responsible party, was banished; further, a senatorial decree was published to the effect that in the future no citizen lacking sufficient means (that is, a net worth of at least 400,000 sesterces) would be permitted to sponsor a gladiatorial show.

Fifty Thousand Miles of Paved Roads

It is estimated that the network of paved roads constructed by the Romans eventually extended for about 50,000 miles.

Eighty Thousand Syracusan Soldiers

According to Diodorus Siculus (14.47), the tyrant of Syracuse Dionysius I had at his disposal in the early fourth century

80,000 infantry
3,000 + cavalry
almost 200 warships, including many quadriremes and quinqueremes — ships with four and five banks of rowers, respectively.

Ninety Thousand Slaves

The number of slaves in fifth-century Attica is impossible to determine with certainty; the figure probably ranges between 80,000 and 150,000. Some scholars suggest that 90,000 may be close. During the Peloponnesian War, some 20,000 Athenian slaves reputedly fled to Sparta.

One Hundred Thousand Sesterces for a Ballplayer

Macrobius (2.6) states that the emperor Caligula often paid 100,000 sesterces to his ballplaying partners. To one of his fellow players, however, a certain Lucius Caecilius, he awarded only 50,000, prompting the latter to comment with some asperity that he had been paid as if he had played with only one hand.

One Hundred Thousand Sesterces Lost in Gambling

The satirist Juvenal describes the gambler who might risk 100,000 sesterces on a single throw of the dice, but yet pleads poverty when the time comes to purchase a cloak for one of his slaves. The emperor Augustus, on the other hand, also enjoyed dicing and gambling, but for far lower stakes, usually one denarius per player on any given throw.

Land for One Hundred Twenty Thousand Soldiers

One of the most unsavory acts of the dictator Sulla was the promulgation of a proscription list (81 B.C.); he needed land for his 120,000 veteran soldiers, and, in many cases, the only means by which this property could be acquired was through confiscation, a task made easier if the owner was recently deceased.

His proscription list reportedly contained the names of 40 senators and 1,600 equestrians (mostly wealthy businessmen). Additionally, he freed 10,000 of their slaves and converted this rabble into his personal bodyguard, which he called the *Cornelii*.

The Four Hundred Thousand-Sesterce Net Worth Requirement

For much of its early social history Rome's populace was divided into two major socioeconomic groups: plebeians and patricians. Gradually, however, a third group emerged, the equestrians (so called, originally, because citizens falling into this category had wealth sufficient to enable them to own a horse). By the second century B.C. this middle class had become both prosperous and influential. Perhaps in an effort to regulate the number of citizens qualifying as equestrians, the emperor Augustus decreed that any Roman wishing to be considered an equestrian had to have a net worth of 400,000 sesterces, a considerable sum.

Tiberius's Six Hundred Thousand-Sesterce Stipend

According to the biographer Suetonius (*Tiberius* 46), the emperor Tiberius was exceedingly stingy, even to the point of refusing to pay salaries to staff assistants who accompanied him on foreign missions. Only once did he deviate from this pattern, when he placed his assistants into three categories, distributing 600,000 sesterces to the men in the first rank, 400,000 to those in the second, and to the third, whom he called his "Greeks," 200,000.

One Million Persians and Other Statistics from Plutarch's Life of Alexander the Great

Plutarch's biography of Alexander the Great contains within its pages many numerical references, including the following:

> 1 million soldiers. King Darius III (reigned 336–330 B.C.), one of Alexander's main Persian antagonists, had under his command 1 million soldiers prior to the Battle of Gaugamela in 331. Earlier (in 334), Plutarch recorded his troop strength as 600,000.
>
> 110,000 Persian casualties. The Persians lost 110,000 soldiers at the Battle of Issus in 333.
>
> 80,000 enemy soldiers and other discouraging statistics. When Alexander had successfully pressed into northern India (327–326 B.C.), his troops refused to follow him farther. They were demoralized by various reports of the dangers that awaited them:
>
>> 80,000 Indian cavalrymen, 200,000 infantrymen
>> 8,000 armed chariots
>> 6,000 armed elephants
>> the necessity of crossing the Ganges River, 4 miles wide and 600 feet deep.
>
> 50,000 soldiers lost in the sand. One of the potential problems posed by an invasion of Egypt—which Alexander undertook in 332—was the matter of desert sandstorms. He had heard that the sixth-century Persian king Cambyses had lost 50,000 of his troops in such a storm when he invaded Egypt in 525.

43,000 soldiers. Plutarch records a number of statistics about Alexander's troop strength and finances when he first crossed from Europe into Asia to do battle with the Persians (334 B.C.). Estimates of the number of his soldiers range from 30,000 to 43,000, with 3,000 to 4,000 cavalrymen. His treasury contained some 70 talents, but he was thought to be 200 talents in debt. Finally, he took with him not more than 30 days' worth of provisions and supplies.

40,000 talents. When Alexander occupied the ancient Persian city of Susa (in 331 B.C.), he discovered great wealth there:

> 40,000 talents in coined money
> 5,000 talents worth of expensive cloth, 190 years old
> Treasure and other valuable items that would require 20,000 mules and 5,000 camels to transport.

30,000 enslaved Thebans. In 336 B.C. Alexander attacked and destroyed the ancient city of Thebes (sparing only certain landmarks, such as Pindar's ancestral home). He sold 30,000 citizens into slavery, and executed 6,000 others.

30,000 students. In 330, while in Hyrcania (near the Caspian Sea), Alexander chose 30,000 young Hyrcanians to be taught the Greek language and learn the Macedonian style of fighting. At the same time he gave a morale-boosting speech to his 20,000 remaining soldiers.

10,000 drachmas for dinner expenses. As Alexander's successes continued, so too rose his banquet expenses, ultimately to a maximum of 10,000 drachmas per dinner.

10,000 talents for a tomb. When Alexander's close friend Hephaestion died, he ordered a tomb costing 10,000 talents to be constructed for him.

9,000 wedding guests. Upon his return to the Persian city of Susa in 324 B.C., Alexander married Statira, the daughter of Darius. Nine thousand guests were invited to the wedding ceremony. At about the same time he liquidated his army's debts, to the amount of 9,870 talents. A little later, when he had advanced to Ecbatana, he sponsored various spectacles and entertainments, with the help of 3,000 newly arrived Greek actors and artists.

1,000 grounds of suspicion. In 330 B.C. one of Alexander's lieutenants, Philotas, was accused of plotting against him; there were, says Plutarch, a "thousand grounds of suspicion" to implicate Philotas. He was found guilty and executed, as was his father Parmenio, one of Alexander's most capable senior officers.

1,000 horsemen. At the Battle of Hydaspes (in India in 327 B.C.), 1,000 cavalrymen and 60 armed chariots stood against Alexander's army. The opposing general, Porus, was a formidable adversary, in particular because of his imposing physical stature — nearly seven feet tall. Alexander respected Porus as a worthy opponent; when the latter was taken prisoner, Alexander not only restored his kingdom to him but also gave him an additional 15 nations to rule, which encompassed 5,000 towns.

A 1,000-talent ransom. Darius offered to Alexander a ransom of 1,000 talents (and his daughter's hand in marriage) if Alexander would release his Persian captives. Alexander refused.

A 400-mile march. In 330 B.C., after occupying several famous Persian cities, Alexander once more started off in pursuit of King Darius, in a 400-mile, 11-day march fraught with deprivations and difficulties of all kinds.

200 galleys. Alexander used 200 galleys during the seven-month siege of the city of Tyre in 332.

The 130-foot monument. When a great admirer of Alexander, Demaratus of Corinth, died, Alexander's army constructed a monument for him some 130 feet in height, with a "vast circumference."

100 hostages. An elderly Indian named Acuphis once asked Alexander how he and his fellow citizens could gain Alexander's friendship. He replied they should select Acuphis to govern them, and send 100 men to him as hostages.

The 50-talent gift and other largesses. So esteemed by Alexander was Xenocrates, one of his teachers, that he gave him a gift of 50 talents. To another of his teachers, Leonidas, he presented 500 talents' worth of frankincense, and another 100 talents' worth of myrrh. He also bestowed a gift of ten talents upon an actor, Lycon of Scarphia. He also gave five talents to a friend named Proteas. A captured house, including a wardrobe worth more than 1,000 talents, was a gift to his general Parmenio. He also presented a gift of 1,000 talents to King Taxiles of India, as a goodwill gesture. When he dismissed his Thessalian troops, he gave them a gratuity of 2,000 talents in addition to their regular pay.

34 casualties. At the Battle of the Granicus River (334 B.C.), Alexander lost only 34 soldiers, while Persian losses were set at 20,000 infantry and 2,500 cavalry. As tangible evidence of his great victory, he sent back to Greece 300 enemy shields.

13 talents. Philonicus, a Thessalian, set a purchase price of 13 talents for Bucephalus, later to become Alexander's famous warhorse. However, Alexander was able to acquire the high-spirited animal free of charge, having won a wager in which he claimed that he could calm and ride him. When Bucephalus died in India at the age of 30, Alexander founded a city on the banks of the Hydaspes River and, in honor of the horse, named the city Bucephala.

The 12-mile hunting net. Several of Alexander's friends enriched themselves with the booty taken during the various military campaigns. One of these, Philotas, had acquired hunting nets that measured in total over 12 miles in length.

12 quarts of wine. During one of his many drinking parties, Alexander proposed a contest to see which of the guests could consume the most wine; a one-talent prize would be awarded to the winner. A certain Promachus won, by drinking 12 quarts of wine. He never got an opportunity to enjoy his prize money, however, as he died only three days later.

12 villages. While Alexander's army was on the march toward King Darius (in 331 B.C.), a small contingent of his soldiers engaged in a mock battle, some pretending to be Persians, others Greeks. The man imper-

sonating Alexander in this "battle" was given a gift of 12 villages for his victory.

10 Indian philosophers. On his journey out of India (to return to Macedonia in 325 B.C.), he took with him ten Indian philosophers, skilled in riddles and sophistry. After listening to them talk, he eventually freed them and, in addition, gave them presents.

The seven-month journey. Seven months' time was required for Alexander to travel the Indian rivers to the sea (325 B.C.).

One Million Sesterces for a Play

The first-century B.C. Roman poet and editor Lucius Varius Rufus reportedly received 1 million sesterces from Octavian in 29 B.C. for a tragic play (*Thyestes*) that he wrote. The play (which was highly regarded in antiquity but is no longer extant) was performed during the games honoring Octavian's victory over Mark Antony at Actium, two years earlier.

The One Million Seven Hundred Thousand–Man Army of Xerxes

According to the historian Herodotus (7.60–80), the Persian king Xerxes invaded Greece in 480 B.C. with an army totaling 1.7 million soldiers (contemporary scholars often claim that the troop-strength figure given by Herodotus is grossly exaggerated). These men came from many different areas and nationalities, located mostly in the Middle East, (modern-day) Turkey and North Africa, as follows:

Nationality	Leader	Equipment
1. Persians	Otanes	Soft caps; chainmail armor; light shields; short spears; powerful bows
2. Medes	Tigranes	Similar to the Persians
3. Cissians	Anaphes	Similar to the Persians
4. Hyrcanians	Megapanus	Similar to the Persians
5. Assyrians/Chaldeans	Otaspes	Bronze helmets; shields, spears, daggers; iron-reinforced wooden clubs
6. Bactrians	Hystaspes	Bows, short spears
7. Sacae	Hystaspes	Tall, pointed caps; bows, daggers, battle-axes
8. Indians	Pharnazathres	Bows, iron-tipped arrows; cotton garments
9. Arians	Sisamnes	Similar to the Bactrians
10. Parthians/ Chorasmians	Artabazus	Similar to the Bactrians
11. Sogdians	Azanes	Similar to the Bactrians

Nationality	*Leader*	*Equipment*
12. Gandarians/Dadicae	Artyphius	Similar to the Bactrians
13. Caspians	Ariomardus	Leather tunics; bows and arrows
14. Sarangians	Pherendates	Bows, arrows, spears; brightly colored clothing; knee-high boots
15. Utians/Mycians	Arsamenes	Leather tunics; bows, arrows, daggers
16. Paricanians	Siromitres	Similar to the Utians/Mycians
17. Pactyans	Artaÿntes	Similar to the Utians/Mycians
18. Arabians	Arsames	Long, flowing garments; long bows
19. Southern Ethiopians	Arsames	Leopard and lion-skin clothing; long bows with stone-tipped arrows; spears with tips made of antelope horn; clubs
20. Eastern Ethiopians (served with the Indians)	Pharnazathres	Similar to the Indians, with whom they were associated, excepted that they wore headgear made of horses' scalps
21. Libyans	Massages	Leather clothing; javelins
22. Paphlagonians/ Matienians	Dotus	Wicker helmets; small shields, short spears, daggers; knee-high boots
23. Mariandynians/Ligyans/ Syrians	Gobryas	Similar to the Paphlagonians
24. Phrygians	Artochmes	Similar to the Paphlagonians
25. Lydians/Mysians	Artaphrenes	Small shields, javelins
26. Asiatic Thracians	Bassaces	Headgear made of fox skins; javelins, light shields, small daggers; brightly colored clothing, with knee-high boots
27. Pisidians	Badres	Small, ox-hide shields; spears; crested, bronze helmets; crimson cloth leggings
28. Cabelians	Badres	Helmets; woollen upper-body armor; light shields; javelins, swords
29. Milyans	Badres	Short spears, bows and arrows; leather helmets

Nationality	Leader	Equipment
30. Moschians/Tibarenians	Ariomardus	Wooden helmets; shields, short spears
31. Macrones/Mossynoe-cians	Artaÿctes	Similar to the Moschians
32. Marians	Pharandates	Plaited helmets; leather shields; javelins
33. Colchians	Pharandates	Wooden helmets; small, leather shields; short spears, swords
34. Alarodians/Saspires	Masistius	Similar to the Marians
35. Persian Gulf islanders	Mardontes	Similar to the Medes

In addition to these contingents, Xerxes was also served by elite troops called "The Immortals," 10,000 strong, under the command of Hydarnes.

The One Million, Eight Hundred Sixty-Six Thousand, Six Hundred Sixty-Six–Sesterce Grant to Freedmen, and Other Largesses of Pliny the Younger

The wealthy Roman gentleman-statesman Pliny the Younger displayed his generosity on a number of occasions, both during his lifetime and in the bequests specified in his will. Some of his largesses are as follows:

1,866,667 sesterces. In his will he bequeathed the 1.8 + million sesterces for the financial support of 100 of his freedmen.

500,000 sesterces for the youth of his hometown. He also directed in his will that 500,000 sesterces be set aside for the support and maintenance of the youth of his hometown, Como.

300,000 sesterces for Como's public baths. A fragmentary inscription (*CIL* 5.5262) indicates that Pliny bequeathed 300,000 sesterces for the furnishing of Como's public baths, and 200,000 sesterces for their maintenance. He also funded the initial construction of these baths, but the sum expended does not survive on the inscription.

300,000 sesterces for Romatius Firmus. Romatius Firmus, a childhood friend of Pliny, was a local politician in Como; his net worth amounted to 100,000 sesterces, 300,000 short of the total required for admission to the equestrian class. To make up the difference, Pliny gave his friend the necessary 300,000.

A farm worth 100,000 for his *nutrix*. Pliny presented his old *nutrix* (nurse, probably equivalent to a day-care teacher) with a farm worth 100,000 sesterces, a *munusculum*, "little gift," as Pliny terms it.

50,000 sesterces for Quintilian's daughter. A certain Quintilian (not the celebrated grammarian) did not have sufficient funds to cover the cost of his daughter's wedding. Pliny came to the rescue with a gift of 50,000 sesterces, as a partial dowry for the young woman. In another instance, he provided 100,000 sesterces as a partial dowry for a relative of his by the name of Calvina.

Additionally, Pliny states in one of his letters (3.11) that he presented an unspecified sum of money to a philosopher friend of his by the name of Artemidorus, at a time when the latter had been banished from Rome by Domitian. In the same letter Pliny relates that seven of his other friends had been exiled or killed in this purge. They were

1. Arria	5. Mauricus
2. Fannia	6. Rusticus
3. Gratilla	7. Senecio
4. Helvidius	

It is apparent from the list of Pliny's benefactions that several of them were earmarked for children or young people; in this regard, he was perhaps one of the first prominent Romans to participate in an emergent early imperial social custom called the *alimenta*: a philanthropic system in which wealthy benefactors provided financial support for needy children. Other noted examples were as follows:

1. A second-century (A.D.) inscription regarding an unnamed African benefactor specified that the interest on his gift of 1.3 million sesterces to his hometown of Sicca be distributed as follows: to 300 boys and 200 girls, with the boys receiving 10 sesterces per month from the ages of 3 to 15, and the girls 8 per month from the ages of 3 to 13.

2. The emperor Trajan gave outright grants of money to various municipalities throughout Italy; these towns, in turn, were required to deposit in their local treasuries an amount of money equal to 5 percent on the grants; this interest money was then to be used for the care of the town's needy children. In the case of Veleia in northern Italy, for example, 263 boys, 35 girls, and 2 illegitimate children (1 boy, 1 girl) were supported in this way on the income derived from annual interest money. The boys' monthly stipend was 16 sesterces; for the girls, the figure was 12. Regarding the 2 illegitimate children, a sum of 12 sesterces was alloted to the boy, 10 to the girl.

It is known that at least 46 Italian towns benefited from the *alimenta*.

Pliny (in his *Panegyric* 26) provides some additional information, notably that nearly 5,000 children were assisted by Trajan's benefactions. He also implies that these grants were not necessarily altruistically motivated, but were intended to nurture youth who would one day mature into strong soldiers or, in the case of the girls, into women capable of bearing healthy offspring.

The Six Million–Sesterce Pearl, and Other Statistics from Suetonius's Life of Julius Caesar

The Roman biographer Suetonius wrote accounts of the lives and reigns of Julius Caesar and his 11 successors. The biography of Caesar, in particular, contains many numbers and statistics. Some examples follow.

6 million sesterces. Suetonius reports that Caesar paid 6 million sesterces for a pearl to give to one of his mistresses, Servilia (the mother of Marcus Junius Brutus, one of those involved in the conspiracy to assassinate him).

150,000 free-grain recipients. During his dictatorship of 45 B.C., Caesar engaged in an ancient Roman version of welfare reform by cutting the number of recipients of free grain from 320,000 to 150,000.

130,000 arrows. After one of the battles against the forces of Pompey the Great, some 130,000 arrows were recovered from the battlefield.

80,000 colonists. Caesar was so concerned about the decline of Rome's population, a decline accelerated by the loss of 80,000 citizens who had left for overseas colonies, that he enacted a number of measures designed to limit foreign travel.

The 30,000 horsemen exaggeration. Caesar was in the habit of exaggerating the dangers of upcoming battles, to instill courage in his men. On one such occasion, he told his soldiers that the enemy (King Juba) possessed 30,000 cavalry, 100,000 infantry, and 300 elephants.

24,000 sesterces. At the conclusion of the civil war (45 B.C.), Caesar gave a largesse of 24,000 sesterces to each of his veteran soldiers.

20,000 citizens. As consul in 59 B.C., Caesar implemented a measure granting land in Campania (south of Rome) to 20,000 needy citizens, who qualified for the grant as long as they had at least 3 children.

6,000 talents. He extorted this amount of money from King Ptolemy of Egypt.

3,200 miles. The circumference of Caesar's province of Gaul was 3,200 miles. From this province he extracted an annual tribute of 40 million sesterces.

3,000 sesterces for a pound of gold. While in Gaul, Caesar had plundered so much gold from the shrines and temples there that he offered it for sale at the rate of 3,000 sesterces per pound, evidently a much lower price than gold usually commanded. During his consulship (of 59 B.C.), he stole 3,000 pounds of gold from the state, and substituted a like amount of gilded bronze.

2,000 sesterces in rent. As dictator in 45 B.C., Caesar offered a full year's rent remission to all tenants in Rome who were paying less than 2,000 sesterces annually. The same offer was extended to Italian tenants whose annual rent was 500 sesterces or less. At the same time he gave a grant of 400 sesterces to every male citizen, as well as 2.5 bushels of grain and 10 pounds of olive oil.

1,000 soldiers. One of the entertainments given by Caesar after the civil war was a mock battle in which 1,000 soldiers, 40 elephants, and 30 cavalrymen participated.

The 365-day calendar. Caesar reorganized the Roman calendar to conform to the 365-day solar year (and as such, it is basically the same calendar format in use today).

300 sesterces. By the terms of Caesar's will, 300 sesterces were to be distributed to every male citizen residing in Rome.

A 200-yard swim. Caesar was renowned for his swimming ability. On one occasion he jumped out of a crowded rowboat and swam 200 yards to the nearest ship, all the while dragging a heavy cloak with his teeth and holding aloft, in his left hand, some documents that he did not wish to get wet.

120 holes in a shield. Stories are told of the exploits of individual soldiers serving under Caesar. One of these, a centurion named Scaeva, counted 120 holes in his shield after a pitched battle.

100 miles per day. He traveled quickly, often covering 100 miles per day (in an era in which traversing perhaps half that distance in a day was considered exceptional).

60 + conspirators. The number of men who formed the infamous Ides of March plot to murder Caesar was set by Suetonius at more than 60. Caesar suffered 23 stab wounds on that day in 44 B.C.

40 days. When Caesar was a young man, he was captured by pirates and held prisoner for 40 days (until a ransom of 50 talents was paid for his release).

A 24-day journey. One of his lost literary works is an essay entitled "The Journey," an account of a 24-day trip from Rome to Spain.

The 20-foot marble column. Shortly after Caesar's assassination, some of his adherents placed a commemorative marble column, nearly 20 feet tall, in the Roman Forum; it was inscribed with the words *parenti patriae*, "to the father of [our] country."

Nine years. Caesar ruled (and plundered) Gaul for 9 years as its military governor (58–50 B.C.).

An eight-legion giveback. Prior to the outbreak of civil war (in 49 B.C.), Caesar had offered a compromise to his opponents wherein he would disband eight of the ten legions under his command. (His proposal was rejected.)

The seven-night comet. Shortly after Caesar's death, a comet was visible for seven consecutive nights; many believed that the comet was Caesar's soul, transmigrating to heaven.

Five triumphs. Victorious generals returning to Rome from battle were often given the ancient version of a ticker-tape parade. Caesar was feted with five such parades, or "triumphs," for his victories in Gaul, Alexandria, Pontus, Africa, and Spain. The Gallic triumphal procession included, inter alia, 40 elephants bearing torches.

A four-hour battle. Within five days of arriving in Pontus (in Asia Minor), Caesar found and defeated King Pharnaces in a four-hour battle in 47 B.C. This quickly decisive confrontation was the occasion of one of Caesar's best known sayings: *Veni, vidi, vici*, "I came, I saw, I conquered."

Three setbacks. In Caesar's nine years in Gaul he suffered only three reverses: once, when he nearly lost his fleet in a storm off Britain; a second time when a legion was defeated at the Battle of Gergovia; and finally when two of his top-ranking officers were treacherously murdered near Germany.

A Ten Million Sesterces Grant

According to Tacitus (*Annals* 12.58), when the town of Bononia was ravaged by fire in A.D. 53, the soon-to-be emperor Nero offered a grant of 10 million sesterces to assist in the rebuilding.

The Twenty-Five Million–Sesterce Debt

Julius Caesar spent so much borrowed money in the 60s B.C. on his political campaigns that he is supposed to have remarked (before leaving for Spain to assume the governorship in 61 B.C.) that he would require 25 million sesterces simply to have nothing at all.

Forty Million Sesterces in Tribute

According to Suetonius, when Julius Caesar organized Gaul into a province in the 50s B.C., he imposed upon it an annual tribute of 40 million sesterces.

The One Hundred Eighty Million–Sesterce Aqueduct Renovation, and Other Statistics from Frontinus's Manual on Aqueducts

The Roman engineer Sextus Julius Frontinus (ca. A.D. 35–104) was appointed to the post of *curator aquarum*, or superintendent of the aqueducts, in A.D. 97. As a result of his experiences in this office, he wrote a manual for his successors, entitled *De Aquis Urbis Romae*, "Concerning the Aqueducts of Rome." This treatise is packed with statistical information on the dimensions, specifications, flow rates, maintenance costs, and related items pertaining to Rome's sophisticated aqueduct system. A sampling of these statistics follows:

180 million. The amount (in sesterces) of money granted to a certain Marcius (in 146 B.C.) to restore Rome's existing aqueducts, and also to construct a new one, which came to be known as the Aqua Marcia.

14,018. In the course of his duties as the *curator aquarum* Frontinus found discrepancies between the amount of water each aqueduct was supposed to be discharging (according to records and specifications), and its actual discharge, as follows (all figures are in *quinariae* per 24 hours, with a *quinaria* roughly equal to 5,500 gallons):

Name of aqueduct	Specified flow	Actual flow
Aqua Alsietina	392(?)	392
Aqua Anio Novus	3,263	4,037
Aqua Anio Vetus	1,541	1,610
Aqua Appia	841	704
Aqua Claudia	2,855	1,588
Aqua Julia	649	803
Aqua Marcia	2,162	1,935
Aqua Tepula	400	445
Aqua Virgo	652	2,504
Totals	12,755	14,018

Many variables enter into these calculations, the most distortive being that Frontinus had no method of measuring the impact of velocity on the discharge figures.

The 14,018 *quinariae* were supposed to be distributed as follows:

4,063: outside the city
     1718 distributed at the emperor's discretion
     2345 distributed to private citizens
9,955: 1707 distributed at the emperor's discretion
     3847 allotted to private citizens
     4401 for public uses, as follows

        279 for military(?) camps
        2301 for public structures
        386 for fountains
        1335 for water basins

(It will be noted that the latter total is 4301, not 4401, one of the relatively common arithmetical discrepancies in Frontinus's manual. It is impossible to determine, however, whether this is the fault of the author or of the manuscript copyists.)

25. The number of different pipe diameters used in conjunction with the various aqueducts, as listed and described by Frontinus. They range in diameter from about one inch up to about nine inches.

17. Frontinus listed his 17 imperial predecessors (that is, those who held the office of *curator aquarum* after the establishment of the Roman Empire). They were as follows, including the dates when they held office:

1. Marcus Agrippa: 32–12 B.C.
2. Messala Corvinus: 12 B.C.–A.D. 13
3. Ateius Capito: A.D. 13–23
4. Tarius Rufus: A.D. 23–24
5. Marcus Cocceius Nerva: A.D. 24–34
6. Gaius Octavius Laenas: A.D. 34–38
7. Marcus Porcius Cato: A.D. 38
8. Aulus Didius Gallus: A.D. 38–49
9. Gnaeus Domitius Afer: A.D. 49–60
10. Lucius Piso: A.D. 60–63
11. Petronius Turpilianus: A.D. 63–64
12. Publius Marius: A.D. 64–66
13. Fonteius Agrippa: A.D. 66–68
14. Albius Crispus: A.D. 68–71
15. Pompeius Silvanus: A.D. 71–73
16. Tampius Flavianus: A.D. 73–74
17. Acilius Aviola: A.D. 74–97

The Six Hundred Million–Sesterce Real Estate Purchase, and Other Statistics from the Res Gestae of Augustus

Shortly before his death in A.D. 14, the Roman emperor Augustus prepared a document (later entitled *Res Gestae Divi Augusti, Accomplishments of Deified*

Augustus) in which he detailed his accomplishments, as the title suggests. The *Res Gestae* contains a plethora of numerical information — some of it no doubt exaggerated — about the reign of Augustus, including the following:

600,000,000. The amount in sesterces that Augustus paid in 30 and 14 B.C. for lands in Italy to give to his veteran soldiers; he also spent 260 million sesterces for land in the provinces, for the same purpose.

400,000,000. The amount in sesterces that Augustus gave to veteran soldiers who returned to their hometowns after their tours of duty; these donatives were made in 7, 6, 4, 3 and 2 B.C.

170,000,000. The amount in sesterces of his own money that Augustus donated in A.D. 6 for the purpose of establishing a quasi-pension fund for veteran soldiers.

150,000,000. The amount in sesterces of his own money that Augustus donated to the public treasury, in a series of four separate grants; the dates of two of these are known to be 28 and 16 B.C.

100,000,000. The amount in sesterces that he donated for various templar sacrifices.

4,937,000. The number of Roman citizens recorded in a census taken in A.D. 14.

4,233,000. The number of Roman citizens recorded in a census taken in 8 B.C.

4,063,000. The number of Roman citizens recorded in a census taken in 28 B.C.

500,000. The number of soldiers who served under Augustus in the 43 years of his reign.

250,000. The minimum number of citizens who benefited from Augustus's donatives and largesses.

35,000. The weight in pounds of gold Augustus returned to various cities that had given it to him as a token of their submission (29 B.C.).

30,000. The approximate number of fugitive slaves captured by Augustus in 36 B.C., during the civil war of 44–31. These he returned to their owners.

10,000. The approximate number of men who fought in the eight gladiatorial shows sponsored by Augustus or by his adopted sons or grandsons.

3,500. The approximate number of wild animals killed in mock hunts sponsored by Augustus in his own name, or in the names of his adopted sons or grandsons; there were 26 such spectacles.

1,800 feet × 1,200 feet. The dimensions of the excavation made for an artificial lake, for the purpose of a mock naval battle. Augustus states that about 3,000 sailors manned the 30 large vessels and numerous smaller boats that participated.

1,000. A donative of 1,000 sesterces per man was paid to veteran soldiers in 5 B.C.; Augustus states that about 120,000 men received these grants.

700. More than 700 Roman senators (of about 1,000) pledged their loyalty to Augustus prior to the Battle of Actium (31 B.C.), the final and

decisive battle against Antony and Cleopatra. Of the 700, 83 had held the consulship, either before or after this battle. In addition, 170 were or became priests.

600. The number of ships captured by Augustus's forces near the end of the civil war with Mark Antony.

400. A donative of 400 sesterces was paid to each plebeian citizen in 29 B.C. from the spoils of the recently concluded civil war. Additional 400-sesterce grants were made in 24 and 12 B.C.

300. A donative of 300 sesterces was paid to each plebeian citizen in 44 B.C., in accordance with the terms of Julius Caesar's will.

240. In 2 B.C. a donative of 240 sesterces was paid to each plebeian citizen receiving public grain. About 200,000 people received these grants.

82. The total number of temples in Rome restored or rebuilt by Augustus.

80. The number of silver statues of Augustus that had been set up in various parts of Rome. He ordered these statues to be removed and the silver melted down.

BIBLIOGRAPHY

Anderson, Warren, tr. *Theophrastus: The Character Sketches*. Kent, Ohio, 1970.

Bailey, D.R. Shackleton. *Cicero*. New York, 1971.

Balsdon, J. P. V. D. *Life and Leisure in Ancient Rome*. New York, 1969.

Basore, John, tr. *Seneca: Moral Essays*. Cambridge, MA, 1928.

Benario, Herbert. "Amphitheaters of the Roman World." *Classical Journal* 1981, pp. 255–58.

Bennett, Charles, tr. *Frontinus: The Stratagems and the Aqueducts of Rome*. New York, 1925.

Boardman, John. *The Greeks Overseas, Their Early Colonies and Trade*. London, 1980.

Bovie, Smith Palmer, tr. *Satires and Epistles of Horace*. Chicago, 1959.

Broughton, T. R. S. *The Magistrates of the Roman Republic*. New York, 1951.

Burton, Harry E. *The Discovery of the Ancient World*. Cambridge, MA, 1932.

Burtt, J. O., tr. *Minor Attic Orators*, vol. II, *Lycurgus, Dinarchus, Demades, Hyperides*. Cambridge, MA. 1954.

Butler, James H. *The Theater and Drama of Greece and Rome*. San Francisco, 1972.

Cary, E., tr. *Dio's Roman History*. New York, 1914.

————. *The Roman Antiquities of Dionysius of Halicarnassus*. Cambridge, MA, 1937.

Cary, M. *A History of Rome*. Second edition. New York, 1954.

Cohoon, J. W., and H. Lamar Crosby, trs. *Dio Chrysostom*. Cambridge, MA, 1932.

Cornish, Francis W., tr. *Catullus*. Cambridge, MA, 1924.

de Camp, L. Sprague. *The Ancient Engineers*. New York, 1974.

Dill, Samuel. *Roman Society from Nero to Marcus Aurelius*. New York, 1904.

Dobson, J. F. *The Greek Orators: The Beginnings of Oratory*. London, 1918.

Duff, J. D., tr. *Silius Italicus: Punica*. New York, 1934.

Duncan-Jones, Richard. *The Economy of the Roman Empire: Quantitative Studies*. Cambridge, 1974.

Dyer, Louis, ed. *Plato: Apology of Socrates and Crito*. Boston, 1885.

Edmonds, J. M., tr. *The Characters of Theophrastus*. New York, 1929.

————. *The Greek Bucolic Poets*. New York, 1912.

Evelyn-White, Hugh G., tr. *Hesiod: The Homeric Hymns and Homerica*. Cambridge, MA, 1914.

Farnell, Lewis. *The Cults of the Greek States*. Oxford, 1895.

Feder, Lillian. *Apollo Handbook of Classical Literature*. New York, 1964.

Fine, John. *The Ancient Greeks: A Critical History*. Cambridge, MA, 1983.

Fiske, N. W. *Classical Antiquities*. Philadelphia, 1847.

Fitzgerald, Robert, tr. *The Odyssey: Homer*. New York, 1961.

Forster, Edward S., tr. *Isaeus*. Cambridge, MA, 1927.

_____. *Lucius Annaeus Florus: Epitome of Roman History*. New York, 1929.

Frazer, James George. *Apollodorus: The Library*. Cambridge, MA, 1921.

_____, ed. *Pausanias' Description of Greece*. New York, 1965. Reprint of the 1913 edition.

_____, tr. *Ovid's Fasti*. Cambridge, MA, 1959.

Friedlaender, Ludwig. *Roman Life and Manners*. Four volumes; seventh edition; translated from the German by J. H. Freese. New York, 1908.

Frost, Frank. *Greek Society*. Fourth edition. Lexington, MA, 1992.

Godley, A. D., tr. *Herodotus*. Cambridge, MA, 1920.

Golvin, J.-C. *L'Amphithéâtre Romain*. Paris, 1988.

Goold, G. P., tr. *Propertius: Elegies*. Cambridge, MA, 1990.

Granger, Frank, tr. *Vitruvius on Architecture*. Cambridge, MA, 1931.

Grant, Michael. *The Army of the Caesars*. New York, 1974.

_____. *Greek and Latin Authors: 800 B.C.–A.D. 1000*. New York, 1980.

_____. *A Guide to the Ancient World: A Dictionary of Classical Place Names*. New York, 1986.

_____. *Myths of the Greeks and Romans*. New York, 1962.

Graves, Robert, tr. *The Twelve Caesars of Gaius Suetonius Tranquillus*. New York, 1957.

Greece and Rome: Builders of Our World. A publication of the National Geographic Society. Washington, DC, 1968.

Green, Peter, tr. *Juvenal: The Sixteen Satires*. Baltimore, 1967.

Greenough, J. B., ed. *The Satires and Epistles of Horace*. Boston, 1899.

_____, et al., eds. *The Conspiracy of Catiline as Related by Sallust*. Boston, 1901.

Gummere, Richard, tr. *Seneca: Ad Lucilium Epistulae Morales*. Cambridge, MA, 1917.

Haigh, A. E. *The Attic Theatre*. Third edition. New York, 1968.

Haines, C. R., tr. *The Correspondence of Marcus Cornelius Fronto*. New York, 1919, 1920.

Harmon, A. M., K. Kilburn, and M. D. MacLeod, trs. *Lucian*. Cambridge, MA, 1915.

Hardy, W. G. *The Greek and Roman World*. Cambridge, MA, 1962.

Harper's Dictionary of Classical Literature and Antiquities. New York, 1898.

Hart, Samuel, ed. *The Satires of Perseus*. Boston, 1875.

Hicks, R. D., tr. *Diogenes Laertius: Lives of the Eminent Philosophers*. Cambridge, MA, 1925.

Hooper, William Davis, and H. B. Ash, tr. *Marcus Porcius Cato: On Agriculture; Marcus Terentius Varro on Agriculture*. Cambridge, MA, 1934.

Hort, Arthur, tr. *Theophrastus: Enquiry into Plants*. New York, 1916.

Howatson, M. C., ed. *The Oxford Companion to Classical Literature*. Second edition. Oxford, 1989.

Humphries, Rolfe, tr. *Martial: Selected Epigrams*. Bloomington, IN, 1963.

Jackson, John, tr. *Tacitus: The Annals*. Cambridge, MA, 1931.

Jebb, Richard C. *The Attic Orators*, volume I. London, 1893.

Jones, W. H. S., Paul Potter, and E. T. Withington, trs. *Hippocrates*. Cambridge, MA, 1948.

Kenney, E. J., ed. *The Cambridge History of Classical Literature*, volume II, *Latin Literature*. Cambridge, 1982.

Kent, Roland G., tr. *Varro on the Latin Language*. Cambridge, MA, 1938.

Ker, Walter, tr. *Cicero: Philippics*. Cambridge, MA, 1926.

Kirk, G. S. *The Nature of Greek Myths*. New York, 1974.

Kravitz, David. *Who's Who in Greek and Roman Mythology*. New York, 1975.

Kunkel, Wolfgang. *An Introduction to Roman Legal and Constitutional History*. Translated from the German by J. M. Kelly. Oxford, 1973.

Lesky, Albin. *A History of Greek Literature*. Translated from the German by James Willis and Cornelis de Heer. New York, 1966.

Lewis, Naphtali, and Meyer Reinhold. *Roman Civilization*, volume I, *The Republic*. New York, 1951.

_____. *Roman Civilization*, volume II, *The Empire*. New York, 1955.

Low, D. M., ed. *The Decline and Fall of the Roman Empire. An Abridgement by D. M. Low*. New York, 1960.

MacDonald, C., tr. *Cicero, In Catilinam I–IV; Pro Murena; Pro Sulla; Pro Flacco*. Cambridge, 1978.

MacKendrick, Paul. *The Mute Stones Speak*. New York, 1960.

Magie, David, tr. *The Scriptores Historiae Augustae*. New York, 1921.

Maidment, K. J., tr. *Minor Attic Orators*, volume I, *Antiphon, Andocides*. Cambridge, MA, 1953.

Mair, A. W., tr. *Oppian Colluthus Tryphiodorus*. New York, 1928.

Matz, David. *Greek and Roman Sport: A Dictionary*. Jefferson, NC, 1991.

Miller, Frank, tr. *Ovid: Metamorphoses*. Cambridge, MA, 1964.

Moore, Clifford, tr. *Tacitus: The Histories*. Cambridge, MA, 1931.

Morford, Mark P. O., and Robert Lenardon. *Classical Mythology*. New York, 1971.

Mozley, J. H., tr. *Statius: Silvae; Thebaid I–IV*. Cambridge, MA, 1928.

_____. *Valerius Flaccus*. Cambridge, MA, 1934.

Norlin, George, and LaRue Van Hook, trs. *Isocrates*. New York and Cambridge, MA, 1928, 1929, 1945.

The Oxford Classical Dictionary, second edition. London, 1970.

Palmer, Arthur, ed. *The Satires of Horace*. London, 1915.

Parker, H. M. D. *The Roman Legions*. Oxford, 1928.

Paton, W. R., tr. *The Greek Anthology*. New York, 1916.

_____. *Polybius: The Histories*. New York, 1922–27.

Pickard-Cambridge, Arthur. *The Dramatic Festivals of Athens*. Second edition. Oxford, 1968.

Platner, Samuel. *Topography and Monuments of Ancient Rome*. Boston, 1911.

The Praeger Encyclopedia of Ancient Greek Civilization. New York, 1967.

Quinn, Kenneth, ed. *Catullus: The Poems*. New York, 1970.

Rackham, H., W. H. S. Jones, and D. E. Eichholz, trs. *Pliny: Natural History*. Cambridge, MA, 1944–62.

Radice, Betty. *Who's Who in the Ancient World*. New York, 1971.

_____, tr. *Pliny: Letters and Panegyricus*. Cambridge, MA, 1969.

Ramsay, G. G., tr. *Juvenal and Persius*. Cambridge, MA, 1918. Revised 1969.

Rolfe, J. C. *The Attic Nights of Aulus Gellius*. Cambridge, MA, 1927.

_____, tr. *The Lives of Cornelius Nepos*. Cambridge, MA, 1929.

_____, tr. *Suetonius*. Cambridge, MA, 1914.

Rossi, Lino. *Trajan's Column and the Dacian Wars*. Ithaca, NY, 1971.

Russell, Donald. *Plutarch*. New York, 1973.

Sandys, John Edwin. *A Short History of Classical Scholarship*. Cambridge, 1915.
Scott-Kilvert, Ian, tr. *The Rise and Fall of Athens: Nine Greek Lives by Plutarch*. New York, 1960.
Scullard, H. H. *Festivals and Ceremonies of the Roman Republic*. Ithaca, NY, 1981.
_____. *From the Gracchi to Nero*. London, 1959.
Selincourt, Aubrey de, tr. *Herodotus: The Histories*. Baltimore, 1954.
Shipley, Frederick, tr. *Res Gestae Divi Augusti*. Cambridge, MA, 1924.
Smith, Clement Lawrence, ed. *The Odes and Epodes of Horace*. Boston, 1894.
Smith, William, ed. *A Dictionary of Greek and Roman Geography*. London, 1878.
Spencer, W. G., tr. *Celsus: De Medicina*. Cambridge, MA, 1938.
Starr, Chester G. *The Ancient Greeks*. New York, 1971.
_____. *The Ancient Romans*. New York, 1971.
_____. *A History of the Ancient World*. Third edition. New York, 1974.
Stobart, J. C. *The Grandeur That Was Rome*. Fourth edition. New York, 1969.
Swanson, Donald. *The Names in Roman Verse*. Madison, WI, 1967.
Swanson, Roy Arthur, tr. *Pindar's Odes*. New York, 1974.
Tarn, William W. *Alexander the Great II: Sources and Studies*. Cambridge, England, 1948.
Tredennick, Hugh, tr. *Plato: The Last Days of Socrates*. Harmondsworth, England, 1954.
Vehling, Joseph Dommers, tr. *Apicius: Cookery and Dining in Imperial Rome*. New York, 1977.
Vince, J. H., et al., trs. *Demosthenes*. Cambridge, MA, 1953.
Walker, Arthur Tappan, ed. *Caesar's Gallic War: Books I–VII*. New York, 1926.
Warner, Rex, tr. *War Commentaries of Caesar*. New York, 1960.
Whibley, Leonard. *A Companion to Greek Studies*. Fourth Edition. New York, 1963.
White, Horace, tr. *Appian's Roman History*. New York, 1913.
Whitehead, David. *The Demes of Attica 508/7–ca.250 B.C. A Political and Social Study*. Princeton, NJ, 1986.
Widdows, P. F., tr. *The Fables of Phaedrus*. Austin, TX, 1992.
Wiedemann, Thomas. *Emperors and Gladiators*. New York, 1992.
Willcock, M. M., ed. *The Iliad of Homer: Books I–XII*. London, 1978.
Zimmerman, J. E. *Dictionary of Classical Mythology*. New York, 1964.

INDEX